So Send I You

A Missionary Story

By: Dr. Delron Shirley

© 2019

Table of Contents

Cover Photo

Even though my mother took only one short taxi ride across the border into Mexico and made a couple short cruise ship stops in the Caribbean, she had a heart for the world – demonstrated by the antique globe pictured on the front cover. As a schoolgirl, one of her most earnest desires was to own a world globe of her own. When she finally obtained this one, it became one of her most treasured possessions. Through it, she owned the whole world! It is my prayer that in *So Sent I You*, you will realize that the whole world is, indeed, yours as well!

The airplane with the banner "So Send I You," was a centerpiece on the table from one of the first missionary events at which I was invited to share a bit of my story. That phrase continues to ring in my ear every time I board an airplane.

Prologue
My Story for His Glory

Over the years, I've been asked a number of times why I haven't written my autobiography. The answer is quite honestly that I've never felt the necessity to write about myself. My mission in life is to write about the Lord – not myself. Yes, I often relate personal testimonies as illustrations in my teachings. This is because I believe that I have no right to give advice to others if the principles that I am sharing haven't worked in my own life. Therefore, I try to validate the teaching with personal stories. And, in fact, it is such testimonies that have prompted some of my readers to ask for a full autobiography. Well, as I am pushing my seventieth birthday – the biblical age limit for the expected sojourn on Planet Earth (Psalm 90:10) – I figure that if I am ever going to take time to write about my life, this would be the time to do so.

As I sit down to recollect my thoughts for this manuscript, two men who have been significant in my life come to mind. One is Dick Eastman, the international president of Every Home for Christ. Just after he turned seventy, he made a comment that there were two problems with reaching such a mature age – first, you tend to forget; second, you tend to remember. What he meant by the first statement is obvious; you sometimes have a hard time remembering the facts that should be included in such a volume as your autobiography. His second point was a bit more obscure, but it is actually very realistic; you tend to remember a lot of details about the events that haven't escaped your memory – details that can be boring to your audience even though they may seem totally significant to you as the storyteller. Well, I pray that I'm able to overcome both of these challenges and will remember the right stories to relate in

1

this book and forget all the unnecessary details that would detract from the purpose and intent behind sharing the testimonies. The second individual who comes to mind is Dr. Lester Sumrall, the bigger-than-life character with whom I ministered for many years. While I was working with him, he released an autobiography whose title I have borrowed – well, truthfully, stolen – for this introductory chapter. Dr. Sumrall always said that he lived seven lives – that his life story fell into seven natural divisions. I have felt somewhat the same about my life – that there are nine logical chapters. Even though I am definitely a "dog person" – even though I did own a pet monkey when I was a boy – I guess I'm like a cat in that I've lived nine lives. Therefore, I've arranged my story in nine topical chapters rather than in chronological sequence.

The only reason that I would take the time to write my life story is that it would be a testimony to the graciousness that God has demonstrated in my life. It is my prayer that the experiences I will share in this volume will be an encouragement and a challenge to each reader to trust God to add adventure and purpose to each day of life.

I Was Born at an Early Age

There, I've done it! As part of one of my classes in Bible school, I have the students share their testimonies in order to learn how to effectively minister from their own personal experiences. When one girl was giving her oral presentation, she began by saying, "I was born at an early age." I assume that she intended to say that she had been born again at an early age but – regardless of her intention – the result was that the entire class burst into uncontrolled laughter to the point that she was unable to continue with her story. At that moment, I decided that if I were to ever put pen to paper to share my life, the opening line would be, "I was born at an early age."

So it was that on June 15, 1949, Planet Earth received its approximately two-and-a-half billionth resident (Amazingly, when my grandson Sheridan was born, that number was triple.) and given the unusual name, "Delron Shirley." My given name is unique since my mother made it up; she thought that the syllables sounded good together. The name was never heard again outside the little town of Belton, South Carolina, until 1965 when an American girl group took the title "Reparata and the Delrons" and recorded their one-time hit "Tommy." To my knowledge, it has never been used again except by a Nigerian student who – in a last-ditch effort to get a scholarship to attend the college where I was serving as dean – gave the moniker to his first-born son. Due to the unusual nature of the name, I've been called almost everything imaginable – to the point that I almost couldn't pronounce my own name correctly after one gentleman butchered it so many different ways while trying to introduce me as a guest speaker. My family name originated in England and came to the southern US during the colonial period. In fact, one of the early governors of Virginia bore this surname. Of course, the

3

name is far more common as a girl's first name than as a last name – resulting in many embarrassing events such as the free subscription to *Seventeen* magazine as part of the periodical's promotion in my high school and being called "ma'am" on hundreds of phone calls, especially since I've always had a rather high-pitched voice. And of course, there has always been the confusion with being introduced as "Delron and Shirley" with many people thinking that Shirley is my wife's name.

When I think about my birth, I am amazingly grateful to God for the way He orchestrated every detail. Having traveled around the world and having had personal interaction with thousands of individuals, I can't think of any other set of circumstances that I could have preferred over the exact conditions through which I was allowed to enter this world. I often think of the possibility of having been born in one of the remote villages I have visited in India or Africa where I could have grown up in abject poverty – not only financial poverty, but also spiritual poverty. Under such conditions, just trying to stay alive would have been the biggest challenge of each day – leaving no time to study, meditate, and explore for truth. Had I been born as one of the two billion people on earth who live their whole lives and go to their graves without ever having heard the name of Jesus, there would be no testimony at all to share – and no hope for an eternal destiny. However, God had a different plan.

Like the Apostle Paul, who wrote in Galatians 1:15 that God had separated him from his mother's womb, suggesting that his life – like those of Isaiah (Isaiah 49:1), Jeremiah (Jeremiah 1:5), and David (Psalm 22:9) – was destined even before his birth, I feel that God handpicked the family and conditions through which I was to enter this life. In fact, Paul even suggested that his destiny was preconceived even before Creation. (Ephesians 1:4) Even though this idea may seem to be a bit audacious, I do believe that God had a plan for my life and that He

4

orchestrated everything in a way to make it possible for the circumstances of my life to be totally aligned to fulfill that plan. Of course, God has a plan and purpose for every individual He places in this world and it is my prayer that in reading some of these stories that reveal how I discovered and began to fulfill the specific plan for my life, God will awaken you to how He has also orchestrated your life for a divine purpose.

Although I could probably try to reconstruct some ancient history about how someone in my family's distant past made the decision to migrate from Europe to America, I wish to start simply with the characters that I personally knew, especially my grandparents. One of the earliest memories I have is that of a preacher (In the middle of the last century in the Deep South, we never spoke of the "pastor" – only the "preacher.") asking me what I wanted to be when I grew up. I remember telling him that I wanted to grow up to be like Papa Timms, my grandfather.   It wasn't until many years later that I learned the backstory to my grandfather's life and discovered that he had made a decision that changed his family legacy.

When my grandfather was barely into his teens, he realized that his parents' lifestyle was not one he could tolerate; so, he collected the few dollars he could get his hands on and walked out the front door of his father's home to start a new life – one that would have no resemblance to the one he was leaving behind. And he did just that! Turning to God as his only source, my grandfather – Harrison "Papa" Timms – eschewed anything that even faintly resembled the environment that he grew up in.

Over his lifetime holiness and righteousness were the non-negotiable standards that he and my grandmother, Carrie "Mama" Timms, set for themselves and their eleven children. As cotton farmers in upstate South Carolina, they worked hard for every penny they were able to bring in and prayed hard for each of those pennies to stretch far enough to feed the family. Yes, working and praying were two things that they were good at!

Papa had a basic education, but Mama was functionally illiterate. She had to leave school at age ten to work in the cotton mill in order to help support her family. In fact, it wasn't until she had reached her sixties and started receiving Social Security that she learned how to write her own name so that she could sign her check each month. Yes, life was hard for them and you could say that all the odds were stacked against them – but they had their two buttresses that saw them through all the hard times: hard work and strong prayers.

In the early 1900s, an unusual phenomenon began to occur around the world. The most well-known manifestation of this phenomenon happened on Azusa Street in Los Angeles, California, but there were similar occurrences happening almost simultaneously around the world: Africa, India, and the backwoods of the Carolinas. This phenomenon was the outpouring of the Holy Ghost (Back then, the term "Holy Spirit" simply wasn't part of anyone's vocabulary; it was always "Holy Ghost.") with all sorts of supernatural manifestations such as healings, speaking in tongues, and people falling under the power of the Holy Ghost. The Pentecostal Movement was birthed from this miraculous outpouring and soon swept across the country and around the world. As soon as the revival flames touched the South Carolina foothills that Mama and Papa Timms called home, this hard-working, strong-praying couple readily embraced it.

Those were the so-called "good old days," when automobiles were a rarity, indoor plumbing was unheard of, electricity in the home was a luxury, and telephones, televisions, and most of what we consider necessities today weren't even dreamed of. These were the days when "central heat" meant a coal-burning potbelly stove

6

in the middle of the room and the most fashionable form of transportation was a horse and carriage. It was into these grim situations that the Holy Spirit fell. And fall He did!

He so mightily overpowered the hungry souls that the stories they left behind are almost unimaginable. Papa and Mama used to tell of times when people would "fall out under the power" and land on the red-hot stove but roll off without a single blister! They would talk about times when people would "swoon" (What we would call today "being slain in the Spirit.") and be in a trance for four or five days. Their family members would have to pick up the affected brothers and sisters, put them on their wagons or buckboards, and carry them home to wait for them to eventually regain consciousness. The heritage that I claim today – the legacy that has shaped my life and the lives my whole family – was birthed out of this fervent move of God in the lives of my grandparents.

Back on the farm, Papa had a pattern of going to the barn to pray every day. Of course, when you have eleven children, there is a certain amount of natural solace to be found in hiding in the barn – even without the supernatural consolation of spending the time with God. His prayer list included his entire brood and all who were to come into the family through marriage and birth. Now, when you start off with eleven children and they all marry and have children of their own, you can imagine how that prayer list must have grown and how much time he got to spend in that barn! But the important thing is that his prayers established a heritage and a legacy that reverberated far beyond that barn in Cheddar, South Carolina. When I was married in 1980, my wife was the one hundredth member to join the family and become a member on Papa's list – even though he had gone on to his spiritual reward years before. I have no estimation on how much more that list has mushroomed in the years since, but I can say that the power of that prayer list has never waned – no matter how many years it has been since Papa has been here to physically call out the names, how many names have been added since his pencil has fallen still, or how many of his descendants don't even know about Papa or his list.

One of Papa's requests was that none of his family would ever die without knowing the Lord – and I can say that, as far as I know, the Lord has honored that request. We have always seen any wayward members come back to the Lord before their deaths. Our family tree has been blessed with an unusual harvest of preachers, Bible teachers, gospel singers, Christian writers, and missionaries. Additionally, even those who did not follow careers in the ministry have made significant contributions in their chosen fields of education and business.

You might have guessed that when Papa and Mama died, they didn't leave behind a fortune to be divvied up among their children. But they left the greatest inheritance that anyone could ever dream of – the godly legacy that prepared the way for us to prosper in this life and enjoy the eternal blessing of the one to come!

Well, that is my heritage on Mother's side of the family tree. Daddy's side was quite different. As nominal Christians, they didn't make church attendance or prayer a central element in their lives. However, I am happy to report that we did see all of Daddy's immediate family come to salvation before they passed into eternity. One of my favorite stories is of my aunt who lived her life with no concern of the gospel but would often say that she intended to get saved someday. She would then add that she wanted to get saved the way they did at "Johnny's church" – referring to Daddy's church. Conversions at the church that she called her home church and that she attended on occasion consisted of simply walking the aisle and shaking the pastor's hand – but not much more, either in emotion or lifestyle change. At our church, on the other hand, we were what you might label as a bunch of Holy Rollers. We jumped, shouted, clapped, and ran around the building. However, contrary to all accusations, we did not swing from the chandeliers – simply because we couldn't afford a chandelier. Had we been able to purchase one I wouldn't put it past some of our members to try to do some aerial acrobatics from it! But there was one other thing about "Johnny's church"; we believed in "praying through." We would cry and repent until we saw life-changing results at the altar. We had the old-fashioned altars – the kind the Wesley brothers would have called "mourners' benches" – where we would come, get down on our knees and seek God until we had a breakthrough. I always thought how appropriate it was that lives were altered at the altars. It was at those altars that we saw many miracles, like the town drunk giving up the bottle and becoming a productive member of the community. It was at those altars where we eventually saw my aunt's errant life miraculously realigned into that of a God-fearing believer. Another of my favorite stories is of a cousin who lived a very wanton life even though she lived right beside a church just like "Johnny's church." For years, she showed absolutely no concern for anything even vaguely resembling godliness until one day she decided to walk across her driveway and into the front door of the church. When she came back out of that door an hour or so later, she was an entirely new person!

Daddy's conversion happened long before I was born. Although he never really talked much about it, I understand it came during a time of revival that swept through our little cotton mill town. The Holy Spirit seemed to invade all the nooks and crannies of our community, miraculously bringing people to their knees in repentance. I've heard stories of home prayer meetings and protracted church meetings in which people were swept into the kingdom, making their "calling and election sure." (II Peter 1:10) Even though I don't know many of the details about that revival, there is one thing that I do know – it produced the most godly man I have ever met – my father.

All that happened in Daddy's family started with him, and for many years, it seemed as if it might also end there; however, he quietly and faithfully continued to pray and believe that he would see his family come to the Lord.

As I said earlier in this chapter, I can only thank God for the handpicked environment into which He allowed me to be born – providing me with the very best of role models to nurture me as I developed through those formative years, a sterling example as I matured through adolescence, and a pattern to look back upon as I grew into maturity.

The other half of the equation was, of course, my mother. She was the pervasive, godly, self-sacrificing influence that nurtured me step-by-step through all the developmental phases of life. As I think back on how her character and love shaped my life, I have to remind myself of Dick Eastman's words about the "remembering" aspect of aging. Before I open the door to so many narratives, let me constrain myself and share just one story that illustrates the kind of influence she was in my life. One night when we were watching television, Mother walked into the den and offered me a glass of orange juice. Even though I had just had a glass a few minutes before, I accepted her offer and drank the juice. It was only after I had finished the glass that I found out that she had gone into the kitchen to get a glass of juice for herself and discovered that there was only one glassful left in the refrigerator. Not knowing that I had already had a drink, she offered the last of the juice to me. It was this kind of generosity and sacrifice that characterized her life and shaped my life every day.

10

I am sure that there were many more times when my parents made decisions that affected the trajectory of my life, but there were two specific occasions that I know were pivotal to my destiny. Both of these events centered around Daddy's decision not to accept relocation offers that could have advanced his career. The first was an offer that came when I was barely old enough to remember the incident. It came just shortly after our family had taken a day trip to Atlanta to visit the zoo. Coming home after being exposed to elephants, monkeys, and all sorts of other exotic species, I learned that my dad had been offered the opportunity to become the plant manager of a factory in the Atlanta area. To my juvenile mind, the only thought at that announcement was an endless safari to the glamorous menagerie that was to me the sum total of Atlanta. You can never imagine how disappointed I was to hear that he had decided not to accept the offer. I know that the decision he had made was basically because he wanted to raise his family in the safe environment of our isolated little burg. I was excited about the much bigger and exciting world beyond our redneck, one-stoplight town, and it was only years, actually decades, later that I realized how such a move to a new environment might have shaped my life. My dad's second relocation opportunity came about the time I was entering adolescence. This time the offer involved a much bigger transition – he was asked to go to Pakistan to become the manager of a factory there. If you think that the allurement of moving to a city with a zoo was something, you can't even begin to imagine how much I craved the opportunity to find out what life would be like in a foreign country! Again, I'm certain that the decision to stay in little Belton, South Carolina, was based on what my dad felt was best for his family. As I look back on the possibilities, I realize that there could have been eternal consequences resulting from such a move. Perhaps the experience of living in a Muslim-dominated environment would have tainted my view of people from other cultures and religions, influencing me into a life far different from the missionary focus that defines me today.

Speaking of other cultures and religions, there is one watershed aspect of my childhood that shaped my interest and eventually directed the course of my life. As I was growing up, I always enjoyed reading the World Book Encyclopedia and National Geographic Magazine. I always took a lot of ribbing about wanting to stay inside and read when I could have been outside playing. Now, don't get me wrong – I did enjoy playing outside, riding bikes, building tree houses and forts in the woods behind our house, and chasing the neighborhood girls out of our backyard – but I also loved to read about other places in the world and about the cultures and religions of the people who lived there. I also loved to watch the "Jungle Book Adventures" on TV every Saturday morning. Hosting the program was a rotund, old fellow. Sitting in his favorite chair, he would reach for a volume of Rudyard Kipling's tales about India – the mystical, mysterious land of elephants, monkeys, tigers, and jungles. How I longed to step through the television screen and find myself seated on top of one of those pachyderms! In my fascination with this wondrous land, I would follow up by reading every word about India and every related topic in the World Book Encyclopedia. As my childish days gave way to maturity, the elephants and monkeys in my mind were replaced with the knowledge of Ganesh, Hanuman, Shiva, Vishnu, Krishna, the caste system, the Atman, confusion, poverty, and despair.

It wasn't until I was an adult that I realized that all that reading was God's way of preparing me for a lifetime of cross-cultural missionary work around the world. I believe that God preordained a path for my life and designed my temperament and interests so that I would be perfectly fitted for the job. He gave me an interest in the world so that I could go to His disciples around the globe and encourage them in their faith. As my understanding of what life is really about matured, I realized that what God had placed in my heart as a young child was not just simple wanderlust to see the world of Jungle Book, but a desire that matched the desire of His own heart – that all the world should know His Son Jesus.

The Holy Spirit began to confirm my inner thoughts through prophetic words, sometimes from total strangers who had no way of knowing what was inside my heart and sometimes by Christian leaders whom I greatly respected and trusted, but all proclaimed the same thing: a global ministry. There were also dreams that widened my vision beyond *Jungle Book* as I saw myself ministering to people of all different colors, dressed in their native attire, from all over the world. Still, any actual participation on my part seemed less likely than my crawling through the television tube to join the "Jungle Book Adventures."

Speaking of becoming a missionary, I actually became a missionary when I was only a grade schooler. One Sunday, a missionary showed pictures of the destitute people he ministered to in India. When I saw those grainy black-and-white photos projected on the screen, I couldn't help but respond by pledging fifty cents out of my one-dollar allowance. The funny thing is that the next Sunday the pastor announced that the missions pledges in that service had topped anything in the history of the church. Of course, I was convinced that it was my half dollar a month that made the difference and it wasn't until years later that I understood better. The truth of the matter was that although my offering certainly wasn't what pushed the congregation over the top, it certainly did push my destiny much closer to the trajectory God was moving me toward. As a youngster, I didn't have the slightest concept that my offering was a seed that would bring forth a harvest – and I definitely had no idea what kind of harvest that it could bring. I doubt that I ever saw any monetary return on that half-a-buck seed, but now I can look back over the more than forty years of ministry in more than sixty nations of the world and marvel at the harvest that has come from that small "mustard seed."

Well, forgive me for getting a bit ahead of myself, I do need to back up at this point and return to the beginning of my story. Not only was I born at an early age, I almost died at an early age. But before we go there, let me make one more comment about the influence of my mother. Of course, it goes without saying that I wouldn't be here without my mother. After all, that's the way we all get here. However, there is even more significance to that statement than might be the case with everyone else. My only sibling is a sister who is six years older than me – but that is not the way Mother wanted things to be. She had hoped for another baby almost as soon as the first one was weaned – but she was disappointed month after month when she realized that her period had passed and nothing had happened. Eventually, she became so desperate that she prayed the prayer that Hannah of the Old Testament had used as she implored God for a baby, "If You will give me another child, I will give him back to You all the days of his life." (I Samuel 1:11) Her prayer was answered and the next month, she realized that she was pregnant with me. So, the truth is that I essentially had no choice in the matter, my destiny was already spoken before I was even born – in fact, before I was even conceived!

But back to almost dying at an early age. My first close encounter with the Grim Reaper was when I was still a baby in my mother's arms. Of course, all I know about that is what my mother has told me. It seems we were driving through the cemetery – an ideal place to face the harbinger of death. But the story is not quite as macabre as it may sound. I think that my parents were visiting a new cemetery that was being opened. Well, anyway, the story goes that I reached up and grabbed the door handle. These were the days before baby seats and seat belts; so, I was sitting in my mother's lap. When the door swung open, I went with it and tumbled out of the car, landing underneath the moving vehicle. Thank the Lord, we were in that cemetery. Had we been on a public street, my father would have been going faster than the ten miles an hour he was driving as we toured the grounds. When the car came to a stop, my mother leapt out to find me in the direct path of the on-coming back tire. I was only an inch from certain death.

My next brush with death has a bit more detail to it. "Help! Help! Help!" I cried. I was drowning and there were no two ways about it. This was my last minute in the land of the living. My parents had taken the family on a Saturday afternoon outing to Broadway Creek. After a picnic of sandwiches, my cousins, sister, and I went for a dip in the swimming hole. There was a place where the water ran over some smooth rocks into a small pool, and we set out to enjoy sliding over the rock and splashing into the water. However, I was really plagued by the warning that I had learned in school that you should never swim within the first two hours after a meal. My teacher had warned that we "would get cramps and drown." Tormented by the idea of the cramps, I reluctantly forced my six-year-old body into the creek to join the older children who seemed to be having so much fun. I couldn't understand the reckless abandon with which my parents had sentenced us to death by the cramps, yet I waded into the water. On my first tumble across the tiny falls, I found that the water in the pond below was almost at the same level as my nose. Even though my eyes were above water, my nose was below the waterline, and I was certain that this was the opportunity for the dreaded cramps to drag me to my death. Instantly, I remembered another bit of information that I had picked up at some time before as I had listened in on the Sunday afternoon conversations between my uncles at my grandmother's house. For some reason, all the aunts and uncles would always gather at my grandmother's house every Sunday afternoon. The men would congregate and talk while the women went another direction and had their own conversations. It was one summer afternoon under the pecan tree when I heard my Uncle Herman say something about someone going down for "the third time." I asked what he meant. My Uncle John explained that a drowning man comes to the surface three times and if he goes down after that, he will drown. That afternoon in Broadway Creek, I began to frantically count my three opportunities to be rescued. Once, twice, and the third time, I stood on my tiptoes to get my nose and mouth above the water line. Screaming for help, I knew that the grasp of death was tightening about me. If I had only known Jesus' words about the "broad way" that leads to destruction (Mathew 7:13), I would have been even more terrified. My father was calling to me to start walking so that I could reach the shallow part of the swimming hole, but I couldn't respond as the fear of my third submersion gripped me. Finally, my sister took my hand and walked me out of the water.

Well, enough death talk; let's get back to some more lively stories. Other than the grace of God being manifested upon my life, I can't explain how I became the recipient of so many good things as I grew up. One really unusual example was the year that I served as the junior ringmaster of the Ringling Brothers, Barnum and Bailey Circus when it came to town. A popular children's television program sponsored a contest in which children were invited to send in their photographs in hopes of being the one that would be chosen to ride into the arena with the circus parade of clowns, elephants, and performers and to stand with the ringmaster as he welcomed the ladies, gentlemen, and children of all ages to the greatest show on earth. A little black-and-white photo and a postage stamp is all I invested, but the return was the thrill of a lifetime and a memory that could never be erased from a little boy's mind. But that wasn't the only contest I happened to win. As a grade schooler, I ran across an ad in our local paper for a nationwide writing contest. There was a simple picture and contestants were invited to write a short story inspired by the drawing. Much to my amazement, I won first place in the nation.

The special privileges continued to fall into my lap: serving as school safety patrol (This special honor allowed me the privilege of wearing a policeman-like hat, badge, and vest as I helped the other students cross the school driveway when the buses arrived at the door), serving as a lab instructor in the chemistry lab (This position warranted the privilege of wearing a white lab coat and walking around the lab drinking coffee that I had made in a Pyrex beaker over a Bunsen burner. I didn't even like coffee, but it was part of the role), representing my school at the state science fair (This special privilege even earned me a write-up in the local newspaper.), and even being a part of the high school Quiz Team that appeared in competition on the local television station (This was a bittersweet match in which I only partially helped in the final elimination round when I was asked where the NASA Mission Control Center was located. I answered, "Texas," even though all my team members were trying to convince me to say, "Cape Canaveral, Florida." Since this was long before the Apollo 13 mission made the line, "Houston, we have a problem," a common expression, I had no idea what city in Texas I should answer when the quizmaster asked me to be more specific and give the city name as well as the state). I was even chosen to represent our local area on a tour of the United Nations headquarters in New York City – including behind-the-scenes tours and interviews with top officials – as part of a student program sponsored by the Independent Order of Odd Fellows. I was also listed in the *Who's Who of American High School Students* – an honor that I also later received as a professional educator. Looking back on all these honors and privileges, I understand that each one was simply another step that the Lord was leading me through to prepare me for a ministry that would require me to stand up in public, take a leadership role, and even put pen to paper to communicate the gospel. Of course, I do have to admit that those were some exciting and fun lessons!

The Adventures of Indiana Shirley

I've introduced you to the godly heritage of my family, but I also need to present another aspect of my family heritage to explain another peculiarity of my DNA. I suppose that every family has at least one or two characters that stand out from the crowd. In my family the most obvious one was my fifth cousin on my father's side, Manse Jolly. Manse was a rebel who refused to surrender when the rest of the Confederate States bowed their knees before General Ulysses S. Grant. He continued to wage his own private war against the Union occupation forces for several years after the war had officially ended. I must admit that I'm rather proud of a man with the spirit it takes to stage one-man raids on an entire army encampment, as my cousin Manse was known to do. With a six-shooter in each hand, he would come raging through the Union camp, blasting everything in sight, and gallop away into the thicket before the startled soldiers could retaliate. With his gun handles notched to keep score of the Union soldiers he had felled, Manse was the terror of the South Carolina foothills. As a fitting conclusion to his story, Manse was swept off his trusty steed by a swollen river at flood stage. Only the rawest of nature's forces could subdue the man that no Union officer or enlisted man could stop.

On my mother's side of my family, we had another newsworthy individual. This cousin engineered one of the most dramatic jailbreaks in history. While incarcerated in the South Carolina State Penitentiary, he convinced his girlfriend to highjack a helicopter and commandeer it to land in the exercise yard of the prison. Before the guards knew what was happening, he raced to the aircraft and disappeared from custody. For several days, it seemed that the whole world was talking about my cousin as he remained on the lam.

This stranger-than-fiction episode eventually became the subject of a made-for-TV movie.

Of course, I wouldn't want to neglect my great-uncle Bramlett who was a real-life hobo. Now, you have to understand exactly what you are talking about when you mention the term "hobo." It doesn't simply mean a tramp or a derelict. It means an adventurer – an adventurer with no money – but an adventurer nonetheless. Uncle Bramlett was the kind of man who heard that there was something to see or do in California or Texas and decided to go check it out. But in the Great Depression, there was no way for him to be able to travel, so he hit the rails. Riding the rails meant finding an empty boxcar and "hitchhiking" to wherever the train was headed. Sometimes it meant even climbing under the box car and hanging on to braking system bars to provide a dangerous, but free, ride to the next stop. Somehow, he always managed to make it back home with the tallest tales to tell about far-away places and unheard of things.

Adventurers! That's what Bramlett was; so were Manse and the cousin with the helicopter, and thank God, that same adventuresome spirit found its way into my bloodstream as well. After all, I became a certified hang glider as soon as the sport was invented. I rafted the New River the same day that Congress declared it a national wild river. I went zip lining across a deep gorge in Nepal long before there actually was such a thing as a zip line. (The locals developed this ingenious technique for getting across the rivers and gorges long before Americans thought of it as recreation. I'll always remember my wife standing on the edge of the gorge yelling that she was going to divorce me if I died while trying it!) I've ridden elephants and camels. I've watched blood sacrifices at Hindu temples and human cremations on the gats along the sacred rivers of India and Nepal. I've swum with dolphins and sharks. I've climbed the

Great Pyramid of Egypt and Australia's famed Ayer's Rock. I've slept everywhere from a two-bit hotel (Literally – I paid twenty-five cents a night for a bed with sheets so greasy that I'm certain they hadn't been washed in forever.) to a maharajah's palace and I've explored the planet from top (Mt. Everest) to bottom (the Dead Sea). I've found myself in some rather precarious situations; such as the day that I awoke in Philippines to find that the region was under martial law due to nearby terrorist attacks during the night and the time in Nigeria that, because of rampant insurgent activities, my car was stopped by military roadblocks every few blocks. I've hiked far up the river bank in Nepal to a clandestine location to baptize new converts so they wouldn't be seen and turned in to the local officials for arrest.

God orchestrated an elaborate tapestry of individuals and circumstances so that He could mold my life for His specific purposes. So, let's talk a little about the adventuresome side of the character that God built into me. I have titled this chapter "The Adventures of Indiana Shirley" after a nickname that I picked up because I was living in Indiana at the time that Harrison Ford portrayed the iconic Indiana Jones – even though many of my Indiana Jones-like adventures happened long before I moved to the state.

When I was in college and seminary, I made a deliberate effort to get summer jobs in different parts of the country. I wanted to experience a lot of different places so that I could decide where I would eventually like to live and work. I spent one summer in Virginia, one in Delaware, and two in Yosemite National Park in California. The summer in Virginia gave me a great opportunity to explore many of the historical heritage sites, such as Colonial Williamsburg, where our nation was birthed and where our national heritage was molded. The summer in Delaware allowed me to spend weekends in Washington, DC, exploring all the monuments surrounding the National Mall plus every level and every wing of every museum in the Smithsonian Institute. I also made other excursions to interesting places like the Liberty Bell and Independence Hall in Philadelphia. My time in California not only allowed me to explore the grandeur of God's creation displayed in Yosemite – giant sequoia trees that dated back to the biblical times, majestic waterfalls, and awe-inspiring rock formations – but also take four cross-country road trips which literally went from coast to coast (the Carolinas to California), taking me to the Grand Canyon, Yellowstone, Monument Valley, the Petrified Forest, Crater Lake, and too many other natural wonders to enumerate here. But more importantly, each venture included some amazing adventures with the Lord.

I arrived in Wilmington, Delaware, on a Saturday, ready to start work the following Monday. The first thing that I did was to check out the phonebook for the addresses of the local churches so I could attend service the following morning. One particular church name seemed to leap off the page at me. Granted, it was printed in bold black type, but there did seem to be something more than just the dark ink that made it stand out. So, the next morning I found my way to the church and located the Sunday school class for the college-aged young adults. When I introduced myself to the teachers, a pleasant middle-aged couple, I mentioned that I had just arrived in town the previous evening. Immediately, the two looked at one another knowingly and then turned back to me and asked where I was staying. I told them that I hadn't found a place yet but would be looking for a rooming house for the summer. They then explained that they had a spare room that they had been renting out to a young man who had just moved out the week before. They went on to say that they had not planned to rent it out again but that it could be mine for the summer if I wished. That incident reminded me of a statement by the great German theologian Karl Barth, "When God is ready to speak and you are ready to hear, He can speak through a phonebook"!

Another powerful thing that happened that summer had to do with miraculous protection. My mother rescued me from the snare of the trap just as the spring was tripped and the jaws were ready to devour me. But the miracle of this story is that she was hundreds of miles away. I was driving from Washington, DC, back to Wilmington, Delaware. in "rush hour" traffic one Friday afternoon when I found myself in bumper-to-bumper traffic racing along at nearly sixty miles per hour. As the flow of traffic moved from the open terrain into the vicinity of Baltimore, Maryland, we suddenly encountered the congestion caused by major city traffic trying to merge into the freeway as they too joined the urban exodus for the summer weekend. Suddenly, the massive congestion brought us to a total standstill. Within seconds, our breakneck pace was brought to an idle – except for the car behind me, whose driver seemed to be oblivious to the traffic jam. Still charging forward at excessive speed, the car plowed into my little burgundy Mustang. My car was slammed into the car ahead of me which, in tum, smashed into one in front of it. Sustaining the full impact of this four-car collision, my little sports car was instantly transformed into a giant metal accordion. I had to climb out the window to escape my prison of twisted metal and shattered glass. Through it all, I came out with only one minor injury – a cut under my chin that required five small stitches. But how did my mother figure into this rescue? Far away, in South Carolina, she suddenly was impressed to pray for me at the exact time of the accident! This was the operation of one of the gifts of the Holy Spirit called the word of knowledge.

When I left North Carolina to drive to California to report to my position as summer intern to the chaplain at Yosemite National Park, I knew that it was just about time to buy new tires for my car. But I felt that the tread on the old tires would last a couple thousand more miles – perhaps even to California. I drove halfway across the continent and into Mexico. Then I turned north and headed for Yellowstone National Park. The tread grew thinner and thinner and my hopes of making it to California on those tires grew less and less. Through all of Arizona and Utah I traveled over poorly paved roads, up and down steep mountain roads and across deserts. On many occasions, I drove for hours without meeting another car – on two tires that were practically bald and the other two not much better. Happily, I had no trouble whatsoever with the tires. However, at the very top of a rugged mountain in Arches National Park, the car "blew its top" – a radiator hose burst. But just as the Lord does things, I was at a campground – just a few feet from a water faucet and just next to the campsite of a man who had tape for patching radiator hoses! I did a temporary patch-up job on the hose and drove to the nearest service station where I had the hose replaced. The next morning, I noticed that another radiator hose was leaking. However, since it was Sunday, there were no stations open. A little more of the patch-up tape kept the hose intact until I reached Salt Lake City. I pulled into the first open service station and just as if it had been planned – and I'm sure it had! – the station was having a tire sale! So, I bought new tires and had the oil changed, since it was exactly six thousand miles since I had last changed the six-thousand-mile oil in the car. But the story doesn't end there. While I was still in the station, a lady came in wanting to buy a pair of used tires. She explained that she couldn't buy a new set right then because her husband was in the hospital critically ill. She had had a blow out on the freeway and needed a replacement for the blown tire and a spare. The attendant told her that they didn't usually carry used tires, but asked her what size she needed. She needed my old tires. So, he sold her the two that still had a little tread. But wait! I still haven't come to the best part. All those coincidences were leading up to the big miracle in the story. Just a few hours after I left the service station, I ran into heavy snows in the mountains of Idaho and Wyoming. There were warnings along the road advising only cars with chains or snow tires to proceed. The Lord had arranged that even though I had only bought regular highway tires and not snow tires, my treads were still like new when I entered the hazardous area! The God we serve sees the end from the beginning and everything in between. He worked out all the details of this trip.

My time in Yosemite was filled with lots of exciting spiritual adventures. One had to do with the bartender in the hotel where I worked. Stu came to know the Lord through a series of what seemed to be accidents and coincidences. When Stu went to visit an old friend who had recently become a Christian, he walked into the house to find his friend listening to a tape on deliverance from demon possession. Rather than turning off the tape, Stu's friend invited him to sit down and listen. Well, to me that was a big mistake; I thought only a strong Christian should study about demons. But, I guess God disagreed! At any rate, they heard the tape to the end. At the end of the tape was a prayer for all demons to be cast out. Just when the name of Jesus was mentioned, the whole house began to shake. The floors moved. The walls rocked. The light swung back and forth. Pots and pans rattled. And Stu repented! Well, it turned out that it wasn't demons leaving the house – it was the first in a series of earthquakes and tremors that hit northern California that summer! Stu claims that it was all planned by God to bring him to Himself.

In addition to all the adventures that I had hiking, rock climbing, rafting, and just exploring, I also got a lot of pleasure out of the wildlife in the park – especially the bears. One of my friends had hiked up to the top of

Nevada Falls and found a quiet place to stretch out for a nap on a large flat rock. After coating herself with a nice thick layer of cocoa butter sun lotion, she reclined for a rest and suntan. About half an hour later, she was awakened by the feeling of a wet Brillo pad rubbing across her face. Trying to not panic, she cautiously opened her eyes to find a big brown bear making a midafternoon treat of her sun tan lotion. Knowing not to startle the beast, she lay there "playing dead" until the monster had licked her clean of the cocoa butter and then lumbered off into the woods. We were constantly having tourists come to report bear damage to their cars, campers, ice coolers, or tents. Many times, they would want to call the insurance company to file a claim. The pat answer from the adjuster was that such damage was excluded from their policies under the "Acts of God" clause. One special story has to do with when the bears were especially active in raiding the cabins that I was in charge of renting out to the park guests. It seemed that the bears were just a step or two ahead of me and were breaking into the cabins a little faster than I could rent them out. Because the maintenance crew had to get into each unit to clean them and repair the damages before I could check new people into them, the guests were beginning to line up in the lobby waiting to be assigned rooms. Eventually, a crowd filled the lobby and began to spill out the front door of the lodge. As I worked through the throngs and around the problems, one lady caught me off guard when she questioned, "How do you do that?" Almost ready to explain the registration and room assignment system to her I asked, "Do what?" "Keep smiling during all this work and confusion," came her reply. Before I had time to think of a response, my mouth spoke up, "It's the fruit of the Holy Spirit. You see, when Jesus is in control of your life, you have love, joy, and peace." I then directed her to read Galatians and handed her a room key.

One other adventure had to do with a cross-country road trip that a college buddy and I did one summer. We left North Carolina, drove to the Grand Canyon, then crossed into Mexico, circled back through New Orleans, and finally found our way back home – basically in one piece. The highlight of that trip was our once-in-a-lifetime privilege of rafting the Colorado River through the Grand Canyon. We experienced the Grand Canyon from every possible perspective by flying into the canyon on a single-engine plane, rafting through the heart of the canyon on an inflated raft, and then hiking out on foot. There were about a dozen people in our party on the actual rafting expedition. We had only one thing in common – the desire to participate in this epic adventure. We were all strangers to one another prior to the trip and had simply joined forces by booking the same dates with the river guide. It was a several-day adventure in which we ran the rapids during the day and camped out under the stars at night – giving us a real opportunity to become well acquainted. One evening as we were sitting around the campfire after cooking our supper on the open flames, one of the team looked out at the gigantic rock formations towering nearly a mile above us on the river bank and began to muse about the millions of years that it had taken the river to cut its path through the solid rock. As soon as he finished his "scientific" discourse, another member of the group began to poetically describe all the impressions that she as an artist had been experiencing as she marveled at the beauty of the monoliths. Finally, I decided to take a turn and began to reference the Bible, speaking of the intricacy of God's handiwork in nature.

There were a number of other notable events on that trip – some funny, some scary, and some spiritual. Andy, my traveling companion, especially enjoyed our trip into Mexico – along the Pacific coast as far as Mazatlán, then inland to Mexico City where we climbed the Pyramid to the Sun and the Pyramid to the Moon, and then back through the heart of the country to reenter the US in Texas. The thing that especially excited Andy was that there were no traffic laws in the country; therefore, he could drive as fast as he wished and he could pass on the curvy mountain roads – even if there were double yellow lines down the middle of the road! Although this was a fun and liberating experience, I still felt impressed to point out all the crosses that were planted along the side of the highway. Somehow, I was never able to convince him that these crosses were memorials to individuals who had lost their lives on that stretch of highway. Well, we eventually made it back into the States, crossing the border late in the evening. Wanting to get to our next destination early enough the following day to have plenty of time to explore, we decided to drive through the night. When it was Andy's turn at the wheel, he seemed to still have some of the Mexican racecar driver blood racing (pun intended) in his veins. When I mentioned that we were back in the USA, where the speed limits were enforced, he responded with, "Yes, but it is the middle of the night, and there is no other traffic." Pretty soon, we saw some flashing red and blue lights approaching from behind us; so, we pulled to the side of the road. It just so happened that there were actually two cars that were speeding along the interstate at that moment, and both of us were being apprehended. When the patrolman stepped out of the car to give a citation to the other driver, Andy said, "Oh, he's ticketing the other guy," and pulled back onto the road. Looking out the back window, I could see the patrolman jumping up and down in the middle of the highway, frantically waving both his arms in the air. I'm certain that I didn't have another calm breath until we crossed the border into the next state. I told you that I had some of my jailbreak cousin's DNA, but actually I think that it was my buddy Andy who really had a serious dose.

28

But there was one really inspirational moment on that trip. We had stopped in some backwoods crossroads in the middle of nowhere for dinner and after enjoying a fairly tasty meal were ready to get back on the road. However, we kept waiting and waiting for our waitress to bring us our ticket so we could pay and get on with our trip. When it seemed that she was never going to come, I finally got up and found her to ask for the check. Her reply was that our dinners had already been paid for. Another customer had noticed us pray over our meal before we ate and was so impressed that a couple college-age boys would pray, especially in public, that he had taken care of our bill.

In a future chapter, as I start talking about the mission work that takes me all over the planet, we will explore some exotic places around the world but, if you'll pardon my getting out of sequence here, there are a few more stories that beg to be included in this "Indiana Shirley" chapter.

Having logged well over a million miles of air travel, you can imagine that I've experienced some interesting things in the air. My wife Peggy and I were boarding a plane for a transatlantic flight when she noticed the man in the seat next to the one assigned to her. He was unshaven and looked rather disheveled in a baseball cap and an extremely wrinkled shirt. She turned to me quietly and said, "You're sitting in the middle today!" As we got to know one another, I asked where he lived. He said that he lived between Detroit and Washington, DC. Well, that's quite a distance, so I asked him exactly what he meant. His reply was that he had two homes – one in each city because he was on the faculty at a major university in each of the cities. When he mentioned the neighborhoods where they were located, I realized that these were some of the really upscale sections of the cities. It turned out that he was one of the leading radiologists in the world and was both a medical doctor and a professor of radiation physics, expert in both the medical and physical factors of radiology. I never did figure out exactly why he was so unkempt when he boarded the plane, but I did learn that he was on his way to Europe to address a convention of radiologists. When I told him that I was a Bible college teacher, he began to ask questions about the Bible that gave me a wide-open door to share the gospel with him.

I was once seated in one of the very back seats of the plane on a transatlantic flight when one of the passengers had a heart attack. In order to give him the necessary medical care, the flight attendants brought him to the back of the plane and created a little bed for him on the floor in the galley. For the next several hours, the area around me was a beehive of activity as the attendants and all the nurses and doctors on the flight hovered around the ailing man. On another flight, before the imposition of the three-ounce limit on carry-on liquids, an already inebriated passenger started to open up a bottle of duty-free liquor that he had brought onboard. There was a heated altercation between him and the flight attendant, and it took numerous threats of arrest before the passenger would relinquish his bottle. That instance was just one passenger. Multiply that by about a hundred to get an idea of the commotion that occurred on a delayed flight into Haiti. Haitians in general are already known for having rather volatile emotions but, since these passengers were from a more privileged class, they felt that they could boss the airline employees around like they were accustomed to doing when dealing with other Haitians from lower classes of society. Needless to say, the departure gate became the scene of a very boisterous protest — essentially, a mini-riot. When we finally did get to board the plane, there was a further delay, and the disturbed passengers refused to take their seats while they passed around a notebook to collect names on a petition to have airline personnel fired and the ticket money refunded. When it was decided that the plane could not fly that day due to its need for maintenance, the protest escalated into somewhat of a sit-in as these angry passengers refused to exit the plane.

On a flight out of London to South Africa, I could see a lot of smoke out the window. When one of the flight attendants stationed himself at the window and got on the phone with the cockpit, I knew that something serious was up. It turned out that we had lost an engine. On one flight back into the States after a mission trip to the Dominican Republic, our plane had to suddenly abort its landing because of winds that would have blown it off course as it approached the runway. On another flight into the Philippines, our plane had to ditch its landing dramatically at the last second as the pilot realized that he had missed the landing strip. The plane was filled with screeches and gasps as the aircraft suddenly took back into the air rather than touching the ground and jolted the passengers about in their seats.

On such days, although I know that it is totally out of context, I claim the promise of Psalm 55: 4-6, "My heart is sore pained within me...Fearfulness and trembling are come upon me, and horror hath overwhelmed me...Oh that I had wings like a dove! for then would I fly away, and be at rest."

One incident that I found comical was a flight out of the island of St. Thomas. The passenger in front of me in the check-in line was complaining about the fact that there was a thirty-minute delay. As we were taxiing down the tarmac in preparation for takeoff, the plane in front of us made too wide a turn as it approached the runway and ran into the grass. Of course, emergency vehicles had to be brought in, the passengers had to be deplaned, and a tow truck had to pull the aircraft back onto the pavement. The whole process took several hours. The one thing that kept me from being frustrated by the delay was my constant musing on what was going on in the mind of the man who had been so upset about our original half-hour postponement.

It was graduation day in June, 1977, and all my classmates and I were waiting to enter Binkley Chapel at Southeastern Baptist Theological Seminary to receive our degrees, wondering – as we were about to go our separate ways – in what strange ways and places God would bring some of us together again. I was talking quietly with Santana Krishnan, a student from India, when he looked at me and said, "When you come to India, I want you to preach at my church!" Prophecy? I was not sure, but as the processional sounded and we started into the chapel, a new excitement stirred in my heart: India!

Not long afterward, I received a letter from a stranger in some foreign country that I had never even heard of before – Sri Lanka. It was only the picture of the country on the postage stamp that gave me a clue that it was the island that I knew of as Ceylon, a country whose pavilion I had visited at the New York World's Fair when I was a fifth-grader in 1965. I remembered seeing the many elaborate exhibits and learning the country was totally dedicated to Buddhism. It turned out that the letter was from a college student who had been born again in this non-Christian environment and had reached out to every Christian organization he could find in hopes of getting materials to help him grow in his faith. One of the ministers he had contacted was my friend Nicky Cruz, the former New York City gang leader whose story was made famous through David Wilkerson's *The Cross and the Switchblade*. When Nicky saw that the letter came from a college student, he wrote back telling him about my ministry among college students. The result was the mysterious letter from the far away island nation of Sri Lanka.

My first mission trip was to Japan, and that's a story all its own which I'll share later. By the time that I was to take my second mission trip, I was ready to take up my invitations to go to India and Sri Lanka – making it into a pretty extensive trip. However, it just so happened that Pan American World Airways offered a special promotional offer right at the time that I was looking at making plans for the trip. What they titled the "Around the World in Eighty Days Fare" allowed the traveler to go anywhere in the world on as many flights as he wished as long as he didn't backtrack and as long as he returned to his starting point within eighty days. This was ideal for me since I could go everywhere I needed to go plus a few extra stops at places that I wanted to visit all for just $999! It looked as if God were making the way, but I still had to have the money. Even at the reduced rates, the trip would wipe out my account that I had been saving for a car. I needed confirmation. As the odometer in my car clicked over to 144,000 miles, I thought about the 144,000 saints in the book of Revelation. Surely, if God stopped counting saints at 144000, I could stop counting miles. Even though the rattles and faulty transmission told me it was time to buy the new car I had been saving for, my heart wanted to use the money for tickets to Japan, India, and Sri Lanka. My mind was in a whirl. I spent Easter break from school checking out new cars. But when I picked up my accumulated mail, there on top of the stack was *Decision Magazine.* "That's what I need right now," I thought, "another decision to make!" Well, the feature article in the magazine was about Billy Graham's recent trip to India. In one of the other articles was the statement, "The major problem with American finances is buying new cars." That did it! *Decision* helped me make my decision. The next day I went to the travel agency to start making arrangements.

Let me remind you that this was in the 1970s – long before the computer age. Back then, there was no information superhighway and airline arrangements were not made over the internet; therefore, I had to go to a brick-and-mortar travel office and talk to a flesh-and-blood travel agent. When I walked into the office, a young lady greeted me rather rudely, "And what do you want?" Since I was just a twenty-something young guy, I assume that she thought I was just going to buy a bus ticket to the next county and that the commission she would make off of my business wasn't worth her time. When I told her that I wanted an around-the-world airline ticket, she became a bit more cordial; however, her rude attitude came back when I began to spell out my itinerary and she asked why I was going to all those places. My response that I was doing missionary work drew out her retaliation, "Well, I hope you're not going there to Christianize them. Their Buddhist and Hindu cultures are beautiful." I responded that I was going to alter their culture and that she should talk to Ted Turner – who was the media mogul of the day – if she were concerned about that. Eventually, she became a little more pleasant to work with and we finalized an itinerary that would send me off around the world on an adventure with Jesus.

Then I shot off a letter to Santana in Madras, India. That's when the trouble really started: ten weeks of cancellations, rescheduling, unanswered letters, and blind alleys. At the end of that time, when I still had not had any response from India, I began to wonder if I had really heard the Lord's voice. I wondered if I would arrive in India with no one to meet me at the airport. I was not prepared to face all that poverty, disease, and starvation alone. But I took the step of faith and kept making preparations. Then the day came, and I boarded the plane.

My first stop was in England where I visited the prehistoric pagan shrine Stonehenge on June 21, the only day of the year that the British government grants permission for people to go inside the fence surrounding the monoliths. The sun-worship cults demanded their religious rights and convinced the government to open the gates on this one day so they could do their ceremonies on this particular day when the sun rises over the central altar. As I was touring the site, one of the sun worshipers stood up and began threatening our group because he felt that we were desecrating the sun worshiper's event by talking. One of the guys in our group – a huge hunk of a man – walked around to the man making all the threats and started cracking his knuckles as if he were ready for a fight. The sun worshiper whimpered and went back to his devilish chants trying to pretend that we weren't there. Our "hero" never had to do anything physical to anybody. He just walked toward our opponent and stood there. His massive presence demonstrated that he was in authority. When he cracked his knuckles, he sent out such a strong message that the challenger simply left us alone. The sun worshiper knew that he had met more than his match. Standing there in the middle of Stonehenge, I got a revelation of what the Apostle Paul meant when he wrote in the sixth chapter of Ephesians that if we had on the armor of God we would be able to stand against all the wiles of the enemy and be able to quench every fiery dart that he would hurl at us.

My next stop was in India. As I flew into New Delhi Airport, my fears mounted. I now had to leave the safety of the plane and face whatever was "out there." Sure enough, the heat and humidity, even at two o'clock in the morning, were unbearable. This international airport was nothing more than a warehouse with a ceiling fan that sluggishly churned up the heavy air. Three-inch roaches scampered happily across the floor. There was even a deranged man who was naked from the waist down walking freely around in the terminal. The customs check was followed by a five-hour wait for the flight to southern India where I reluctantly deplaned again, this time in Madras. I could identify with Saint Thomas, patron saint of the city; I too was a doubter! I actually feared the unknown!

If you don't mind, let's take a little detour here so I can tell you about my friend, Santana. He had been a professor of linguistics at the University of Madras when Voice of America radio recruited him to come to America as their official spokesman for India. Since he spoke almost all the major languages of the country, he was the ideal candidate for the position since he could do the broadcasts in all the languages rather than needing several people who spoke only one language each. But his linguistic skills were not the most interesting aspect of this unique man. He was a Hindu married to a Pentecostal woman. You have to understand that in India, there are very strict rules and customs that keep people segregated into their social groups. Pentecostals don't marry Baptists – much less, Hindus. His was a unique situation to say the least. Upon coming to the US, he began to attend a Presbyterian church, where he accepted Christ. Then, he felt called into the ministry; so he enrolled in the Baptist seminary that I also attended, where he received the baptism in the Holy Spirit. Upon graduation, he was invited by the Church of South India to move back to India to become the director of their evangelism department. Things can't get more unusual than that: a Hindu man with a Pentecostal wife getting born again in a Presbyterian church and educated in a Baptist seminary where he became a charismatic in order to take a leadership role in the Church of South India. His position as the director of the evangelism department gave him oversight of all the church planters, evangelists, and nation missionaries for the denomination, and he knew that there was one thing that was necessary for them all if they were to be successful in their assignments – to be filled with the Holy Spirit. As part of his plan to accomplish that, he invited me to come to

Madras to speak on the topic at a conference for all the ministers on his staff.

Now, let's go back to the fact that Santana did not meet me in the airport. This incident happened in the 1970s – a couple decades before email or even fax. There were only two ways to communicate between the US and India – telephone and "snail mail." The telephone system at that time in history went through transatlantic cables under the ocean with one cable between New York and London and a second one between London and Bombay. It was a major accomplishment to find a time when both cables were free at the same time so that a call could be patched through both lines at the same time. I remember one time when I missed a flight when coming home from India and had to negotiate for almost twenty-four hours before getting a connection to tell the people at home that I would not be on the flight. Of course, if you don't have a phone number, it doesn't matter how complicated the phone connections were – and this was the case for me. Santana had recently moved back to India and did not have a phone number to give me. Therefore, the only way I could communicate with him was through the postal system – and it took two weeks to get a letter from the US to India. That's where the problem arose – after I booked my ticket and sent Santana the itinerary, the airline changed their flight schedule and there wasn't sufficient time for my last-minute letter with the new schedule to get to him in Madras. Therefore, I arrived at the airport with hope but no real assurance that he knew about the change and would be there to collect me. In the humble excuse for a terminal, I searched every face for the slightest indication that someone knew about me or at least cared that I was there.

Someone did! A baggage porter rushed up to help me with my bags. Begging for a few rupees, he insisted that I give him my suitcase to carry. As I clenched the handles of my luggage, I kept insisting that I didn't have any place for him to take the bags and there was no need for his services. Eventually, I realized that there was no hope of being picked up; so, I asked the porter if he could arrange hotel accommodations and a bus to the hotel. With my head still spinning, I soon found myself bumping down the road to a hotel in downtown Madras. As we rumbled through the streets of Madras, I got my first glimpse of that mysterious and mystifying world of India, including images that will never fade from my mind: cows in the middle of the traffic, people bathing on the side of the road, and a beggar dipping water from a pothole in the middle of the street. One accident and two fistfights later, the driver deposited me at my destination. It was about two o'clock in the afternoon by the time I arrived at the hotel – twelve hours after I first set foot in India.

My stay in this hotel turned out to be a miracle in a number of ways. First, it was the answer to a prayer that one of my friends had prayed over me before I left the US. In fact, I had almost laughed in his face as he prayed for me to find all the "conveniences and amenities" I would need while on the trip. I thought, "Surely, there was a time when India was a glittering jewel in the Far East, but today she has lost her luster." I could only imagine her as a great, gaping wound, filled with millions of starving, diseased beings who somehow had been deprived of their humanity. I had heard countless stories of the people living, eating, sleeping and dying in the streets. I could fill a volume with pictures of starving children in India which had been sent to me by charitable organizations asking for money. So, as my friend prayed that in India I would find "conveniences and amenities" to make my visit as a missionary pleasant and profitable, my mind was filled with vivid scenes of flies swarming over food arid dunghills. But in this little hotel, the Lord liberally answered my friend's prayer for "amenities in India."

Even though I was paying only a few dollars per night, the hotel was one of the most deluxe properties I'd ever seen. It had the elegance of any hotel property in the US but here, in the land where I expected utter poverty, I found dinner on a silver platter for less than two dollars. Exhausted from the long flight, the torturous ordeals in both airports, and jet lag, I decided to go straight to bed. Unfortunately, my rest lasted only a few minutes when I was jolted out of sleep by the most unearthly commotion I had ever heard. Jumping out of bed, I wasn't even sure what planet I was on, much less which country I was in. Like the father in the "Night Before Christmas" poem, I sprang from my bed to see what was the matter. Away to the window I flew like a flash, tore open the shutters and threw up the sash. And what to my wandering eyes did appear was not a miniature sleigh with eight tiny reindeer – rather it was a Hindu funeral happening right outside my window. The waling, mourning, groaning, and lamenting of the event confirmed the Apostle Paul's evaluation of those who are without Christ – "aliens from the commonwealth of Israel, and strangers from the covenants of promise, having no hope, and without God in the world." (Ephesians 2:12)

The traumatic awaking left me totally alert and unable to sleep again; so, I decided to try to find my friend. I looked for his name in the phonebook, only to find that there were several pages of individuals by that name. I tried the Church of South India, only to get someone who could not speak English. Finally, I decided that there was no way for me to locate him nor for him to find me, and I gave up. So I just settled in to try my best to enjoy this first visit in India while I awaited my scheduled departure several days later. The next morning, I took a walk down the street just to see what India was all about. Two blocks down the street from the hotel, I noticed a building across the street with a huge sign that read, "Church of South India National

Headquarters"! I don't even remember looking for traffic as I bolted across the street and dashed into the front door. I tried to look at least a bit civilized as I rushed up to the receptionist and asked if she knew how to contact the director of evangelism. To my amazement, she pointed me to an office just two doors from her desk. There, in a city of millions of people, hundreds of hotels and guesthouses scattered in every sector of the metropolis, the Lord had put me in the one hotel that was only a couple blocks from my friend's office!

But this was only the beginning of the adventure. Because of that miracle, I was able to keep the commitment to teach at the evangelism conference. I'm not sure of all that God did in those meetings, but there is one story that I will never forget. A little white-haired Indian man had been trying year after year to evangelize his remote village in Tamil Nadu state in southern India. Yet, his Hindu neighbors' hearts and ears were closed. That is until he learned the principles of the Great Commission, that signs and wonders should accompany the proclamation of the kingdom. Returning to his village with a new power from his new relationship with the Holy Spirit, he found that an old lady in the village had been gored by a water buffalo. He politely asked if he could pray for her in the name of Jesus. When she consented, he laid his hands on her and commanded that she be totally healed. Instantly, her crippled legs received strength and her mangled body was straightened. Since the whole village had seen the woman's condition after the attack and then saw her miraculous recovery, everyone immediately believed that the old man's message was real. The village that had rejected his testimony year after year was converted overnight.

Every detail of my stay in Madras was so amazing that it had to be God's direct intervention. With this miracle experience of "where God guides, He provides" fresh in my mind, I flew to Colombo, Sri Lanka, expecting to meet the college student with whom I had been corresponding for over five years. I did not know that he had moved out of the country or I would not have come at all. But God knew! As I scanned the waiting crowds, I was excited in my ignorance. "Lord," I prayed, "what new adventure awaits me here?" Two smiling faces greeted me. One belonged to the president of Lanka Bible Institute in Kandy, a hundred miles away, the other to a teacher in the school. My pen-pal friend heard that I was coming just before he had left the country, so he contacted an evangelical group to host me during my stay. They were unable to make any arrangements for me so they, in turn, contacted these two individuals who greeted me enthusiastically as a brother in Christ from America.

When God is running the show, the details fit perfectly. I arrived on the day and the hour they had to drive another brother the hundred miles from their city to the airport. They had been notified, through a typographical error, that I would arrive one hour later than the flight was actually scheduled. And it "just happened" that my plane was one hour late. It also occurred that my flight leaving Sri Lanka several days later "just happened" to be scheduled for the day and the hour they had planned to again drive the hundred miles from Kandy to the airport to pick up a missionary returning from New Zealand.

I found Sri Lanka to be like a *Tarzan* movie set, lush with tropical broad-leaf foliage, the air filled with the jungle sounds heard on TV but never quite believed. Rice curry and fresh tropical fruit satisfied my tummy while prayer and praise satisfied my soul. I stayed with the Bible college instructor, his wife, and daughter. The day before I arrived, they had moved from a one-room apartment into a six-room apartment. The paint wasn't even dry. He had recently resigned as director of a large international campus ministry when he received the baptism with the Holy Spirit. Since that time, he had been ministering on campuses in Kandy for over seven months without support except for a small salary he received for teaching one course at the Bible institute and a few free-will offerings. He had been invited by six different churches and missionary groups to be pastor or missionary, but each time he said, "No," knowing that his calling was to the college students. He had received a prophecy that God would send him a man to help him get started in the right way on the campuses. When we met, he acknowledged that I was that man. God had sent me halfway round the world to tell him about Full Gospel Student Fellowship (I'll tell you about it in a following chapter). He accepted the position of Director of the Full Gospel Student Fellowship in Sri Lanka with a vision of spreading out into all Asia. Flying out of Sri Lanka, I recalled the question I had asked the Lord when I first arrived, "Lord, what adventure awaits me here?" My mind was boggled. I never did see the student who was the reason for my trip in the first place. Instead, my trip fulfilled several prophecies given in Sri Lanka as well as those given to me. The Lord had done far above anything I could have asked or thought.

After we were married, Peggy and I returned to India and Sri Lanka for six weeks in which we traveled and ministered extensively in both countries. Our adventures included sleeping on the floor in the airport when our flight was delayed because of a giant sandstorm in the Rajasthan Desert. One odd thing about that experience was that the airline crew in Delhi actually loaded us on the bus to go to board the plane – simply because it was time for boarding. When we arrived at the designated spot on the tarmac, there was no plane awaiting us – in fact, the plane had not even departed from Amritsar! So, they took us back to the terminal, unloaded the bus and directed us to walk a short distance to the terminal entrance. As the guide was directing us, I could see that we were actually crossing an active runway with a plane taxiing toward us. Motioning to the attendant whose back was to the approaching aircraft, I warned him of the situation. That was one time when the word "terminal" almost took on a new meaning! Other adventures on that trip included developing the missionary quality of learning to enjoy our rice with a side of flies. In Sri Lanka, we ate rice for all three meals each day. And the flies – they were our constant companions, especially if there was food involved. When the food was served with a basket or net to cover it, the protective shield would literally look black from the mass of flies that would land on it. When we removed the cover, the flies would swarm and inevitably light in the rice. It has been said that the hand is quicker than the eye, but it certainly is not true that the hand is quicker than the fly! We also had the privilege of staying in an historic hotel that was once both a brothel and major transit point during the Opium Wars in China.

One of the highlights of that trip was the interview we had with Mother Teresa. During our trip to Calcutta, we made our way to the convent where she lived. Because of her busy traveling schedule, we could only pray that we had picked a day she was at home. As we entered the simple, clean, concrete building, we immediately sensed the presence of God. What a sweet spirit was in that place. We never expected that we would actually have the privilege of talking with this great woman. We thought that perhaps we would get a welcome from one of the sisters there and a tour of the facility. A nun warmly welcomed us and replied that Mother was busy in a meeting, but if we could wait a minute, she would ask Mother if she could see us. In just a few minutes, the door opened and she entered the room. This saint of God had dropped all that she was doing to visit with strangers who had shown up at her door unannounced and without an appointment or invitation! Her welcome to us was as heartfelt as if we were her closest friends or outstanding celebrities or officials. But that was Mother Teresa. To her, every human being was of ultimate worth – royalty or street beggar, it seemed to make no difference to her.

Mother Teresa graciously shared with us about her work around the world and her original call into the ministry to the poor in Calcutta. She then invited us to the Home for the Dying. Peggy was overwhelmed with emotions and told her – with tears – how she wished that she could visit this wonderful work Mother was doing but had to decline. Peggy explained to her that she thought she was dying from all the pain and misery she was experiencing from what we had seen on the city streets. She went on to tell Mother that she had never seen anything like this. Mother just patted Peggy's hand and told her that this was a normal reaction for a first visit. She said that many come from other countries to help, but many find it too hard to live and face what Calcutta has and they end up leaving. She said again, "That's okay, dear. I understand." The glow in her eyes was a window straight to the heart; it told us that she really did understand. She knew not only the hurt of those on the street, but also the hurt of those from the outside who were strangers to this level of anguish.

On a future trip to Calcutta, I did have an opportunity to visit the Home for the Dying where volunteers from around the world were caring for the destitute of the city. Then I made my way to the door where I had been welcomed before. This time, a handwritten note was posted, "Mother is not able to receive guests. She is in prayer." Apparently, only God Himself was more important to Mother Teresa than the humans who made a constant trail to her door and into her life. As we talked about all that she had accomplished around the world, we never felt the slightest bit of pride or feeling of accomplishment from her – just the overwhelming, gnawing feeling about a job that still was not yet done.

The outstanding quality of our conversation with Mother Teresa was that she turned the discussion away from herself and began to ask us about the mission work that had brought us to India and the neighboring country of Sri Lanka. After a few more minutes, she politely mentioned that her staff were waiting for her in a meeting. We asked if we could have a photograph taken with her before she left. When the picture was developed, Peggy and I both laughed at the way we were stooped just like the aged saint. It was only later that we realized what had actually taken place. Mother Teresa was gentle and gracious, yet at the same time, she had such a powerful personality that we had actually begun to take on her qualities in just those few minutes. We could only pray that her faithful caring and loving would become evident in our lives as well. Her parting remarks to us were in reference to the necklace Peggy was wearing. It was a metal piece that had a little dove symbolizing the Holy Spirit. "I see that you have the Holy Spirit. I do, too." Her life and works certainly proved it!

Following a conference for leaders from all over Latin America in Peru, I had the chance to check off one of the major entries on my bucket list by fulfilling a lifelong dream, visiting the ruins of the ancient Inca city, Machu Picchu. The visit necessitated a three-day stayover in Peru — one day to travel to Cusco, one day to see Machu Picchu, and one day to travel back to Lima to catch the flight home. After arriving in Cusco in midafternoon, my adventurous spirit took me into the city for a little freelance exploration. I began by catching local transportation into the city center — a minivan that was already packed with twenty-five passengers when I boarded but took on more and more customers at each stop. Even though I was totally at a loss in trying to discern what the conductor was saying at each stop, I kept riding until the van entered an area of town with cobblestone streets and a few touristy-looking shops. Assuming that this was where I wanted to go, I paid the seventeen-cent fare and jumped off the bus. One funny little incident that occurred while shopping was that the clerk in one store was looking through a big stack of plastic bags for one that was the right size for the small gift I had picked out. In the middle of her frantic quest, her small baby stuck her hand into the pile and grasped one bag. When she pulled it out, the bag was exactly the size that the mother needed.

Soon it was time to eat, so I ducked into a little hole-in-the-wall diner and ordered "pollo," the only Spanish food name I knew. When the waitress began to make a lengthy explanation in Spanish, I knew that I had a problem. As I was trying to communicate with sign language, a young man stepped up and asked in perfect English — even with a bit of a British, rather than a Latin, accent — if I needed help. He then explained that the restaurant was out of chicken but suggested their fried trout that was on special for the equivalent of less than two and a half dollars. By the time I had finished talking with the helpful stranger and turned around to take my table, another gentleman had taken my seat. With no other empty tables in the place, the stranger motioned that I sit with him. Thankful that Peggy wasn't there to stop me from breaking all the cardinal rules of foreign travel (eating in a local dive, ordering fish in a foreign country, and eating fried food), I enjoyed one of the most delicious meals of fried lake trout with a mug of complementary tea made from the leaves of the coca plant (the source of cocaine).

Now it was dark and time to head back to the hotel, so I tried to catch a cab. Unfortunately, every taxi had passengers, and there didn't seem to be any hope of finding an available one. After walking to the corner and breathing a quick prayer, I looked up to see that the car that had stopped at the red light right in front of me was a vacant taxi. The following day was a full day of adventure with a 6 AM departure by car to the train station a two-hour drive away. The road wound its way past the majestic white-capped Andes Mountains, through quaint villages and alongside the vast fields of the local substance crop, potatoes. The scenery was graced with the traditional Andean women dressed in top hats, flared skits, and braided pigtails. In one particular area, the local form of transportation was the three-wheeled taxi — motorbikes adapted by adding a cab with two passenger seats — a common sight in India and Nepal.

At the train station, I boarded the passenger coach for the hour-and-a-half trip through the gorge to the Machu Picchu bus station where I then transferred to the bus for the half-hour drive up the serpentine mountainous trail to the eight-thousand-foot elevation archeological site. Following a thorough tour of the expansive site, I headed back to Cusco via the bus, train, and automobile trip in reverse. One added blessing of the day was that, on the train trip, I was assigned the seat next to the bishop of the South East Diocese of the Methodist Church. We had a lengthy discussion about what God is doing around the world since the bishop had just been in Lima for the Methodist world convention on evangelism. My one last adventure before heading home the following morning was a surprise syrup that the hotel served with its French toast — coffee flavored. Well, after all, it is South America.

In a later chapter, I'll share about the many years that I spent working in Nepal, but let me take a few sentences here to tell a couple interesting stories of things that happened in transit on my various trips to Nepal. One route that we often took to get to Kathmandu forced us to overnight in Seoul, South Korea. Since this was home of Yoido Full Gospel Church (the world's largest congregation) and Prayer Mountain (a retreat center dedicated totally to prayer), the stopover gave me a chance to take my team members on a little spiritual sightseeing adventure. However, a couple of those adventures turned out to be a lot more adventuresome than I had planned. Because the food in many of the places that we traveled to in Nepal wasn't safe, we always carried little packets of tuna with us for emergency meals. Since I had been to Prayer Mountain before and knew that the only food available there was from a traditional Korean soup kitchen, I had warned the team members to be sure to bring their tuna for the day that we were to spend at the retreat center. Unfortunately, Peggy struck up a conversation with a Christian Korean man on the plane who told her how good the soup was, so she had passed the word around among the team members that they didn't need to bring their tuna. When it turned out that no one could force themselves to swallow the swill that was offered on the cafeteria line, we all spent the day in fasting as well as in prayer! On another occasion, our team got split up on the buses that take guests from the church to Prayer Mountain, and some of them didn't understand that the last bus of the day retuning to the church left at 6 PM. I was able to make reservations for all the people who were in the group with me for the last bus, but I was not able to include the ones who had gone ahead on a different bus. Eventually, I found the other two ladies and told them that they had to get on the bus with me or else they would have to spend the night at Prayer Mountain and miss the flight the following morning. There was a problem in that there was only one seat left on the bus. The driver was insistent that he could not overload the bus because he had to pass through several checkpoints on the journey because the route took us very close to the demilitarized zone between North and South Korea. He was relentless that he could lose his job if the guards at the checkpoints cited him for having too many passengers. Eventually, I agreed to become a stowaway by crawling under the seat so that it would appear that there were no more passengers than seats!

Another route that we could take to Nepal required an overnight in Bangkok, Thailand. This stopover was actually more inconvenient than the transit in Seoul since we had to make a transfer from the international terminal to the domestic terminal and the airlines would not automatically transfer the luggage. Therefore, we had to collect our bags and keep them with us until we could check them in for the domestic flight the following morning. Further complicating things was that the late evening arrival into Bangkok and the early morning departure made our stay too short to go into town for a hotel due to the time it would take to travel each way and negotiate hotel check-in procedures. Therefore, we wound up spending the night in the airport terminal – sleeping in the waiting area on the cartons of literature that we were bringing into Nepal. On one particular trip – long before there were security screenings (This was especially true in foreign countries.) – we were settling down for our night in the airport when my sister remarked, "Well, since we are going to be here for the next several hours, at least something exciting could happen." At that point she curled up and fell fast asleep. Not long afterward, an argument between two Thai men broke out directly over her. One of the men brandished a pistol and threatened to shoot the other man. Police had to intervene and haul the men out of the terminal. Amazingly, my sister slept through the whole incident. I, of course, accused her of having wished the excitement upon us and then taunted her with the fact that she was the one who asked for it and then missed the whole thing.

I've had the privilege of visiting Russia on two different occasions – once when the Iron Curtain was just beginning to come down and a second time after the country had twenty years of capitalism to recover from the austerity of seventy years of communism. Both visits were to the same city, but under two different names – Leningrad under communism and St. Petersburg under capitalism. Before my first trip, I had never dreamed that I would walk streets of the Soviet Union. To me Russia was Nikita Khrushchev taking off his shoe and banging the table in the United Nations in 1960. It was Sputnik that I had watched twinkle in the skies as a child – fearing that, since Russia had a satellite before America – they would someday make good Khrushchev's threat, "We'll bury you!" The USSR was a forbidden land – frightful, foreign, and foreboding. But all that changed when I had the opportunity to walk its streets, taste its foods, meet its people, and pray with its believers. Having arrived in the harbor by boat, Peggy and I walked quickly through customs and security without delays or interrogations; no questions were asked. With a quick glance at the passport to confirm that the photos matched our faces, the officer waved us ashore and wished us a pleasant visit. Once officially on Soviet soil, we were met by our hostess, a Christian lady married to a Russian Jew. Having formerly worked as a tour guide with the official Russian tour agency, she was totally knowledgeable and capable of showing us around. As an English teacher, her command of the language was flawless. Although her husband spoke no English, he was very talkative and most informative through his wife's translation.

Lines for gasoline were usually two or three blocks long. When they did manage to get to the pump, they were rationed only forty liters. Outside every shop, we saw lines of at least thirty to forty people waiting their chance to buy goods. It was sad to see the little package each person was holding in his hand when exiting the shop after having waited so long to get in. In addition, each shop carried only one or two items, so the people had to wait in line after line to buy first meat, then milk, then bread, then eggs – all of which were rationed in unbelievably small quantities. The stores contained hardly any merchandise at all. A porcelain shop we visited had around half a dozen items on the shelf. A food store carried about four pieces of meat, a couple flats of eggs, and a couple pitchers of milk. Life – or should I say, "existence" ? – for these people seemed so foreign to us. The conveniences that seem so natural to us were simply nonexistent. After selling a kilo of apples, the vendor did not offer a bag to carry them in. Instead, the customer had to find enough pockets to hold them. To him, there was no problem of recycling the paper or plastic bag – there was no bag to begin with. A pair of blue jeans was available for about two full weeks' salary for a white-collar worker in Russia. Our guide summed up the situation by saying simply, "We eat when we can get food." Even in what could be considered a nice restaurant, we found that many items on the menu were not available and that the napkins had been cut into tiny squares so that one napkin could be stretched to service a full table of guests. Leningrad of the eighteenth and nineteenth centuries was a showplace on the Baltic. The palaces of the czars and emperors were gilded with incalculable wealth in gold. The magnificence of the architecture and art of the city was second to none in the sumptuous society of European nobility and royalty. Those palaces, cathedrals, and museums stood as memorials to the Russia that once was. Alongside golden overlaid cathedrals, stood decaying apartment buildings, rusty buses and streetcars, and a crumbling society. All this is a testimony to an era without God. We toured magnificent cathedrals that had been taken from the congregations during the communist revolution. Some had been made into warehouses; others were factories; others were used as schools; some were museums; one had been used as a skating rink; and one had become the Museum of Atheism. When I returned twenty years later, I found a bustling economy and a strong, viable Christian community.

Because of my desire to reach the pastors who don't have a lot of opportunities for formal Bible education, my treks around the world have taken me to some of the most remote areas imaginable. I got to one church where I preached in India by riding on the back of a donkey cart. I arrived at the village only to discover that I was preaching over a loud speaker system that demanded that everyone in the village hear the message even if they didn't choose to come to church. In Kerala state of India, I traveled as far as the passenger train would take me and then boarded a logging train to travel to the end of the line, followed by an on-foot trek to what seemed to be the very end of the earth. I eventually wound up in a village so far away from modern civilization that the local women didn't wear anything above the waist and all the people stopped and stared at me as if I had just arrived on a spaceship from another planet.

In Uganda, I visited a village where a ninety-plus-year-old lady came for prayer because she had never seen a white person before. It was hard to imagine that she had never had the opportunity to meet a Westerner – even an aid worker or a doctor – at any point in all those years. On another trip to Uganda, I asked my host to take me into the remote part of the country to see what God was doing at the grassroots level rather than staying in the capital city like many missionaries like to do – and did I ever get a grassroots experience! To define what is meant by "remote," I was in an area where the people still live in mud huts with thatched roofs. The only significant building in the most remote village where I ministered was the church – a simple but spacious block building. Even though the area was very remote, the pastors and leaders from over a hundred churches found their way to the church to be part of the meetings. The meals were cooked on the ground in big kettles on outdoor fire pits.

On the way back to the city, a problem with the battery in the car occurred. All that was needed was a jump, but the problem was that it was impossible to get even that simple help because there were no other cars nearby. After some considerable searching, someone finally found one of the villagers who had a battery in his hut that he was using as an electrical source since there was no electricity in the village. Great! Now there was a battery available, but it would do no good without jumper cables. I suggested "jury rigging" some makeshift jumper cables from a piece of the electrical cord from the sound system and generator which had been used in the meetings. This seemed like a simple matter of cutting and stripping the wire; and it would have been if only there were a few simple tools available. After a futile search through the village for a knife, someone offered a hacksaw. It is still a mystery as to how the people perform the simplest of daily tasks such as preparing meals without a knife. Once the wire was ready, the next step was to strip the insulation off the wire so that it could be connected to the battery posts. In spite of all my adamant insisting that it not be done that way, the cables were stripped with the repairman's teeth!

I've dealt with an ocassional dog and lots of rats in attendance in my services as well as scorpions, rats, and even a cobra in the house where I was to sleep. So, now you see how remote "remote" can be.

In many of the places where I've stayed, life is very basic. Sometimes there is water; sometimes, not. Usually, there is no electricity. When there is electricity, there may or may not be a bulb in the light fixture. When there is no electricity, there may be a candle stand but no candle. Such was the case in Haiti on the morning I was to leave to return home after my mission there. Since I had an early flight, I had to shower, shave, and pack before daylight. Wisely, I had filled a bucket of water the night before in anticipation that the water would not be working when I got up the next day. Unfortunately, I had made only one provision for light in those pre-dawn hours – a flashlight. This was an unfortunate decision because the batteries went dead almost as soon as I crawled out of bed. After stumbling around in the dark, crashing into the door, and banging my toe against the step-up between the bedroom and the bath, I attempted to use lighted matches to find my way around. This, of course, was not a very functional solution since I could not shower while holding a match. I actually wound up burning my fingers before I could collect more than two items to pack into my duffle bag. Eventually, the ingenuity of a true missionary kicked in, and I flipped on my laptop and used the glow from its screen to illuminate the room so I could wash, shave, and pack.

In the Congo, I stayed at a very nice little guest house with Wi-Fi, electricity, and hot and cold running water. By "cold running water," I mean that when I wanted cold water, I had to run to get it out of a plastic bucket in the bathroom. When I wanted hot running water, I had to run and boil some on the stove. By electricity, I mean that it randomly came on and went out every now and then. This wasn't a major problem except if the outage occurred when I needed to put in or take out my contacts. The Wi-Fi worked when the electricity did and could usually be picked up in the room. Sometimes, I had to go out to the front yard or even walk across the courtyard to the office building to get a signal. But eventually I had to leave my "luxury" accommodations to travel to the village where there was no Wi-Fi and only a trickle of cold running water. There I had to take bucket baths and flush the toilet with a bucket of water. The bathroom light didn't have a switch; I turned it on by connecting two wires that stuck out of the socket. Since the electricity was from a solar panel, it was not strong enough to charge the laptop or camera battery; therefore, I could only work and take pictures as long as the batteries lasted. The lights were too dim for me to shave, and the place was too dusty for me to wear my contacts. After my stay in the village, I headed back to the city. Who would have ever thought that I would consider it a blessing to be going back to a place where I had to boil water for a warm splash bath, flush the toilet with a bucket, never know when the electricity would work, and hope for Wi-Fi connection?

There is one other really humorous story that I must share while we are on the topic of the primitive conditions. This event occurred in Haiti. I had two other missionaries with me – a single guy and a single gal. Although we had separate bedrooms, we did have to share the bath. One evening, the young lady was taking a shower – well, actually she was just splashing herself with water from the five-gallon bucket – when she decided to wash her hair. After shampooing, she thought that it would be easier to stick her head right into the bucket for the rinse than to try to splash enough water over her head to thoroughly rinse her long hair. Unfortunately, she lost her balance when she tried to lean over to submerge her head. With her head stuck in the bucket filled with water, she was actually in danger of drowning; so, she began to yell as best as she could with her head under water in a plastic bucket. The young man and I both heard her pleas for help but neither one of us was about to barge into the bathroom knowing that she was in there naked. After what seemed like a long eternity of indecision concerning what to do, we finally heard her announce that she had managed to get her head out of the bucket. You'll never know how relieved I was that I didn't have to explain to her family why I let their daughter drown in Haiti!

Along with international travel comes international cuisine – a combination of blessings and curses. During my first ever sermon in Nepal, I had to hand the microphone to the local pastor and rush off the platform to avoid throwing up right in front of the whole congregation! On one of my trips to Uganda, my team and I had to kill our own food. After slitting the cow's throat with a really dull knife and then skinning and butchering the poor beast, we turned the meat over to the local tribesmen who mixed it with vegetables and God-only-knows what else to stew all day long in a caldron over an open fire. When we were finally offered the concoction for supper that evening, I felt that I should have apologized to the poor cow. I wouldn't have felt too badly about slaughtering the animal if it were for steaks, but it just didn't seem right that the poor thing had given its life for this indigestible brew. In my travels around the world, I've eaten literally everything from A (alligator) to Z (zebra) and everything between – octopus, ostrich, rattlesnake, squid, yak, and lots of things that I felt better about leaving them unidentified. But I have to tell you just a couple stories.

On one particular trip I was with a team in Japan just after McDonald's had gone international. Since one of their first international franchises was in Tokyo, all the team members were begging to go there for a meal. Well, actually there was one girl who was from a town on the US-Mexico border who really loved Mexican food. When everyone else claimed to be having a "Big Mac attack" – a popular slogan from the McDonald's ads that were running at the time – she countered by claiming to have a taco attack. When we finally did find the McDonald's, everyone except me rushed in to satisfy their craving for American fast-food cuisine. I ducked into a little Japanese restaurant across the street and enjoyed a delicious local meal. When the team reassembled, I taunted the young lady by telling her that she should have stayed with me since I had tacos. At first, she didn't believe me. However, I went on to describe that I had

56

had a plateful, followed by a second, and then refused the offer for a third refill. By this time, she was green with envy. At that point, I volunteered that the Japanese word "taco," means octopus. At that, she turned green for a totally different reason!

In Egypt, I took a group to a very nice restaurant where the waiters were constantly offering us fresh hot pita bread to go with our meals. The bread was so delicious that everyone ate a number of pieces. After the meal, I stepped outside the restaurant and waited next to the bus for everyone to come out. It was then that I noticed a little lady squatting on the ground making patties of dough and baking them on a little stone oven. As the members of my group came out, I pointed to the unsanitary conditions and joked with them that she was cooking the bread that we had had just been eating. About that time, the backdoor of the restaurant opened and out came the waiter to collect another tray of pita bread from the lady! But that's not the end of the story. Immediately after the meal, we headed to Israel – across the Siani Peninsula on a bus with no toilet facilities and a busload of people with upset stomachs!

Another dining experience that really stands out took place in Scotland when I was invited to a traditional ceilidh, a formal ball complete with bagpipes, kilts, and Scottish dancing. Of course, the highlight of the evening was the meal – complete with haggis, a Scottish delicacy of sheep heart, liver and lungs mixed with onions, oatmeal, and spices cooked inside the sheep's stomach!

Of course, there is much more to get accustomed to in foreign countries than just the food. There are the customs and the way the nationals do things. My first experience in dealing with foreign mindsets was in Japan where I was to minister in a meeting which we anticipated would draw about fifty people. Since the venue we had would seat about two hundred, I spread the fifty chairs out with plenty of "elbow room" on each side and plenty of "knee room" between the rows. My objective was to make the room seem fuller by spacing the chairs. As soon as I walked away, the Japanese pastor came behind me and shoved all the chairs together into a tight configuration that took up about a fourth of the room and left the rest as empty space. Since the Japanese are accustomed to living compacted together in limited spaces, my arrangement was just not acceptable to them.

It was also in Japan where I had a very challenging language encounter. One of the men on our team decided to tell a joke to a group of pastors, "What goes 'Ha, Ha, Ha, plop?'" The answer was, "A man laughing his head off." Of course this expression did not even come close to translating into Japanese; so, the locals were left standing there mumbling, "Laughing head off? Laughing head off?" and the man who told the joke turned to me and said, "Well, you have been here more than I have; you explain it," and walked off!

In Haiti, I became part of a couple of weddings by total surprise. There was an empty slot in the agenda at the conference where I had been speaking and I had puzzled all week long as to what was in store for that Thursday afternoon session. Still filled with questions, I walked into the tabernacle at the appointed time for the session and noticed immediately that the room was being decorated for some formal event and that there was a different group of folks gathering, all of whom were dressed, as they say, "to the nines." My guess was that there must be a wedding about to happen so I decided to excuse myself and come back after the wedding. As I started toward the door, an English-speaking gentleman grabbed me and surprised me with the notification that I was supposed to speak at the wedding! It was an elegant affair with extravagant pomp and elaborate choreography as the bridal attendants entered the hall. Unsure as to whether the bride and groom were even aware that this unknown foreigner was to take part in their ceremony, I gladly added my insights to their nuptials. By the time the ceremony was over, I realized that it was too late for the afternoon meeting that had been scheduled to follow the wedding; so I headed back to the missionary apartment for dinner and a little rest before the evening session. A few minutes later, I answered a knock at the door to find the interpreter insisting that I hurry back to the church. There was another wedding going on, and I was requested to speak at it also! I hastily finished my dinner and rushed back to the sanctuary to address the second couple. This wedding was less extravagant but was plagued with all the customary Haitian delays, such as failures with the sound system. Finally, just as the couple was about to be officially declared legally united, the lights went out. By this time, the sun had set, so the ceremony was engulfed in total blackness except for a few random blue and green glows from cell phones that the guests throughout the audience flipped on. Eventually someone found a candle and finally a kerosene lantern in order to light the sanctuary sufficiently for the marriage certificate to be signed. At long last, the generator was restarted so everyone could witness the couple's first kiss and wish them well as they exited the church and entered their new life together.

At a wedding in the Congo, they added kabobs, samosas, and sausage to the usual Congolese menu of fufu, boiled potatoes, French fries, rice, greens, peas, fried sardines, fish heads, chicken that was impossible to chew, beef that was remarkably tender compared to the chicken (I think that the cows should give the chickens some lessons.), sweet hushpuppies, roasted peanuts, onions, cooked cabbage, cucumber salad, tomatoes, and fruit including luscious pineapple, mango, finger bananas, and regular bananas. The actual wedding ceremony lasted about an hour and a half with lots of singing, preaching, praying, and even an offering. The sermon was sort of a hodgepodge of stuff about man, woman, and marriage but the highlight came when the preacher talked about the wife's role as being submissive. He said that if she is in the kitchen cooking and the husband calls her, she should drop what she was doing and go take care of whatever he wants. At that point, I was surprised that the affirming response came from the women – all of whom started clapping, shouting, and doing an African whistle with their tongues. The vows were in Swahili, French and English – and stressed the submission point. At the reception, I sat next to a young man who spoke great English because he had gone to college in Kenya where the educational system is in English. When he asked me what I thought of the wedding, I commented on that part of the ceremony, and he said that that is exactly how it ought to be because it is African culture. I then asked him if it was biblical culture and went into a bit of the explanation of Ephesians chapter five, but he didn't seem to "get it" at all. The other amazing thing about the wedding was that no one – including the bride and groom – smiled during the entire ceremony. Apparently, the ceremony was too serious to enjoy.

Also while in the Congo, I went to the home of one of the church elders for dinner. We had a great meal and a good time together, but I was concerned because the wife and some of the kids didn't eat. Finally, I told my host that I didn't intend to be rude or break African protocol, but I thought that we should invite the wife and children to join us. I didn't understand exactly how the children were divided – some ate and others didn't. His reply was that they will eat. I responded with, "Yes, I know that they will eat, but I would like for them to join us now." He then told them to get their food, and they got up and went to the serving table. The wife started to serve a plate and pretended that she had to check something in the kitchen. She disappeared for a while and, even when she did come back, I don't think she ever finished the serving on her plate. I'm not sure what happened with the children. But at least I tried. The whole event reminded me of the first time I took Peggy to India. When we were seated for a meal, there was no chair for my wife. The response that I received when I asked for an additional chair was that she would not be eating with us but would have to go into the kitchen with the rest of the women. Of course, I insisted that she be allowed to join us – which happened, but only because of the color of her skin.

The Christian gatherings in Haiti are basically songfests. Some of their enthusiasm for singing is a cultural result of their slavery heritage. During the colonial days, the slaves used music as their way of communicating to one another. Fearing that the slaves might instigate a revolt, the masters forbad them from gathering in groups to be addressed by a speaker. To get around these restrictions, they passed messages through hidden meaning in the songs that they sang while they worked and in the evenings when back in their compounds. In addition to this natural propensity toward musical communication, they simply believe in speaking to one another in psalms, hymns, and spiritual songs as commanded in Ephesians 5:19. The joy of their salvation erupts in song every time they gather. Their melodies of worship echo all through the night and from their pre-dawn prayer vigils. Their jubilant harmonies burst forth every time people meet. At least half of every gathering consists of singing as each one volunteers to sing a special number by dropping a little slip of paper into a hat from which the emcee would pick the next performer, apparently their cultural substitute for sharing testimonies and prophetic teachings. Even though some of the time I felt as though I were at an "un-talent show" and wanted to applaud simply because the song was over rather than because it was such a good presentation or how much I cringed each time I saw another piece of paper drop into the hat, I couldn't help but appreciate the way they all want to take part in the service – not perform out of a desire of being seen but from a true expression of the gratitude for the work that God has done in their lives.

Upon my arrival in Nigeria – after pushing and shoving my way through all the commotion and chaos of the barrage of begging, bantering, and bartering that is characteristic of airports in third-world countries – I found my way to the exit where I was met by a delegation. Typical of African culture, they sent an entire entourage rather than just one person to greet me. As they say in Africa, it takes a whole village. One of the ladies greeted me with, "Dr. Shirley, I see that you have gained some weight since you were here last." I replied with, "Well, I have put on a couple of pounds, but I didn't think it showed." Her response was, "Well, at your age, it doesn't matter." Within the first two minutes that I had been in her country she had insulted me twice – calling me fat and old. At least she didn't call me ugly! Of course, she was not intending to insult me; rather, she thought she was complimenting me. In a culture where food is so limited that the people find it difficult to have enough – much less enough to gain excess weight – being overweight is a sign of prosperity. Likewise, in the conditions where adequate nutrition, proper sanitation, and good health care are unavailable or too expensive for the general populace, living to be an older person is a sign of prosperity and divine favor.

Understanding the differences in customs and culture are imperative to getting along in foreign countries. Unfortunately, I have not always been as well-informed as I was with this lady. Once I was sitting in a restaurant making plans with my host in Sri Lanka when the sound system began to blare, drowning out our conversation. I asked the waiter to please turn off the music since it was interfering with our discussion. His response was that the song was their national anthem which they patriotically played at that specific time each day. With proverbial "egg on my face," I had to apologize for being so insensitive.

I've had a couple other rather embarrassing moments as the result of being the international guest during communion services and, therefore, being invited to the front of the line where I was not able to observe the others before I had my turn. In Sri Lanka, I stepped up to the pastor and received the bread and wine while standing, only to observe that everyone else behind me knelt down before taking the elements. I'm sure that everyone realized that it was an act of ignorance rather than arrogance, but still it made me feel awkward. In Hungary, I was handed a huge hunk of bread which I popped into my mouth and began to chew, forcing myself to swallow it so I could then receive the wine – all along thinking to myself that this was the biggest piece of communion bread I had ever seen. It was only after I turned to walk back to my seat that I realized that the piece of bread was not intended for me but was supposed to have been broken and passed to those in line behind me. And then there was the time in India when I was glad to be the one in the front of the line since there was one cup of wine that was to be passed to everyone in the congregation.

One cultural practice that I enjoyed in Japan was the ofuro – a hot tub bath that was usually taken at the end of the work day, with many workers stopping at the public ofuro on their way home from the factory or office each afternoon. The procedure is to wash while squatting on the floor in front of a little faucet. After rinsing with a bucket of warm water, each bather then steps into the hot tub – and by "hot tub," I mean water that makes me want to rename our American hot tubs as "warm tubs" – for a relaxing soak. Now, there is only one issue with the whole procedure – the cleaning crew who constantly work in the bath to keep the floors mopped up. Since the cleaners are all women and the bathers are all naked, the whole experience can become a bit uncomfortable. On one occasion, I had a guest with me who was not aware of what was about to happen once he was undressed. When the cleaner showed up, he ducked behind the lockers – exactly where she intended to mop next. He then hurried to another corner – again, her next targeted area to clean. It seemed as if she were deliberately chasing him. After several futile attempts to avoid her, he found himself cornered with nowhere to escape.

Of course, as the old expression goes, "The shoe can also fit the other foot." Sometimes it was the people that I have visited who had a problem adjusting to me. In the Turk and Caicos Islands, my team and I were the first outsiders they had ever invited to minister in their church. We learned later that everyone was very nervous about having "white people" come to their meetings. They confessed that they were afraid we might not fit in with their native culture; however, they also added that they realized as soon as we walked into the church for the first service that we were just part of their same family that they had never met before!

Back to the topic of food, I once took cases of vitamin-enriched rice to Nepal to distribute to the people. Some of the packages were chicken-flavored, but others were beef-flavored. No matter how much a blessing it would have been for the people to have free food, they all refused the beef-flavored packages – in spite of the fact that there was no actual beef content in the rice!

And then, there are other cultural norms that are nothing more than camouflaged socio-economic prejudices. While visiting with a missionary in an Asian country, we engaged a porter to carry our luggage from the train station to the bus line we were going to take to get to the missionary's apartment. To my amazement, the missionary insisted that only one porter be hired to carry the baggage. The two of us had been struggling to haul our bags from the train, but now he expected one frail-looking old man to take on both our loads. I couldn't believe my eyes as I watched the little man struggle to hoist the bags on his head and then stagger under the load. Even though I tried to tell the missionary that the load was too much and that we should call on the services of a second porter, my pleas fell on deaf ears. After sympathetically watching the poor man stumble up the stairs with his heavy load on his head, we finally reached the bus stand where my friend offered the man a few coins. When the porter began to insist that he deserved more because he had carried so many bags, my friend refused and sent him away. I'll never forget the sense of injustice that welled up inside of me as I watched the poor little man disappear in the sea of faces at the bus stop. The situation grew even worse when my friend suggested that we have lunch at an American-style restaurant located in the city. When the waiter served us our hamburgers and Cokes, the missionary reached into his pocket and pulled out several American dollars as a tip. The waiter had carried only a couple pounds of food on a tray while the porter had struggled under a load of more than a hundred pounds on his head. The waiter had only walked a short distance from the kitchen to the dining room while the porter had staggered for blocks and climbed a steep set of stairs. Yet the waiter walked away with more than a week's wages in the local currency while the porter gained barely enough to buy a bowl of rice for his next meal.

In addition to remote places, my adventures have also led me to places all around the globe where the Christian faith is not welcome – and, in some instances, is persecuted. There was the time in the British Virgin Islands when all the local Rastafarians gathered right outside the church with their blaring music to try to interrupt the service and dissuade my wife from preaching. And then there was the time when an angry woman stood up and began to yell during our open-air rally in a gypsy village in India. It was only after the top elder of the community intervened that she was quiet enough for us to continue with our ministry.

In one country, I was billed as a "world-renowned speaker" in order to protect me from possible charges of violations of my tourist visa. They couldn't put my name on any of the printed materials in case the poster were to fall into the hands of authorities, who are opposed to Christian work. In one Islamic nation, I was invited to minister to a colony of foreigners who were serving as teachers and nurses; however, there were severe restrictions against sharing the gospel with the nationals. Some of the locals seemed to like to come and gather in the nearby rooms when the Christians were meeting so that they could hear the gospel through the open doors. If they were ever interrogated or if I were questioned, we could honestly answer that they had not been in the meetings.

When I first traveled to Myanmar, there were very strict regulations. I could not stay in the country more than forty-eight hours, and I could only visit a very limited number of places. Over the years, the country has become much more accepting. However, real freedom has never been fully granted and government restrictions placed on Burmese believers tend to fluctuate. On some of my visits, we were not granted permits to hold the conferences until the last minute, effectively preventing us from properly announcing the meetings and therefore blocking those we were inviting from being able to make plans to attend. The believers I work with there have been told to limit the amount of singing and number of meetings or else they will be cited for disturbing the peace. I have seen people arrested and hauled off to the police station for such minor offenses as jaywalking. I had been told that I couldn't be seen in public with certain leaders lest they come under scrutiny because of their association with Westerners and I have been made to walk several blocks to snap a photo because the driver was afraid to stop his car too near certain government buildings. On one visit, I was not permitted to hold the seminar in the church but was forced to move it to a public location such as a downtown hotel. I had to limit the number of pastors who were permitted to attend the seminar, I was not allowed to use microphones or tape record the teachings, and the pastor in charge of the meetings closed the curtains halfway through the seminar, commenting that there were people watching us from outside.

Just prior to one of my missions to Myanmar, the nation experienced a tragic bloodbath and was suddenly thrust into upheaval. In spite of all the confusion in the country, I felt led to go ahead with my plans to hold a pastors' conference – even during this time of upheaval and unrest. It was not until two months after the trip that the full significance of that trip came into focus. Eight weeks after I had preached at the church in Yangon, the pastor suddenly collapsed and died right in the middle of preaching the Sunday morning sermon. This was, of course, a tragic event, however it is a wonderful testimony that he was working for the Lord right up to the last second. I felt that there was some special significance to the fact that I had accepted his invitation to come to Burma at this particular time after not being able to visit him for nearly six years. I was there as one of his last guests – if not the last one – before his death! But that's not the end of the story – I had taken him a copy of Last Enemy, my book on death, because his father had recently passed away. I will always believe that reading this book not only comforted him during the time of loss of his father but also prepared him for his own journey into eternity.

When the opportunity arose for me to visit the nation of Niger while on my way to Nigeria, my contact in the country arranged for me to get acquainted with a few of the nation's Christian leaders. I discovered that although evangelical Christians comprise less than one percent of the population of the nation, there is a vital and growing church in the country. Although the nation is essentially totally Islamic, the people are open to listen to the presentation of the gospel and there is very little organized persecution of believers. However, there is still a social stigma about converting from the Muslim faith which keeps many who are open to the gospel from making a public confession of faith in Christ. This obstacle didn't seem to be an overwhelming barrier as I saw results at every church where I ministered. Each altar call brought only one new convert per service forward to publicly pray the sinner's prayer; but this one-by-one growth is one way the Lord adds to His church daily, and each individual salvation causes a celebration in heaven as well as here on earth.

My first journey into Bhutan was the culmination of many years of prayer and believing. Since the early days of my work in Nepal, I had had a desire to also be part of the frontline team to bring the gospel to this remote and restricted corner of the world. Finally, the connection was made so that I could go in and minister to the emerging church in this Himalayan kingdom. Known as the "Land of the Thunder Dragon" and also labeled as the "Kingdom in the Clouds," Bhutan is a tiny Buddhist country of less than seven hundred thousand population nestled between the two giants of India and China. Until recently, the country practiced total isolationism from the outside and even forced all the citizens to wear the traditional dress – gho for men and kira for ladies. Today, Bhutan is becoming more and more in contact with the outside world through tourism, which has become one of the country's major revenue sources.

Because of the openness to tourism, my son Jeremy and I were able to enter the country as tourists. We, therefore, had to carefully play the role of tourists by being sure to visit at least one tourist site each day. When we returned to the hotel each evening, the staff would always ask us where we had been and what we had seen that day. Perhaps the hotel employees were just being courteous. However, they may also have been informants who were keeping track of their guests' activities. There was no way to know for sure. When I met with believers, caution was always evident in the way that I was asked not to bring my camera with me, how they always held quiet discussions in corners, how the Bible was referred to as the "holy book" (a term which would not distinguish it from a Buddhist text), and how the ladies covered their faces when a stranger entered the room. Though some travel restrictions had been imposed which prevented many of the Christians who were planning to meet with me from being able to come, there were a number of believers who gathered from many regions of the country for some training and to receive the teaching materials that we were able to bring into the country. One symbolic event during our visit was the hike that Jeremy and I took to the top of a mountain overlooking the capital city of Thimphu. Standing among tens of thousands or possibly even hundreds of thousands of Buddhist prayer flags that had been strung around the peak, I noticed that many of them had collapsed due to weathering. As I walked among the fallen flags, my heart was quickened with the words of I Samuel 3:19 which says that God did not let any of the prophet's words fall to the ground. No matter how many of their flags wind up in the mud, the words of our God will never fail.

In a secret meeting room, every inch of space was crammed with young women, breast-feeding babies, school children, high school and college age young men, a handful of adults, and one grandmother. They all sat on the floor and huddled as closely as possible to accommodate the latecomers. Joy radiated from every face as they raised their hands in praise and worship. Unless you were able to talk with them and learn their stories, you would never guess the hardships they had endured and continued to face. My interpreter told me that he had once held a respectable position with the government but, not only had he been fired as soon as he was exposed as a Christian, he had also been sentenced to a three-year prison term. Fortunately, the sentence was reduced to just seven months, but he did come out of incarceration jobless and ostracized. Another brother shared with me that he had once been somewhat of a Saul of Tarsus who helped persecute believers by serving in the position of keeping the official records of all who were reported to be converts. Now, he was more of a Paul the Apostle who was promoting the faith. Another one of these underground believers told me that the congregations have to relocate every three or four months because of the complaints by neighbors in the apartment complexes who accuse them of having too many people coming regularly and making too much noise with their singing. The complaints from the neighbors can result in serious consequences if they reach the proper authorities.

Because our ministry was to people who were already believers, we were not violating any laws since Bhutan officially has a policy of religious freedom — meaning that it is not a crime to engage in one's own personal religious expression. However, involvement in converting individuals or promoting your faith among members of other religions can result in very severe retribution. As international guests who were participating in conferences that did not officially violate any laws, we were not in any personal danger; however, we were constantly aware that we had to be careful with everything we said and every move we made so as to not endanger any of the local believers. In fact, after we left the country, many of our friends did suffer intensive interrogations as to why they were associating with Westerners. Because the house church meetings are open to believers and anyone that they would want to invite, their very existence makes them subject to the scrutiny of the officials and targets for persecution. Both in the public conferences and in the underground house churches, we found that the believers clung to every word we shared, treasuring the opportunity to learn more about their position as more than conquerors in Christ. Hungry for biblical teaching, they sat for hours on end and then testified that they needed more such systematic training and biblical exposition. In addition to biblical teaching, their services were uniquely centered around prayer. Intense, earthshaking prayer introduced every session, erupted in the middle of every service, and brought each meeting to a close.

Before I conclude this chapter, I need to introduce you to a friend who did some of the most incredible missionary exploits that I have ever known. She flew to India one time because the Lord told her to deliver a message to Indira Gandhi. With no possible connection to the Prime Minster, she acted on simple faith. The morning after her arrival in Delhi, she struck up a conversation with another guest at the hotel – only to discover that the lady was the personal secretary to Mrs. Gandhi! On another occasion, she traveled to a remote island nation in Micronesia and led the entire royal family to Christ. But one day, she came to me in tears. A friend of hers had accosted her with the accusation, "You're not a missionary! You've just got a spirit of travel and adventure!" When I heard what the woman had said to my friend, I responded, "But you couldn't be a missionary without a spirit of travel and adventure! God made your temperament so you could do all the amazing things that

He has planned for your life." With that story, let me suggest that God knew what He was doing when He gave me DNA not only from my saintly grandfather Papa Timms but also from my hobo uncle, Bramlett.

Now it is time for us to rewind a bit back to my teen years. When I left my parent's home at age eighteen to go to college and beyond, I guess my mother knew that there were to be lots of adventures in store for me, so she gave me a printed copy of the ninety-first Psalm – about the Lord's constant protection. That psalm became my life's passage, and even today I keep my old family Bible on my desk open to that page. In the remaining chapters of this book, you'll see that the promises of that scripture have never failed.

The Ole North State and Beyond

From the very earliest age that I could even consider where I wanted to go to college, I never had another school in mind other than Furman University. My mind was made up years before I actually had to pick a college. I was unquestionably certain that the die was cast when I was selected by the university to represent my high school as a Furman Scholar, and then was awarded a scholarship! But one day my high school guidance counselor asked me to come to her office because she had some information about a scholarship program that she felt I would qualify for. I took the information and made the submission – still feeling that I was headed to Furman no matter what results I might get from the scholarship program. When it turned out that I was offered twice as much funding as from Furman at a school with a much lower tuition base, I decided to take time to seriously consider changing my mind. I did decide to enroll in the Pulp and Paper Science and Technology program at North Carolina State University (NCSU) with the intention of going there for two years to get the basic required courses out of the way and then transferring to Furman for my junior and senior years so I would have a degree from the school of my dreams. After all, was I really interested in studying pulp and paper science and technology and then spending the rest of my life in a paper mill town where everything smelled like sulphur? So, after graduating as a member of the first class from Belton-Honea Path South Carolina High School, I headed north of the border to Raleigh, North Carolina, to become a freshman "Wolfpacker" at NCSU.

One of the first things that I did upon arriving in the "Ole North State" was to find a church to attend on Sunday. It turned out that one of the leaders in the church that I located was a research chemist at Research Triangle Park, a science complex affiliated with the three major universities in the area – North Carolina State University, the University of North Carolina, and Duke University. Dr. Zakules was a perfect role model for me because he embodied everything that I had always aspired to be – a strong Christian and a brilliant chemist. He and his family "adopted" me, providing a ride to church each Sunday and often inviting me to their home. But there was one other thing that my mentor introduced me to – the Full Gospel Businessmen's Fellowship International. This organization was an interdenominational group of men from the business and professional sectors who really loved Jesus and were filled with the Holy Spirit even though they may not be members of Pentecostal churches. For the first time in my life, I discovered Baptists and Methodists – and even Catholics – who spoke in tongues and prayed for people to be healed. It was an entirely new and eye-opening experience for me. But before I get too involved in that, allow me to back up to the Sunday morning rides to church.

The first Sunday that I was to be picked up for church, I was standing at the curb when one of the guys from the dorm walked by and asked me where I was going. I replied with a very non-committal, "Out." As soon as the fellow student walked away, I thought to myself, "And exactly whom do you think you are fooling? It's ten o'clock on a Sunday morning, you're wearing a suit and tie, and you're carrying a Bible. Where else would you be headed other than church? Why try to hide it?" I was really embarrassed by my lack of boldness, but didn't have any suggestions as to what I should do to overcome it. This is where the Full Gospel Businessmen's Fellowship International (FGBMFI, for short) came into play. The next weekend, I joined my friend from the church at the meeting of the local chapter. Since they held their meetings at a hotel that was just a block from campus, I was able to walk there without having to ask for a ride. When I met these men and began to hear their stories of how co-workers, friends, and occasionally random strangers had shared the gospel with them, I began to feel that it really wasn't all that hard or intimidating to witness to others about the Lord. So, I decided to go back to my campus and not hide my faith like I had just done the previous Sunday morning. Within a few weeks, I had found a couple other students who wanted to go to church with me. Before long, there were more than would fit into my friend's car, and we had to recruit more drivers to come by the campus every Sunday to pick us up. Shortly after that, the pastor decided that there were enough college guys coming every Sunday that there should be a special Sunday school class just for the students from the campus.

Of course, this whole experience was a lesson in the power of unashamedly sharing the gospel, but there was also a side lesson that came out of that Sunday school class as well. I learned of a student on campus who was the son of a pastor from another city; so, I made a point to invite him to the class. Even though I extended several invitations, he never responded. That is until the day that there was a guest evangelist speaking at the church. Since the evangelist was a friend of his father, the student came to church with me for the first – and only – time on that specific Sunday. When the guest speaker got up to preach, he acknowledged the presence of his friend's son and commented on how good it was to see that he had been busy on the campus bringing so many young men to church with him. I assume that the student had been in communication with the evangelist and fed him a line about how active he was spreading the gospel at the university, but that was no concern of mine because the important thing in life isn't who gets credit in the eyes of men. It is only how Jesus credits us that counts.

There was one personal experience on one particular frosty autumn night that set the stage for all that was to come in my life as a university student. My 1969 Mustang sat in the parking lot of Bragaw Dormitory. On this night the windows of that flashy coupe were totally fogged up from the heavy breathing and passionate activity taking place inside. But wait! I have to go back and tell the backstory that leads up to this evening before we open the door to the little sports car and expose what's going on inside.

You see, I grew up in a very strict Pentecostal environment where we were taught that to be friends with the world made you an enemy of God. (James 4:4) In fact, we were so strict about not associating with "the world" that we were almost afraid to be too friendly with Methodists, Baptists, and Presbyterians. For certain, we would never even think of becoming friends with Episcopalians or Catholics. But now that I was away in college, I was developing friendships with other students who were not only those "questionable" Presbyterians and Episcopalians – but also with some students who drank, steamed up the windshields of their cars on a regular basis, smoked pot, experimented with LSD, and who knows what else. This was quite a challenge for someone who had grown up with the motto, "We don't smoke, drink, or chew – or run with them that do!" The mantra of my church leaders was, "Holiness, without which no man will see God." (Hebrews 12:14) Our strict code of modesty required that our girls wear skirts for physical education class rather than the school-issued gym shorts. Of course, there were plenty of regulations that had to do with hair and make-up – taboos that kept the women so "unpretentious" (Okay, let's be honest – so ugly.) that it's a wonder they ever got married. But now that I was away from home I had developed friendships with classmates who broke all those rules. Well, actually, they weren't technically breaking any rules because they didn't grow up under such restrictions. Nonetheless, I found myself running with a crowd that I would have never envisioned before. Although it was never said in so many words, I could always know what was acceptable and unacceptable behavior by one simple test: "If it's fun, it's sin." I remember not being permitted to eat at a popular pizza shop because they served beer. Even though no one at our table would be drinking, the fact that there would be alcohol on the premises made the establishment off limits to our church leadership.

We lived by a very regimented observance of religious duties. For instance, we honored the Sabbath Day by never doing any form of work – not even washing clothes on Sunday. I remember one weekend when my mother needed some clothes cleaned for Monday morning. She stayed up past midnight to use the washing machine even when the only actual work she was going to do was tossing the clothes into the machine and taking them out to transfer them to the dryer. Another example was our dutiful tithing. I remember hearing one man testify about how his car broke down on the week he had failed to pay his tithes, costing him the same amount of money that he would have given to the church had he paid his tithes. He concluded with, "So, God got His tithes anyway." Even though I was just a young child I remember thinking that there was something wrong with that picture. Unless God was running the local auto garage, I could not connect the repair bill with the man's tithing. Looking back on that incident now, some sixty years later, my reaction has a different slant: "Those were the good old days – when you could get your car repaired for one tenth of a week's wage!"

In keeping with our ongoing labors to maintain holiness I recall one particular sermon in which the pastor was trying to encourage the members to be faithful in their church attendance by being present every time the church doors were open. He waxed eloquent in describing how many temptations and struggles were waiting in the outside world to ensnare us and said that we could never get enough of what it takes to resist the world, the flesh, and the devil in just one service on Sunday morning. Definitely we needed that extra dose from the Sunday night service. And, by the time we had rubbed shoulders with the world for the first three days of the week, we needed the "booster shot" of the midweek service in order to make it through to the next Sunday.

So this brings us back to the steamed up windows in my Mustang. I hate to disappoint you, but the passionate activity in the front seat wasn't the "making out" with my girlfriend that you've probably been imagining for the past several paragraphs. It was a passionate, hours-long prayer struggle. I had wanted a private place to do some deep soul-searching, and the only place that I knew I could be totally alone would be in my car away from all the other campus activity. That night I wanted to settle a deeply troubling heart-level question, "Was there something wrong with me? Was I not a real Christian?" I was afraid that I was missing something because I didn't find the Christian life to be a constant struggle, as all the preachers in my life had always said it should be. After all, here I was, friends with "the world," and that must make me an enemy of God. Yes, I understood that my friends who slept around and used drugs were plain and simple sinners, but I was questioning why I didn't see anything wrong with my friends who claimed to be Christians even though they didn't comply with all the rules and regulations that I had always been taught were obligatory.

I couldn't help questioning if somehow I had deceived myself into believing that I was okay because I didn't find my life to be an uphill struggle. Perhaps, I was the dead fish that I had heard so many sermons about – the one who was floating downstream while all the live

78

fish were busily swimming upstream against the current. That night in my little sports car with the steamed-up windows, I finally came to some powerful realizations. I suddenly understood something about the whole "holiness without which no man shall see God" teaching. I realized that Jesus had given us another avenue for seeing God – to have a pure heart. (Matthew 5:8) I also realized that He had given us a better approach to fulfilling all the laws and requirements of God – living in love rather than trying to count the pennies in our tithing or monitoring what is being served at the other tables in the restaurants we are eating in, or even calling in the "modesty police" every time we get dressed. (Mark 12:30-31)

Reflecting back on my grappling that night in the dorm parking lot, I can see one significant component in my life that got me to that place. And, amazingly, that very same aspect of my life is what took me through the struggle and out the other side. That astonishing element was my relationship with my parents. Because I had seen my parents continually demonstrating sacrificial love for me, I had grown up with a deep-seated love and respect for them. My father worked two jobs in order to supply for his family: a comfortable home, nice clothes so that we never felt awkward in school, fun vacations so we could grow up with happy family memories, and a college fund to ensure that we would have the very best opportunities for making our own future. In fact, during my senior year in high school, when I was applying for college, I received lower scholarship offers than some of my classmates who were less academically qualified. The explanation that the scholarship committee gave me was that my father had saved up too much money in my scholarship fund. The irony is that he actually made less money than my classmates' fathers. He had just lived sacrificially in order to provide for me. My mother and father had been purposely frugal – bypassing things that they wanted for themselves, going to work when they physically were not able, and generally pinching every penny so they could see that their children not only didn't lack anything as we were growing up but also so that we had sufficient for our futures.   As I observed this kind of selfless love from them, I developed a heart relationship in which I never wanted to disappoint or disobey them.   I wasn't afraid of breaking their rules; I was afraid of breaking their hearts.   Because I had learned to see life through the eyes of that kind of love, I was not struggling with "the world" because I was not drawn to participate in its temptations even though I was constantly surrounded by them.   So, it was because of growing up in this sacrificially loving environment that I was drawn to the place of a disconnect between my life experience and the religious ideology that I had inherited. That night in the front seat of my car, I realized that true Christianity is exactly the same – it's not about breaking the rules of our Heavenly Father, but about breaking His heart.   The Father so loved us that He gave His own Son for us, and Jesus so loved us that He gave His own life for us.

As I was looking for more Christian friends on the campus, I discovered several Christian fellowships and began to attend one of them since a couple of the members of that group lived in my dormitory.   Even though I became active in the organization's activities on campus, I was always a bit out of place because of their stance on the baptism in the Holy Spirit and the operation of the gifts of the Holy Spirit.   They taught that the spiritual gifts were not for the present day and actually believed that anyone who spoke in tongues had to be possessed by demons.   The funny thing is that the leadership of the group assigned one of the students who lived down the hall to spy on me to see if he could collect enough evidence to prove that I was demon possessed. I understand that he reported back to them six months

80

later that he had not found any evidence that could be used against me and that he told them he actually thought that I was a better Christian than anyone in their group. Of course, I knew nothing about any of this until the spy received the baptism in the Holy Spirit a couple years later and came to me to confess about his surveillance assignment.

While I was active in this group, I attended one of their regional conferences. I actually had a great time and enjoyed all the sessions. However, I did use my free time that weekend to do a bit of extracurricular activity. Since they had an extensive display of books for sale, I took the opportunity to look through the materials that would be considered the foundational documents of their beliefs. My objective was to find out exactly why they taught that the gifts of the Holy Spirit are not for the present day. One book said that these supernatural gifts ceased as soon as the New Testament was completed. Another proposed that they passed away at the death of the last apostle. Even though there would be just a few years' difference between the time that John made the final pen stroke in the book of Revelation and the day that he passed away, there was still a bit of a discrepancy. Another author suggested that the gifts continued on until the end of the second century – adding a little more than a hundred years to the timetable. One book even suggested that the gifts still occur in very remote places where missionaries are just beginning to penetrate. Armed with the results of my investigation, I was ready the next time someone confronted me over my belief that God still fills people with the Holy Spirit and does miracles today; I simply asked, "Well, if the leaders that you follow can't even agree on when these gifts stopped, how can you say for certain that they really did stop?"

Before I get into the next big part of the story of my time at North Carolina State, allow me to fast-forward a couple years to the time when Billy Graham held a crusade in the football stadium on our campus. All the Christian organizations got together to promote the event with each one taking a specific role – one group was responsible for getting ads in the campus newspaper, another was responsible for handing out fliers around campus, and my group (which is the next part of the story) was responsible for putting up yard signs (like "for sale" signs or election placards) around campus. Everyone in the planning meeting got a good laugh out of the announcement of our assignment since we were the ones that believed in the signs. (Mark 16:17)

Even apart from the organized Christian fellowship, my roommate and I were very excited about sharing the gospel with our fellow students and inviting them to our dorm room for a Bible study and prayer group, which suddenly mushroomed beyond dorm room capacity. In addition, we began to have co-eds becoming interested. Since this was before the days of open dorms, girls and guys were strictly prohibited from entering the other's dorms. We tried a remote-control Bible study with the ladies on one end of the telephone while we passed the receiver around among the guys as we did our study and discussion.

Of course, that didn't work very well, so we decided to approach the college administration about using a classroom after hours. The response was that we would be permitted to use any campus facility we needed if we were recognized as an official campus organization. Only two obstacles stood in the way of our recognition – a constitution with by-laws and a faculty advisor. Now, the legal document was not a problem to write up, but where would we find a faculty member on our secular university campus who believed in the Bible and living in the Spirit? We decided to dedicate two weeks of prayer to the matter. In about the middle of our prayer vigil, I received a church newsletter from one of the local Pentecostal congregations. One of the items was a welcome to their recent visitors, including their names. One name leapt off the page. It was a professor from the school. Like a flash, a group of us were off to his office to talk with him about the faculty advisor's position. It turned out that he had just recently accepted the professorship at our campus after completing his Ph.D. work. When job offers all over the country began to close for one reason or another, he began to feel that God had a special reason for sending him to NC State – the only position still open. Even though this was <u>his last choice</u>, he felt that it was <u>God's first choice</u> for him. Now, six months later, he was really struggling with why God had put him there. What was his purpose? Why hadn't God shown him yet? When we shared our story and our request, tears came to his eyes and he fell to his knees with uplifted hands to thank God for putting him in the right place at the right time.

Thus was born Full Gospel Student Fellowship, an official campus ministry with all the rights and privileges of any other university organization. As the influence of the group grew on campus and began to spread to other colleges and universities, the Full Gospel Businessmen's Fellowship adopted us as a "daughter" organization and helped us do all the legal work to become an officially recognized not-for-profit organization by the governments of North Carolina and the United States of America.

Let me remind you that the time period of all these events was a turbulent time in American history – the civil rights movement and the Vietnam War. (I barely missed being drafted when a moratorium was announced just before the young men with my draft number were called up.) I remember sitting in my dorm room window watching the whole of the south side of the city go up in flames on the night that Martin Luther King Jr. was assassinated. A year or so later, student protests over the Vietnam War reached a climax, resulting in riots and university closures all across America. After students took over the administration buildings on a number of major campuses and the National Guard had to be called out to maintain peace – most notably at Kent State University in Ohio – the administration of NCSU, in an attempt to prevent any violence on our campus, made a decision to grant amnesty to all students who wished to become involved in peaceful reform. It was at this time that I was leading a Bible study in my dorm room when an army of protestors marched past the building chanting, "All we are saying is, 'Give peace a chance.'" As their mantra echoed through our Bible study group, I stopped teaching and bellowed out, "Give the Prince of Peace a chance!" Instantly, everyone in the group was on his feet with a new desire to demonstrate to our fellow students that there was a way to world peace and unity – Jesus Christ!

Those were also very special days in totally other ways as well. You might even call them "glory day" as it seemed that God was doing some really extraordinary things – first the Jesus Movement, with the Charismatic Movement following hard on its heels. All across America, young people – from the hippies of Haight-Ashbury to Ph.D. candidates on the university campuses – were being swept into the kingdom of God by the thousands. All around the world, nominal Christians – from Baptist housewives to Roman Catholic priests – were experiencing the miraculous, renewing power of the Holy Spirit. The move of God was like a tsunami, and the wave seemed to be cresting at NCSU.

Almost overnight, we saw hundreds of students coming to know the Lord. When I look back on all that the Lord did in, for, and through my life at North Carolina State, I realize that the day the high school guidance counselor called me into her office and shared with me about the scholarship possibility was actually a divine appointment and a pivotal point in my life. Had I not

84

made the decision to go to NCSU, my life would have been much different – and so would have been the lives of so many others for whom God arranged our paths to cross.

One example was Kirk, the biggest drug dealer on our campus. After the Lord touched his life, he became the biggest Jesus dealer on our campus. When his customers would come to him to buy pot or LSD, he would smile and say, "You know, I've got something that will make you higher than you've ever been." When his clients would ask what he was talking about, he would reach under his bed where he used to store his drugs and pull out a Bible. Within a few minutes, another soul would be born into the kingdom. There is one particularly interesting story involving this young convert. He and I were sitting in the parking lot late one evening having an in-depth discussion when one of his customers came up to the car. He was pretty "high" at the time so I was really questioning if anything that we said had any effect on him. Eventually he walked away and I thought that was the end of the story. However, a few months later there was a knock at my apartment door. I opened the door to find a college student who looked like he could have been one of the Wolfpack linebackers standing there, but – totally out of character for a man his size and built – he was crying like a baby. When he regained enough composure to talk, he blurted out, "What can I do to be saved?" – the same question that the jailer in Philippi asked Paul and Silas when the earthquake destroyed the jail. I, of course, welcomed him inside and asked him how he had wound up at my apartment. His story was that his girlfriend had become a Christian at one of the Full Gospel Student Fellowship meetings and had threatened to break up with him if he didn't also get born again. So, she had sent him to me for prayer. My roommates joined me as we shared the gospel with him and led him to salvation and then into the baptism in the

Holy Spirit. At the end of the prayer, he looked at me through his tears – now, tears of joy – and said, "I know you. You talked to me about God in the parking lot last spring!"

This sort of hunger for God was not an anomaly; it was prevalent all across the country, and members of our fellowship were connecting with students on other campuses who wanted us to come share with them and help them begin campus fellowships like the one we had started at NCSU. In fact, we eventually had twenty-two affiliate campuses with Full Gospel Student Fellowship chapters. We organized weekend retreats where the groups from the various campuses could come together for fellowship and praise, and I visited each campus on a regular basis to lead Bible studies. Of course, we had some interesting experiences both on the campus at NCSU and at our sister campuses. For example, at Appalachian State University, I had no more than walked onto the campus when I was greeted by three young men who asked me the same question as the guy who showed up at my apartment door, "What must we do to be saved?" They had seen the lives of their friends on the campus radically changed by coming to Christ, and they wanted the same life-changing experience in their own lives.

St. Andrews University was one of the first colleges in the US to become totally handicapped-friendly, with all the required amenities such as wheelchair-accessible bathroom stalls and sidewalks with ramps. So, as you might expect, a number of the students that I got to know there had various physical challenges. One particular student who was wheelchair-bound was very passionate in his faith and readily received the baptism in the Holy Spirit when I shared with him. After praying with him, I suggested that I'd also like to pray for his legs to be healed. His response was, "The Lord gave me this wheelchair to keep me humble." At that point, I looked back and replied, "I thought that humility was the work of the Holy Spirit, not a wheelchair." The quizzical look on his face let me know that my words had "struck a nerve"; so, I suggested that he meditate on them until I would be back on campus a couple weeks later when we could pick up on the discussion. When I did return, I asked him if he had been considering the statement that I had left him with on my previous visit. He said that he had and that he had decided I was right. I then reached down and took his hand, and he stood up and started walking! He had been more crippled in his mind than he had in his legs.

At Pembroke State University, the Lord was ready to do a work but it took a series of "coincidences" to make it happen. Along with some of the students from nearby St. Andrews University, I visited the campus to see just what it was that our Lord was about to do. Not knowing any students, we went to the office of the Director of Student Affairs. We explained what was on our hearts, but he couldn't allow outsiders to start any movement on campus. Quite by accident, he happened to have met some students whom he felt might be interested in the fellowship so he sent us to their rooms. Well, after several unfruitful attempts in the dorms, we wound up in the library. The first person we saw in the library was reading a Bible. Praise the Lord, an open door! Within a few minutes we were in a heavy conversation about the Lord, and students at the nearby desks were straining to hear the conversation. Soon, a couple asked if they could join in with us. One student introduced himself as the biggest agnostic on campus. A few minutes later, he was a believer! The other turned out to be an art student who had dedicated her talents to the Lord just a couple of days before! From the "accidental" meeting in the library, a great movement began on the campus and the Full Gospel Student Fellowship's newspaper got a great new editor.

And then there was Donna at the Wilmington campus of the University of North Carolina. It was a dark and stormy night – well, actually it wasn't stormy and it wasn't any darker than any other ordinary night; however, the events of that evening seem to fit so perfectly into one of those "dark and stormy night" stories that I just couldn't resist that intro line. Actually, the evening began as a rather ordinary one. While a group of students from the fellowship were visiting the Wilmington campus, we had decided to stay with a friend who managed an old beachfront hotel in Wrightsville Beach since it was only a few miles from the school. The old building had long since seen its better days and was soon to be bulldozed down to make way for the parking lot for a modern condominium. After checking into our rooms, we headed back to town for a Bible study on campus.

About halfway through the study, a young lady sort of floated into the room. With an out-of-this-world daze in her eyes, she looked around and asked, "What is this place?" We responded that it was a Bible study and that she was welcome to sit down and join us. Her reply was that she was just walking down the hall when "the spirit" told her to come in – so she took a seat and glared around the room as we completed our session. After the meeting, several of the students talked and prayed with her until it was time to leave the room. At that point, one of the students who was traveling with me suggested that our guest come back to the hotel with us for some further counseling. She decided to accept the invitation and we jumped into the cars for the trip to the beach. As soon as we parked and headed toward the building, I began to feel the uncanny sensation that I was walking into a horror movie. The eeriness continued to mount as we entered the back door. Inside, the kitchen was vibrant with an unearthly presence. On the table we found a large box with a note attached. It was from a young man who had just received Jesus into his heart that day. It explained that, with his new life, he wanted to totally break from the old one that had involved a lot of occultism. The box contained all his occult books that he wished to destroy but was afraid to do by himself. His request was that we burn them for him.

Eager to rid the house of the unholy manifestation, we grabbed the box and headed for the fireplace. In that it was winter and that this relic of a hotel was anything but airtight, a roaring fire was already waiting for us in the lobby. All the lobby furniture was huddled around the fireplace as a retreat for all the guests as we tried to defend ourselves against the chilly ocean breezes that blew almost as freely through the hotel as they did on the windswept sand dunes outside. Our group, including the new guest, grabbed seats close to the open fireplace as we began to toss the occult books into the flames. Our new friend, in an almost hypnotic voice, began to talk about each of the books as she pulled them out of the box, "This is an expensive book, you can't burn it. This is a nice one, why do you want to destroy it?" We all knew that something was wrong, but no one knew what to do or say. Upon our insistence, every book made it to the inferno, but the evil presence remained. It was at that point that we realized the demon was in the co-ed from the campus, not the books – so we began to try to cast it out.

Notice that I said "try." None of us had ever done that before, so we were novices using the trial-and-error method. At one point, we asked the young lady if she wanted Jesus to come into her heart so that she could go to heaven; the response was, "Oh, heaven will be boring – just sitting around playing a harp." At that instant, I realized that I had not been talking to the young lady at all, but that my conversation was with a demon that was speaking through her. I demanded that the spirit be quiet so that the girl could hear and respond. Calling her name, I commanded her to answer me and to receive

Jesus into her heart and join me in commanding the demon to leave. She did – and she was free! No longer did she stare with hollow eyes into space. No longer did she speak in a monotone. No longer did she move catatonically. Suddenly she was a vibrant, vivacious young girl. But, she had one major problem – she didn't know where she was or how she had gotten there. Looking at her watch, she exclaimed, "How did it get this late? I've only been gone about ten minutes!" In actuality, she had been in the hotel lobby at least two hours plus all the time she was in the classroom on campus. The spirit that had been controlling her had actually obliterated all reality from her consciousness, and she had been living in the twilight zone under its domination. She was free at last and has continued to live a free and productive life.

Back at North Carolina State, I had other experiences with the demonic – including Robby, a young man who came to me for counseling and prayer. Under terrible bondage of low self-esteem, he refused to look up. Recognizing this as a demonic torment, I put my hand under his chin and forced him to raise his head and look me straight in the eyes. After ministering deliverance to him, I took him with me to a fellowship meeting. Before long, people who had known the lad for several months began to come up and welcome the newcomer to the group. They had never seen him with his head up and did not recognize him as the same person they had known for months.

One interesting experience was the time that couple of students from the fellowship group decided to attend a presentation by a psychic at the campus. When they walked into the auditorium, the psychic – who up to that point had been doing supernatural feats such as bending metal objects with his mental powers – announced that his spiritual forces had been disrupted and suddenly cancelled the rest of the program!

A bright young high school student contacted me for advice and counseling on his new life in Christ. As we corresponded over a period of several months, he suggested that he and his father would be happy for me to visit when I was in the area. It turned out that I was scheduled to visit a college campus not far from their home, so I arranged to drive down a day early and spend the night with them. I had no idea what awaited me as I walked through their front door. There were several strange items that caught my eye. For example: a lady's dress was hanging on a coat rack in the entrance – even though the father and the mother were divorced and she had not lived in the home for many years. When the father showed me to my room, he explained that everything inside had been brought intact from a Mississippi River boat that had served as a floating house of prostitution in the 1800s. I was to sleep in a reconstructed brothel.

It was only after dinner and after my young friend retired for the night that I found out that the father was the head of the local gay rights movement. He was one of the few who had come out of the closet in the 1970s. It was a very uneasy conversation, but we spent some time discussing what the Bible says about homosexuality and that Jesus was willing to release him if he wanted to be free. A crocodile tear and a weak confession later, he asked for me to lay hands on him for deliverance. I soon discovered that all he wanted was for me to get close enough for him to lay his hands on me! The instant that he reached out for me, I screamed out, "In the name of Jesus!" and he was hurled backwards across the room. At that point, I left him sprawled across the furniture and retired to my room. It was the most restless night of my life. All night long, there was the sound of clawing on the walls and door. I knew that demon spirits were trying to attack me, but I was convinced of one fact more concretely: I was under the shadow of the Almighty, and those things would not be able to penetrate God's protective wing. (Psalm 91:1-4) The next morning, I left for my college meeting, realizing the difference between that house and my own. (I'll share the story about the demon in my house a little later in this chapter.) In each, there was demonic manifestation. In one, it was not tolerated and it had to leave; in the other, it was welcomed and it had taken total control.

One incredible postscript to that story is that, when I arrived for my college meeting, I found that my host had left his apartment door open for me even though he was in class at the time I was expected to arrive. So, I went in and made myself at home. While resting on his sofa, I drifted off into a sound sleep from the exhaustion of the night's spiritual warfare. Suddenly, I was jolted to reality as the radio came on and began to blare an evangelist's fifteen-minute show into my ear. When the man finished his quarter hour of edification and exhortation, the radio shut itself off and I drifted back to sleep. Later my host arrived and I recounted the events of the past twenty-four hours. I ended the story by describing how neat it was that he had the radio set to turn on and off for the program and that the message was a blessing to me after the challenging encounter. With eyes like saucers, my host explained that he had not set the radio and, in fact, it wasn't even programmable!

Of course, most of the supernatural encounters I experienced on the campuses were not with demons, but with the Holy Spirit. One fellow student, after talking with me about the baptism in the Holy Spirit, was so concerned that I was in error over this Holy Ghost doctrine that he went home to pray for me. Down on his knees, he began to intercede that I would find the truth and be released from error. The major problem he encountered was that he could not say the word "error" because, by that point, his own language had been changed to unknown tongues.

Ray had gone to one of the college campuses in the mountains of western North Carolina to try to "straighten out" his friend who had just received the baptism in the Holy Spirit. As they talked, it turned out that the friend "straightened out" Ray. Having realized that he also needed to be filled with the Holy Spirit, Ray began to pray as he drove down the steep and winding mountain road back toward Raleigh. Suddenly, the Holy Spirit came upon him, and Ray received the baptism in the Holy Spirit while driving down that mountain. He was so overjoyed with his experience that he threw his hands into the air and began to praise God in his new language. Only God could have gotten his car safely down that twisty mountain road! And then there was Gene who had grown up in a Pentecostal church and was very desirous of receiving the Holy Spirit baptism. In fact, he had been praying for this blessing for thirteen years. One afternoon, while trying to lead a fellow student to salvation, Gene was confronted with the question, "How do you know that it will really work?" His answer was, "You have to accept it by faith." Just then the Holy Spirit spoke inside of Gene's heart, "Yes, and that's how you have to receive my baptism – by faith." The "better idea" light bulb suddenly flashed on inside his spirit, and Gene understood why he had been hindered for so many years. That evening, he released his faith and was inundated by the most spectacular flood of the Holy Spirit that I have ever witnessed. For the next two days, he could not talk on the phone, answer a question in class, or order a meal in the campus cafeteria. He literally found it impossible to force himself to speak English. I guess it was all the praise that had been pent up in him for more than a dozen years suddenly rushing out!

Another story along this line actually has two parts. The first has to do with a trip to the laundromat. I thumbtacked a tract on the bulletin board where people could leave public announcements such as items for sale or rooms for rent since it was an ideal place to connect with the university students. A few days later, my roommate and I did a little door-to-door campaign in our dorm to invite the students to our Bible study. One student from a couple doors down the hall accepted our invitation and came to the group the following evening. At the end of the meeting, my roommate offered him a tract to read. His response was, "I've seen this pamphlet before – in the laundromat. I took it from the bulletin board and read it. In fact, I was so impressed by the message that I stuck it back on the board in hopes that someone else would read it and be helped by it as much as I was." Our new friend continued to come to the Bible study and attend our fellowship meetings but somehow wasn't ready to receive the Lord. And this is the second part of the story – that is until the day at one of the fellowship meetings when he happened to be seated next to Larry who began to speak in tongues as he was praying. At the end of the meeting, he asked me about Larry, saying that he must be from Italy. When I answered that he was not, my new friend said, "But he speaks Italian. I know Italian when I hear it spoken because my grandparents are from Italy, and I have learned to recognize a number of Italian words from hearing them speak to one another in their native tongue." At that point, I explained that what he had heard was the miraculous gift of speaking in tongues – using a language that you do not know but is given to you through the power of the Holy Spirit. At that point, he realized that Christianity was more than a philosophy or a religion to guide our lives. Acknowledging that what he had seen was a manifestation of the supernatural power of God, he readily decided to be born again.

Probably the most dramatic experience of the supernatural occurred when I had organized a retreat for Full Gospel Student Fellowship groups from several of the North Carolina campuses at one of North Carolina's

94

Atlantic Coast beaches. The retreat weekend was planned as a teaching conference, yet a number of the participants wanted to use the time to do beach evangelism. Tension began to rise as the students began to split into two camps – those who wanted to evangelize and those who wanted to be taught. Sensing the turmoil in the atmosphere, I picked the top leaders of each group – three from each side. Leading them to an attic room in the ocean-side house we had rented for the weekend, I said, "We're going to the Upper Room until the Holy Ghost falls like He did on Pentecost." After a short season of prayer, one young man began to prophesy. After a few sentences, be abruptly stopped in mid-sentence. Across the room another young man picked up the message, finished the sentence and added several more lines. But he too stopped in mid-sentence. Again, the message was picked up without missing a word and completed by another of the participants in our prayer group. He also stopped in mid-sentence. Again and again this happened until everyone in the room had taken part in the prophetic word. One prophecy, spoken by seven of us – bouncing back and forth between leaders of two opposing sides of the argument – confirmed that the original plan for a training conference was God's plan for our weekend. The body was brought into harmony and given excellent direction through the Holy Spirit's gifts. To confirm the word, a rainstorm blew in that evening and drenched the coastline for our entire stay. No beach ministry could have occurred after all!

One of the lessons that became very clear through those supernatural encounters was that it is absolutely necessary to be sensitive to the Holy Spirit's direction so that He can truly be in control of our lives. One experience that clearly proved this point occurred at one of our campus weekend retreats when a prophetic word came forth in which the Spirit reiterated three times that the Lord is God and that His people should kneel before

Him in worship. As soon as the prophecy had ended, the moderator of the meeting took the podium, "We've all heard the Holy Spirit's admonition, so let's stand up and praise the Lord." Fortunately, I was in the position of leadership within the fellowship so that it was not out of order for me to step up and correct the moderator by reminding the people that the Holy Spirit had directed us to kneel – not stand – and to worship – not praise. No matter how sincere he may have been, he was wrong and would have led the people astray because he had not been sensitive to the voice of the Lord in the prophetic message.

Let me share one other experience that happened just so perfectly that you would think it must have been planned. This experience occurred at a Saturday morning prayer breakfast. After the meal, one man pulled a chair into the middle of the floor, sat down in the chair, and asked for prayer. In those days, the common form of ministry was what they jokingly called the "hot seat." Since the Bible directs the laying on of hands for healing, it seemed only reasonable that the more hands you could get on you, the better your chances for healing would be. Thus, the sick person would take a chair and be surrounded by the entire group and dozens of hands would suddenly bring blessing to the sufferer.

Well, this morning an unusual scenario was just about to unfold. One of the leaders of the group had just returned from a Kathryn Kuhlman meeting where he had experienced being slain in the Spirit. He insisted that the poor man stand up rather than sit down just in case God wanted him to "fall under the power" as he received his healing. Before the sufferer could get to his feet, another man who had been under some strong positive confession teaching interrupted with a statement that he should be calling himself healed; otherwise, he would remain sick whether he fell on the floor or not. Instantly someone else began to encourage him to rebuke the devil. Someone also asked if he really believed when he prayed. Next, another brother interjected some statement about claiming a Bible verse. Before long, other men in the room were busy talking about unconfessed sins, not being a bold witness, and unforgiveness as hindrances to receiving healings. Suddenly a scream like a Native American war whoop pierced the air. We all jerked to attention just in time to see the sick man suspended in midair about three feet off the floor. The supernatural power of God had sovereignly hit the man with no laying on of hands, no falling on the floor, no Bible verses being quoted, no positive confessions made, no devils rebuked, and no sins confessed. The jolt of God's power had totally healed the man, and he was leaping for joy. This was a real miracle in that his back had been so seriously injured that he could barely walk – much less jump!

Having mentioned Kathryn Kuhlman, I have to share one exciting story about this great woman of God. In case you may not know about this iconic figure from the last century, Kathryn Kuhlman was a dynamic healing minister who held some of the most powerful crusades and healing campaigns imaginable – so powerful, in fact, that you didn't just go to one of her meetings; you had to "arrange" to be there! You couldn't just open the door and walk in; you had to plan to be there several hours in advance and stand outside waiting for the doors to open. On one occasion, four or five other students from our fellowship and I had made all the necessary "arrangements" to be in a Kathryn Kuhlman meeting. We had been waiting in line for an hour or so when we noticed some people in wheelchairs and crutches who really needed to be healed. I turned to my friends and said, "Those folks back there who really need healing are so far back in the line that they aren't going to get in. Why don't we give them our spot?" They took our place in line and we moved to the back of the line. When the doors opened, they went in and we were left standing outside because there were more people in line than there were seats in the auditorium. Then an amazing thing happened – the head usher came up and said, "If you don't mind sitting on the floor, I've got a place for you." He brought us in and seated us in front of the front row. We were so close, we could have reached out and touched Miss Kuhlman! That was one time when the last really did get first place. When we were willing to give up our places so somebody else could have a guarantee of getting into the building, we wound up being in the very front.

Those little promptings from the Holy Spirit – like, "Give up your place in line," proved to be very significant in the unfolding saga of what God wanted to do in and through my life. For example, after the university actually assigned our campus fellowship an office on campus (Remember that I said that we had all the rights and privileges of any other campus organization.), we set up office hours which we publicized on campus in case anyone wanted to come by for prayer, and many students did stop in during those posted times. On one particular day, however, I just felt an uneasiness in my spirit even though it was my assigned time to be in the office. Even though I didn't want to neglect my responsibilities, I felt a stronger urge to stroll around campus; taking the longer way to the office and making a stop at the nearby post office. On my walk, I met a couple of students that I hadn't seen for a while. I casually talked with them and invited them to our fellowship meeting that evening. I found out when they came that night that my steps had truly been ordered of the Lord. One young lady had been backslidden for about six months and was working as a dancer in a topless bar. She had been deliberately avoiding contact with Christians, but my words were all it took to draw her back to fellowship and the Lord. The other student had been going through a very serious temptation and just needed the encouragement of a brother. He wouldn't have come to me in the office for prayer, but the Lord had led me to him.

Even in ways that might not seem so "spiritual," the Holy Spirit is always ready to give direction. During exam week one semester, I found myself so busy with work, a Bible study group, and other ministry, that I really couldn't study for one of my exams. The day of the test, I found myself ill-prepared. That morning, another student and I got together to study. In a quick review of the text, we ran across the listing of the characteristics of the Chinese civilization a thousand years ago. We read over the list and sort of got stuck there. Finally, we wound up memorizing the list and letting some other facts go unstudied. When we got to the exam, the main question was, "Discuss the ancient civilization of China"! Another example occurred when I was arranging the list of guest speakers that we wanted to invite to speak at our fellowship meeting one year. I marked a possible date next to each name and began to write letters inviting each speaker for a specific date. Accidently I marked the wrong date in one of the letters. I felt the Holy Spirit's direction to simply shuffle the entire list of dates rather than to rewrite the letter. When the replies came back from the speakers, each one said that he could come on the suggested date and, almost to the man, each mentioned that this was the only date he was available!

And then there was the Christmas when the students decided to buy a gift for the faculty advisor. We took up an offering for the gift, and a couple of us headed down to the store to pick out a present. The only gift that really seemed right was a wall plaque of the praying hands, but it left us with a little spare money. Looking at the extra money, we felt that inner nudge of the Spirit to get the plaque personalized with an engraved inscription. When the final bill was figured, it matched the offering to the penny! Perhaps this seems to be a small example, but it is the sort of ground in which the seed of faith grows best.

But one experience was so dramatic that it was obviously a set-up by God. One Christmas vacation, I was trying to get off campus and head home for the holidays. It seemed as if everything that could go wrong did. I had to turn in some papers at an office. When I got there, the office was closed for the next two hours. I had some books I needed to return to a lady in town. When I got to her house, the women's prayer band was meeting there. So, I was delayed until a break in their meeting. Well, one thing after another came up, but finally I was ready to leave – two or three hours behind schedule. I guess I should say that I was behind <u>my</u> schedule because I was right on target on <u>God's</u> timetable.

When I finally did leave school, I was only about half a mile from campus when I picked up a hitchhiker. As soon as she got into the car, she made a comment about a "God loves you" sticker that I had on my dashboard and began to pour out her soul to me. She explained that up until two weeks before she had been an atheist who didn't believe that there was a God or that she had a soul. However, a big "accident" had changed all that. She and some friends were tripping on LSD. Everyone else came down, but her trip went on for a couple more hours. During the whole time, she could tell that there was some real difference between her and her friends. The only thing that made sense to her was that she must have died during the trip, but she wanted so desperately to live. Finally, her trip ended and she knew that she was still alive. From down in her innermost being – a place that she did not even know was in her – a voice cried out, "Thank God, I'm alive!" At that moment, she knew that there is a God because something inside of her acknowledged His existence. She also recognized that she must have a soul because of the "something" inside her that recognized God's existence even when her mind refused to believe in Him. Through all those delays that seemed to me to be accidents, the Lord had arranged that I be there at just the right moment to introduce her to the God she was seeking!

Of course, not everything that happened on campus was always "spiritual." There were lots of just fun events like the wonderful spring weekend when about a hundred of the students from the fellowship gathered at a seaside lodge for a spiritual renewal retreat. The schedule was filled with Bible studies, prayer sessions, testimony times, and teaching sessions. Very little free time for the beach had been scheduled. No one really minded because we were all there because of a genuine desire to grow in our faith and deepen our experience with the Lord.

On the other hand, we were still kids in our early twenties and we had been corralled on campus all winter. So, needless to say, the precious little time we had for the sun, surf, and sand was exactly that – precious and little! So, when Butch announced that he had something special that he wanted to present and asked the leadership if he could have part of the free time for his presentation, you can imagine the less than joyous response that reverberated through the crowd. It turned out that his special presentation was a slide show from his recent trip to Israel. At that point, I was reminded of the existentialist's presentation of the afterlife in which a man found himself in a locked room with an elderly couple and their stacks of slides of their grandkids and their travels around the world. When he exclaimed to the warden that he realized that he was in hell, the warden's response was that there was another room exactly like this one upstairs in heaven. Well, the student giving the show may have been in heaven, but no one else in the room shared his elation. His photographs were not exactly on par with *National Geographic*. In fact, he had a series of shots of the thirteen steps that Jesus had climbed at Caiaphas' house. Butch had a shot from each one of the steps. In addition, he had taken many of the pictures at a forty-five-degree angle in order to get a wider shot. The result was that he had to turn his projector on its side to show the diamond-shaped photos. We all tried to politely encourage our brother, but can't describe how happy we were when his bulb blew up and we could head for the beach!

While we are at the North Carolina coast, let me share the story of another visit I made to Wrightsville Beach. As I walked through the door of the church where I was to preach, I was welcomed by one of the ushers who grabbed me in a Pentecostal bear hug of a greeting. Since he was a very tall and rotund man, when he pulled me to himself, he actually picked me up off the floor. There I hang – suspended between heaven and earth – when suddenly the anointing of the Holy Spirit fell upon this man. He began to dance and spin, and – as I was being whirled about in midair by this total stranger – he began to tell me my life story. He proclaimed that I was to go around the world to teach the gospel. My ears really perked up at that because I had never been out of the country except short excursions into Canada and Mexico! Since that time, I have visited over sixty nations around the world and in most of them I have held teaching sessions to help establish the local believers in their Christian faith.

One summer between college terms, I worked in a corrugated board factory, making the shipping containers that large appliances are packaged in. My job was to take the huge sheets of corrugated board, fold them over and shove them into a giant stapling machine that would stitch them together. This piece of equipment was very loud and drowned out every other sound as it stitched the flaps of the big containers; so, as the machine's operator, I essentially lived in his "own little world" of isolation from the rest of the factory. Every morning before I reported to work at seven o'clock, I would memorize a Bible passage to meditate on while running my noisy machine. At nine o'clock, the factory workers had a fifteen-minute cigarette and coffee break. Since I didn't need cigarettes or coffee, I used my break time to memorize a second passage to mediate on for the next portion of my shift. When our eleven-o'clock lunch break rolled around, I didn't need the full thirty-minute break to eat my lunch so I memorized a third scripture to meditate on for my next stint at the stitching machine. When the one-o'clock whistle signaled that it was time for our afternoon break, I still didn't need cigarettes or coffee so I memorized a fourth set of verses to meditate on during the final leg of my day. I believe that I grew more spiritually that summer than during any other period in my life because I spent eight hours each day doing nothing but meditating on the Word of God. That summer in the cardboard box factory was a highlight in my spiritual journey and growth.

As some of the leadership of the fellowship graduated and had to move off campus, we realized that we needed to find a home base for the ministry; so, we decided to buy a house just a few blocks from the campus. It was in a rather interesting location, just next door to a mental hospital and on the edge of a rather rough part of town. With the location came some interesting experiences, such as the night that the police burst into the house chasing what they thought was an escaped patient from the asylum and the night when the house was robbed as we all sat upstairs watching television. Since there were several students living in the house, we all assumed that the noises we heard were just one of our other roommates in the other part of the house.

But before I get ahead of myself by sharing too many of those stories, I need to tell you what happened before we even moved in. I was alone as I swept away years of dust out of the large attic room. Suddenly, I felt an evil presence as I worked my way across the middle of the hardwood floor. Clutching the broom a little tighter, I looked around to locate the source of this unwelcome invader. My attention was drawn upward to the light fixture directly above my head. I noticed immediately that there was a sort of secret cubbyhole above the light where a horizontal platform for mounting the fixture had been suspended from the slanted ceiling. After locating a chair, I climbed up to investigate that mysterious compartment. Inside, I found the most horrible cache of pornographic literature imaginable. After removing the literature, the demonic presence left the room. Later, a group of us prayed over the house and asked that God anoint the building so that people would be aware of the Holy Spirit's presence when they came in. We wanted to totally replace the evil with good. In fact, one student even prayed that the very doorknobs would be anointed! We knew that our prayer had taken effect the day a man knocked at the front door to ask what kind of house it was. He claimed to have felt the presence of Jesus as he walked down the sidewalk in front of the home.

One other incident that occurred as we were fixing up that old house was the removal of a lot of old lumber and building supplies that had been stacked up on the second-floor balcony. When I picked up an armload of wood, I was alarmed to find that there was a wasp nest inside. As the wasps began to swarm, I threw down the boards and ran toward the edge of the balcony – which, by the way, did not have a guard rail. When I got to the precipice, I realized that even though I was on the second floor of the building, I was actually three stories up since I was on the back of the house where there was garage beneath the first floor. I also had a second revelation in that same split-second – I couldn't fly! I was trapped between a swarm of angry wasps and a three-story leap. It was impossible for me to escape. There was no way for me to safely get back to the screen door that would allow me safety inside the house. At that instant, I commanded, "Wasps, let me through, in the name of Jesus!" Miraculously, the whole swarm of wasps flew in the other direction – allowing me access to the door and shelter inside.

For the next several years, I was "housefather" over the students who came to live in the fellowship's house. I was tasked with enforcing the house rules which included everything from not leaving dirty dishes in the sink to not murdering the other residents. As you can imagine, trying to be the one to keep order over a bunch of college guys gave rise to a full litany of interesting experiences. I came to be known by the nickname, "The Ant" because when I would catch anyone slacking off, I would always quote Proverbs 6:6-11, "Go to the ant, thou sluggard, consider her ways and be wise, which having no guide, overseer or ruler, provided her meat in the summer and gathers her food in the harvest. How long wilt thou sleep, oh sluggard, and when wilt thou arise out of thy sleep. Yet a little sleep, a little slumber, a little folding of the hands to sleep, so shall thy poverty come as one that travaileth and thy want as an armed man." I was hoping to develop in them some self-motivation and self-direction so that they could function effectively even if there was no one standing over them every minute saying, "Do this. Do that. Do the other."

Before I share this next story, I must remind you that this was before the days of cellphones so the student in question here had no way of communicating to me that he had been taken to the hospital after a minor accident. When he arrived home several hours after curfew, I had to be awakened to let him in. Opening my second-floor bedroom window, I accused the young man of every sin in the book and soundly scolded him for every imaginable crime. When the "culprit" finally got a chance to explain, I simply replied, "Just save that scolding for some time when you sin and I don't catch you!"

One of the house rules was the "four dirty dish law" that was designed to allow the residents to leave three dishes in the sink but required them to wash up after themselves when they had four dishes. I've already told you that this was before the days of cellphones, but it also predated microwave ovens. The principle was that a student could make a sandwich with only three dishes (a plate, a knife, and a glass) but would have to use at least four dishes (a plate, a fork, a cooking pot or pan, and a glass) if he made a real meal. One of our residents soon decided that he could bypass the rule by washing off his fork and leaving just the pan, the plate, and the glass in the sink. Of course, I confronted him with the question of how he ate his food without a fork – especially since he was not an Indian who ate with his fingers. Such was the life of "The Ant"!

I mentioned earlier that the fellowship house was on the edge of a rather "shady" neighborhood – a situation that caused a couple interesting events. When one student moved in, I warned him that he should not leave his bicycle outside if he hoped to have it to ride to school the next morning. He answered that he had it chained up. Unfortunately, when he went out the next morning to jump on his bike to go to class, all that he found was his front wheel chained to the back steps. Since he had not put the chain through the frame, one of the neighbors had simply loosened the nuts to the front wheel and taken the rest of the bike. On another occasion, someone used one of the hedge bushes in our backyard as a hiding place from which to attack one of the ladies in the neighborhood. It was this second incident that occasioned the following episode.

In order to make our property a bit safer I decided that I needed to get rid of the hedge bush, but there was one big problem that I didn't foresee – I didn't realize that a poison ivy vine had grown up inside the bush. When I grabbed the hedge bush with my bare hands to pull it out of the ground, it refused to yield; so, I squatted down, wrapped my arms around it and, using my leg muscles, yanked it up by the roots. Since it was a very hot summer day, I was working without a shirt and only wearing a pair of cut-off jeans. The result was that almost my total body – legs, arms, and chest – was covered with poison ivy. The worst part of this whole story is that this happened just a couple weeks before I was to leave on a mission to India, and the reaction to the poison ivy made me too sick and weak to make the trip. One night, while I was lying in my bed writhing with agony from the itchy blistering rash from the poison ivy, I literally became almost delirious. In my distorted mental state, I lapsed into the spiritual realm. Suddenly, I saw beyond the physical and recognized that the attack against me was spiritual; the physical ailment was only a manifestation of all the Hindu spirits which were whirling around me, piercing me with pitchforks and spears. Instantly, I realized what I had to do. I had to rebuke the spirits and take authority over them. In clearing out the spiritual realm, I would have victory in the physical. This was a powerful lesson to me in knowing how to "put my foot down" and tell the devil that he had no authority over me.

Because of my work with college students, a well-known evangelist invited me to serve as his youth director. His plan was that I would travel the country with him and hold youth rallies while he preached in the adult crusades. For a kid just out of college, this was a real honor and an open door for a great ministry. But something inside – the Holy Spirit – said, "Wait two weeks." So, I asked for two weeks to pray before I made the decision. During those two weeks, the man was caught in adultery with a lady in Canada. Like dominos, other cases of adultery began to pop up all across the country. How wonderful it was that I was able to save my reputation by not becoming a part of such an organization!

I suppose that by now you have figured out that I didn't leave North Carolina State University after my sophomore year to finish my degree at Furman University. In fact, I stayed on at NCSU for graduate school in the chemical engineering department working on a research project that had to do with water pollution control within the paper industry. As an unexpected side benefit, we discovered that the process that I was helping to develop not only substantially cut back on the water pollution but also eliminated a major portion of the air pollution within the industry. Things were going well. I held a highly sought-after specialized degree and now I was gaining additional experience as part of a cutting-edge research team. For me, the door was open to some very lucrative jobs and I seemed to be positioned for a very comfortable future. However, God had something much different in store for me.

About mid-way through graduate school, the Lord directed me to switch from my chemical engineering career plans to teach in a Bible school. I knew that I would have to have a degree from an accredited theological school in order to fulfill this directive; however, there were no recognized Full Gospel schools back then. Because Southeastern Baptist Seminary was just a few miles from my home and their tuition was incredibly reasonable for off-campus students, I decided to check out the school. I applied and was accepted; but I never told anyone what I was up to. About this time, I was invited to be interviewed on a Christian television talk show. After the interview, the program host and I went to the chapel to pray over the prayer requests which had been called in during the program. One of the engineers from the studio joined us, but instead of praying over the call-ins, he wanted to pray over me. He began to prophesy and spoke out, "Do what's in your heart and don't be afraid of the doctrines of men." Well, this was a real word from God because – as a tongue-talking, devil chasing fanatic – I was concerned about sitting under Baptist doctrines for the next several years. Southeastern was the most liberal seminary among the most conservative Southern Baptist schools – a perfect setting for me because they were open to new ideas even though they held to biblical foundations. On the orientation day at campus, I sat in the balcony of the chapel and counted a dozen students whom I had led to the Lord, prayed for to receive the baptism in the Holy Spirit, or discipled through the Full Gospel Student Fellowship ministry that I had done on their secular college campuses. Long story short – I was able to initiate a charismatic movement on campus that even involved some of the faculty by the time I finished my degree.

While working in Yosemite National Park the summer before my final term in seminary, I was approached for a full-time position. It was an absolute dream come true – living and ministering full-time in one of nature's wonderlands. It was toward the end of the summer, and I had to make a decision quickly whether to accept the offer or return for my last semester of seminary. It was then that I met a gentleman named Dick Mills. He was vacationing in the park and had been coerced by some of the local believers to minister to them in a home fellowship. Dr. Mills had a most unusual ministry of looking at individuals and giving them Bible verses that were God's directions or encouragements for them at the moment. As I entered the park ranger's living room where Dr. Mills was to speak, Dick turned to me and said, "Young man, you have a decision to make within the next ten days. Don't you?" I replied in the affirmative, and he responded that God would speak to me through Isaiah 30:20. Then he went on with the meeting. Flipping my Bible open I found the indicated verse and read, "Thine eyes shall see thy teachers." Instantly I knew that I was not able to complete my studies by correspondence as I was considering because I had to be in class to see the teachers. During my final year, the members of the charismatic group I had started on the campus were able to arrange a campus meeting with a leading Baptist minister who was also a well-known charismatic figure. It was the largest attended meeting on campus that year short of the graduation and brought significant positive attention to the move of the Spirit.

One of my seminary classes consisted of a life-changing trip to Israel. But before I tell you about that experience, I have to set the stage a bit. From the third century AD, the Western Wall had been considered as the abode of the Shekinah, the physical presence of God, and it became a special place of prayer. Called the Wailing Wall, or the Western Wall, it is of special importance to Jewish life today. When the wall was captured by the Israeli army in 1967, the senior chaplain of the armed forces declared, "We have taken the City of God. We are entering the messianic era for the Jewish people." Even an "irreligious" Israeli said that he "shook with uncontrolled emotion" as he stood at the wall on that occasion. This was the spot where I experienced the most impactful encounter of the pilgrimage.

Four years of saving and planning had finally brought me to what the rabbis claimed to be the center of the universe. Two nights before, I had stood on the terrace atop Mount Olivet and had, to some degree, experienced the emotion of Jews throughout history as they looked longingly upon their spiritual capital. Many had been pilgrims, eager to visit their sacred sites; I, too, was a pilgrim eager to view the holy shrines. Many had been refugees and exiles returning to the ruins of what was once their treasured city; I, too, was a sort of a refugee from the twentieth century hoping to return to the first century and taste its atmosphere and essence. Many had been irreligious, gainsaying merchants; I too, in a sense, was a self-seeking merchant – I had come as a tourist who would trample the streets, taking photographs, eating the best meals, and perhaps even insulting the residents with my Western lifestyle. Many had been spiritually bankrupt people of the land hoping to find spiritual reality in the temple; I, too was looking for spiritual renewal. As we moved along our schedule of tours, we finally came to the Old City of Jerusalem. My spirit shouted with the Psalmist, "I was glad when they said unto me, Let us go into the house of the Lord. Our feet shall stand within thy gates, O Jerusalem." (Psalm 122:1-2)

At the Western Wall, I suddenly became no longer a tourist; I was a worshiper. My whole perception of the Holy Land changed as I reached up to touch the massive stones. Around me, I was aware of the true importance of the Torah, whether in reading and recitation or in just being in its presence. I was also aware of the still-lingering significance of the temple as a symbol of Shekinah, and – therefore, hope – in spite of the agonies of the past and present. Later that day I became even more acutely aware of what the Western Wall must mean to the Jews as I visited the Garden Tomb. There, I was spiritually reminded of the reality of the resurrection. To the Christian the ruins of an empty tomb proclaim, "He is not here: for He is risen." (Matthew 28:6) At the Western Wall, the Jews feel that they have come as close as possible to the presence of God. At the empty tomb, I felt that I was in the actual presence of the risen Lord!

Back in the US, I completed my master's degree at the seminary and decided to go on for the doctoral program. However, there was one hurdle that I had to jump in order to qualify – I had to pass a competency test in German. The requirement was put in place because so much of the theological scholarship in the first part of the twentieth century was written in German. The easiest way for me to learn the language was to take a class at my alma mater, North Carolina State University, which was less than an hour's drive from the seminary. Since I still lived in Raleigh, I found taking the classes at the campus convenient – well, somewhat. I started my day by teaching at a high school in the outskirts of town, followed by driving to the seminary and taking a couple classes. After class, I would drive back to Raleigh and park at a hotel where I had worked while in college. Since I was only taking one class, I didn't want to pay for a university parking permit so I requested permission from the hotel manager to use a spot in their lot each day. I would then speed-walk about a mile to my German class, arriving just as the class was ready to begin.

Of course, I was exhausted from the hectic pace I had kept all day – and I usually dozed off for a couple minutes as soon as I was relaxed in my seat. On one particular day, the professor began the class by telling a joke in German. I woke up just before he got to the punch line and immediately caught the gist of his story. Since the rest of the students in the class were busy trying to translate through the whole story, none of them was able to catch the point. I was the only one who laughed at the story. Of course, the instructor recognized that I had slept through most of his story and told me later that he was amazed that I was able to understand the joke. Well, at least, I had learned enough German to get into the doctoral program.

Unfortunately, the next step was not a joke. My major professor – the man who really determined if I would make it through the program – became more of a tormentor than the mentor he was supposed to be. Every encounter I had with him was a confrontation rather than a confirmation. It seemed that he saw his

112

mission in life as hindering me, rather than helping me as I worked to earn my degree. No matter how hard I tried, the situation didn't seem to improve. That is, until the day he made an off-the-cuff statement that let me see into his personal self. I realized that he was having trouble at home and that he was bringing his frustrations and anxieties from home to the office. For some unknown reason, I had become the brunt of his emotional release. When I realized what was happening, I mentioned to him that I was going to pray for him and his family. Instantly, his attitude changed and our working relationship took a one-eighty! Magic? No, it was the blessing of God because I finally got my vision in proper alignment. From the moment I started praying <u>for</u> him rather than <u>about</u> him, I was seeing him the way God wanted me to see him. When I was able to stop seeing him <u>as</u> a problem and begin to see that he <u>had</u> a problem, I began to see him from the viewpoint of God. It turned out that I actually didn't finish my doctoral program at Southeastern, but that's a story for another day.

My first mission trip was to Japan with a Japanese friend from seminary. He would go back home to minster during each summer break and always asked me to join him. The first summer I politely nodded when he extended the invitation and promptly dismissed the idea. The second summer I also politely thanked him for the invitation and ignored the request. When he made the offer the third summer, there was something different about his invitation, he concluded the request with, "and I've already booked your tickets." (No, he didn't pay for them; he simply put them on hold under my name.) Well, that was enough to make me decide to be serious about the request. As I prayed about it, I gave God all the excuses I could think of as to why I shouldn't go. When I got to, "I'm not adequate," He responded with such a distinctly clear reply that to this day I still wonder if it might have been an actual audible voice. When God speaks, He can say just a few words but convey volumes of meaning. That is exactly what He did that day. His words were, "I know that you're not adequate. That's why I'm sending you." The commentary on the actual words communicated that if I were adequate I'd go in my own ability rather than relying upon His ability working through me.

Well, I did go to Japan that summer and had one of the most unusual experiences imaginable. I was scheduled to speak for a week at a youth camp in a rather remote area where no one spoke English. Of course, that many years ago, very few Japanese outside the major cities were bilingual. My friend was to serve as my translator; however, his wife fell seriously ill and he had to take her back to the hospital in Tokyo. The result was that I was stranded for the full week and couldn't minister in any of the sessions. When my friend came back at the end of the week to pick me up, the director of the camp asked him to translate a message of thanks to me for being with them for the week. In the salutation, he said, "We've learned so much from you." I interrupted to ask how, since I had not ministered. The response was that they had learned from the Spirit in me. Thank God, I was inadequate!

Late one night while driving home through the downtown streets of Raleigh, the Lord spoke to me through, of all things, the traffic signals. Since there was no other traffic around me, I could see that for blocks ahead of me there lay a virtual obstacle course of traffic lights, some green, some yellow, but the ones that I was really focused on were all those red lights, keeping me from getting home where I could put my tired body to bed. But, as I drove, every light turned green as I approached; so, I just kept driving along at the same speed all the way down the street. The traffic system had been carefully programmed by a traffic engineer, and all the lights were synchronized. As long as I carefully observed the speed limit, I did not have to stop for a single signal. In the middle of the night, the Lord spoke to me. He assured me that He was the Traffic Engineer who had planned my life and if I continued going steadily at His speed each obstacle in my path would become a green light and an open door. I was only to concentrate on the green lights close at hand and entrust the red lights to Him. The amazing thing about this revelation was that just a few weeks later I was invited to go to Sri Lanka to hold a youth training conference. Even though the Lord did a number of miracles as I was in the process of trying to raise the funds for the trip, I was still five hundred dollars short of what I needed. However, I received a note from a friend along with a five-hundred-dollar offering. He explained that he had saved the money for a mission of his own but that the Lord had directed him to send the funds to me instead. He concluded by sharing the words that the Lord had spoken into his spirit about the offering, "Red light for you, but green light for Delron." Of course, the miracle is that my friend knew nothing at all about my experience that night.

As we often say, I've saved the best for the last. The events that I'm about to share here did occur chronologically very close to the end of my time in North Carolina. One night, several of the guys from the campus fellowship (By this time we were all out of school and most of them were employed in rather significant positions.) were sitting around in my apartment when my roommate, commenting on the fact that we were all in our late twenties and still not married, said, "What we need is a Christian singles bar." I responded that we didn't need a bar but that we could possibly have a Christian coffeehouse. I mentioned that I had heard an announcement on the radio about a Christian coffeehouse that was opening in the next town and volunteered to check it out. I followed up with a visit the next weekend, only to discover a roomful of thirteen-year-olds, and Peggy, a twenty-eight-year-old lady who was there for the same purpose that I was – to check out the scene for her peer group. It turned out that she was part of a group of female twenty-somethings who were looking to meet some eligible Christian guys. I got her phone number for my roommate and assumed that that would be the end of the story; however, it turned out to just be the beginning.

Yes, a coffeehouse did develop out of that connection. A local church gave us the use of a basement room which we cleaned up, painted, decorated, and christened as "The Ark." Every Friday night, we had praise and worship, music, food, and fellowship. However, I suppose I should change the "we" in that sentence to "they" since I got a new shift at work that prohibited me from ever attending the Friday night meetings. The other thing that we did was to have a Bible study every Tuesday evening. Since we couldn't use the church facility during the week, we held the study in Peggy's apartment. The funny thing about that arrangement was that she had other commitments on Tuesdays so she gave me a key so I could hold the meetings even without her being there. It was actually pretty ironic that the two of us were essentially in charge of the whole coffeehouse ministry yet we never saw each other. It was even more ironic that I had a key to her apartment even though we were essentially only casual acquaintances. In fact, our relationship was even less than that since I actually didn't like her because of what I described as her "brassy" personality. She was a strong, domineering individual – not at all like the "Southern Belle" kind of woman I admired.

This non-relational relationship went on for about a year until one day when I was trying to organize a mission trip to Puerto Rico. I was especially interested in recruiting Peggy as part of the team since she had lived and worked in Mexico for two years and spoke a little

116

Spanish. I had a chance to chat with her about the idea before a concert one evening. Unfortunately, as she was explaining to me that she would not be able to get off work for the trip, the lights went out so that the concert could begin. So, rather than trying to find my way back to my seat in the dark, I took an empty chair next to her. During that concert something began to happen – it was chemistry, but not the kind that I had spent my life studying! Although the reaction was immediate in her case, I was not affected as quickly. In fact, Peggy became very frustrated over the fact that I was not also feeling the same emotions that had taken over her; so, she decided to take some aggressive action. She and several of her friends went to Florida for a week and spent the time praying and fasting about several issues – one of which was my lack of interest in her. Rather than parking her car at the airport, she had asked if I could keep it for her; so, I had to pick her up at the airport upon their return. As I was driving her back to her apartment, I invited her to join me for a carry-in dinner that my church was having that week. She accepted, realizing that showing up with me at the church function was essentially an engagement announcement.

And yes, it did turn out that way since everyone started matchmaking from the minute that they saw us walk in together. Her prayers and fasting had been working because I was beginning to have feelings for her, and I actually told her that I was in love with her on our third date. However, we decided to take a full year before talking about marriage since we had come from such different backgrounds and wanted to make sure that we could successfully adapt to each other's personality and fit into each other's world. There were definitely some bumps in the road, like the time I came home from India and confessed that I had not pined away like a love-sick puppy. Instead, I was so focused on everything that I was doing on the mission that I barely thought of her.

Of course that didn't go very well – and it went even worse when I said that I didn't want to waste money on a fancy wedding when I could see how the money could be better used to help the impoverished people around the world. After breaking the engagement for a few days, we finally came back to our senses.

But then came another hurdle. After we worked through those issues, we went to our pastor and asked him to perform our wedding – only to have him refuse. He said that he knew me well enough to expect that I would wind up living in a mud hut in Africa and that he was not willing to take the responsibility of marrying Peggy to me unless he was sure that she could also live in a mud hut. Therefore, he sent her home to pray until she was able to make that kind of a commitment. Several days later, the Lord spoke to Peggy through the words of Ruth when she committed herself to her mother-in-law Naomi, "Whither thou goest, I will go; and where thou lodgest, I will lodge: thy people shall be my people, and thy God my God: Where thou diest, will I die, and there will I be buried: the Lord do so to me, and more also, if ought but death part thee and me" (Ruth 1:16-17) – the words that eventually became our wedding vows.

Then another hurdle arose – Peggy's mother was to be part of one of the very first groups of Americans that were allowed into China when it opened its doors again after almost three decades of isolation. But her trip was scheduled for the exact time that we had planned for our wedding. We rescheduled the wedding for my spring break rather than after the close of the school year, meaning that we didn't get to go on our honeymoon until three months after we were married. In fact, it was actually while we were on our honeymoon that we realized that Peggy was pregnant with our first child! That put us in a really tough spot since Peggy was basically supporting us since I was only working part time in a chemistry lab – a job that had been just right while I

118

was still in school and she had a full-time job. But the fact that she would not be able to continue working at the demanding job she had and that we would have another mouth to feed really complicated things. I had, of course, been making lots of applications for teaching positions in Bible schools since I knew that that was the direction God had directed me. When I had initally said that I felt that this was God's plan for my life, some friends told me that it would be an impossibility, for several reasons: there were very few Pentecostal Bible colleges; they would not hire outside of their denominational ranks; and they wouldn't hire a novice because their practice was to take the pastors who were retiring from their churches and put them on the faculty.

I found a list of all the Pentecostal Bible colleges in the country and sent them resumes; however, as the response letters started coming back, I was beginning to feel that my advisors were right. Letter after letter said that they were impressed with my credentials but wanted someone with experience. I kept wondering if it wasn't the proverbial dog-chasing-his-tail situation. I had to have a job in order to get the experience that I needed in order to get a job. One school actually told me that they would hire me in two years when one of their current professors retired. To that, I wondered what I would eat for the next twenty-four months. Of course, I wasn't too concerned because of the prayer that I had prayed when I sent out the resumes, "Lord, I only need one job. If I get several offers, I'll have to make the choice; if I only get one offer, I'll know that You made the choice."

However, as it the time drew closer for the next school year to begin and that one offer had not come back, I was beginning to have my doubts. But that's where the next chapter picks up.

My Life with a Dinosaur

It was August, and I still hadn't received a favorable response from any of my applications and resumes; so, I figured that nothing was going to happen that year since it was so close to time for schools to open. Therefore, I settled into the work that I had taken as a technician at a chemistry lab; after all, I now had a new wife and a baby on the way that I had to support. But then the phone call came. It was the business manager from Dr. Lester Sumrall's ministry and he was asking me to come to South Bend, Indiana, for an interview. Of course, I accepted the invitation, and Peggy and I booked the next available flights. Since South Bend was only about a half-an-hour drive from Peggy's parents' home, we were excited to be able to spend a few days with them as well as having the one and only promising interview for a teaching position. Everything went well in the meetings with Dr. Sumrall and his staff, and Peggy and I both knew in our hearts that I would be offered the position; however, we didn't know exactly what that position was to be.

It turned out that I was being interviewed not just for a teaching position but for the dean's office – to actually run the whole school! When I questioned why they had waited until the last minute to fill such a key position, Bro. Sumrall's manager began to spin a most amazing story. It seems that there had actually been another person hired for the position – a man with years of experience. Oh, how I hated to hear that word! It was the one thing that I lacked and had, therefore, kept me out of the running for all the positions I had applied for, even this one. Everything was in order for him to step into the position. He had been scheduled to arrive in town on Thursday and preach at the church that evening so the local congregation would have a chance to get acquainted with him. He was to move in over the weekend and start work on Monday. When the Thursday evening service began, he had not showed up; so, someone called to see if there was a problem. His response was that he had decided not to take the job. He had not even had the common courtesy to let anyone know! Two weeks before opening day, and the school had no one at the helm! Since the only other resume they had on file was mine, I was their only other option. The offer that I was presented was that they wanted me to start work "yesterday." Of course, Peggy and I had things to take care of back in North Carolina: we both had to quit our jobs, we had to get out of the lease on our apartment, we had to pack our belongings, and we had to move everything to Indiana. We wouldn't be able to arrive until after school had started. I wasn't really sure how they were going to get through opening day without a dean, but I soon discovered that it wasn't such a gargantuan task as I would have assumed.

It was only after I got settled in that I learned a significant part of the school's history that had been somehow overlooked during the interview. The former dean and Dr. Sumrall had had a "falling out" the previous school year. The dean had taken all the students with him and opened another school in another town! The only students remaining at the campus were a handful of local residents who were taking part-time classes and those students were enrolled in only two or three classes. Essentially, I had inherited a desk and a stack of letterhead stationary. It was up to me to create everything else and turn World Harvest Bible College back into a viable school.

Okay, I'm sure that you are puzzled by my unusual title for this chapter. A dinosaur!!?? I couldn't believe my ears – one of Lester Sumrall's most trusted friends and employees had just described this great man of God as a dinosaur!!?? In his advice to me as rookie on the staff at the Lester Sumrall Evangelistic Association, this veteran staff member had told me, "You'll be working with a dinosaur." He went on to explain that there was probably no other living preacher who had worked hand-in-hand with and ministered alongside such great Pentecostal pioneers as Smith Wigglesworth, George and Stephen Jeffreys, Lillian Trasher, Donald Gee, Stanley Frodsham, Howard Carter, Finis Dake, Carrie Judd Montgomery, Victor Plymire, and Lewi Pethrus. Indeed, he was a link between generations; when all the "founding fathers" of the present-day move of God had gone to their rewards, he lived into the next generation almost as a living dinosaur – but certainly not as a fossil, for he continued to be an active and moving force until the closing years of the twentieth century. As I was praying about accepting the offer to join Dr. Sumrall's staff, one trusted friend offered me some advice, "Remember that the man is already sixty-seven years old. You want to consider the question of job security in an organization founded on one man's ministry, especially when the man is already past retirement age." The problem was that my friend didn't realize that Lester Sumrall would continue to minister for another sixteen years and that the organization would continue, and even expand, after his death. You see, he didn't know that the principles of faith were foundational within the life and ministry of the "dinosaur" Lester Sumrall.

One advantage of living with a dinosaur is that dinosaurs tend to flock together. Therefore, I had the privilege of getting to meet many of the great men and women of God that were part of Dr. Sumrall's generation – men like Dr. Yonggi Cho, Benny Hinn, Oral Roberts, Kenneth Copeland, and Kenneth Hagin. I have stories to tell about all these experiences, but let me limit myself to just one. When Kenneth Hagin was preaching at the church, I was sitting off to the side just soaking in the ministry until he came to the altar call. At that point, I got up and moved to the front of the auditorium in case he might need assistance directing the people who were coming up for prayer. I assumed that Bro. Hagin thought I was really eager to respond to his message on "These Signs Shall Follow Them That Believe" since I had come to the front before he had even really called for people to respond. So, he rushed over to me and began to pray for me. Even though I wasn't really asking for prayer, I know that I received a new anointing that day and began to see a significant upturn in the number of people who were healed when I prayed for them.

Working for and with Dr. Sumrall was an adventure of faith. I soon became his "left-hand man." Yes, we often refer to someone's trusted assistant as his "right-hand man," but Dr. Sumrall directed that I sit next to him in the chair on his left side in all our meetings, so I assumed that I should have a different title. Even though I was a brand-new employee, I soon discovered that he trusted and respected me. One day, Bro. Sumrall asked me to help him remember a rather important issue that he needed to discuss with one of his other employees. Since he knew that he would be with the other gentleman the following day at a specific time of the day, Dr. Sumrall asked me to arrange to come by that specific place at that specific time to remind him about the matter that needed to be handled. When I stopped in to remind him of the topic, the gentleman he was with became rather indignant because he was a long-standing employee and I was essentially still "wet behind the ears" within the ministry. He confronted Dr. Sumrall directly as to why he had asked an underling to bring the message. Being the great statesman of the kingdom of God that he was, Brother Sumrall responded without a second's hesitation, "I don't have any underlings!"

However, I didn't gain that same kind of respect from everyone immediately. I will always remember the day when a lady came by my office to apply for school. When she walked into my room, her mouth dropped open and she exclaimed, "You're just a kid!" Even after I assured her that I did have a doctorate degree, she again erupted, "You're just a kid!" Even after I told her my age, she continued with, "You're just a kid!" No matter how firmly I tried to steer the conversation back to the college, its curriculum, or anything academic, the only thing that would come out of her mouth was, "You're just a kid!" After as cordial an interview as I could possibly manage, I closed the conversation and thanked her for coming by. Of course, I never saw her again. After all, how could we possibly expect her to enroll in a college that was directed by a kid?

Even in a ministry where the Word of God and faith were foundational, I soon discovered that not everyone had caught on to these principles; for example, there was a group that met each morning before work to share requests and then lift up the needs in prayer. Each day they would go around the circle and list all the needs, then one member of the group would be asked to intercede. He would then reiterate all the needs as he mentioned them in prayer to the Lord. Finally, my day came to lead the prayer. I agreed only if they would allow me to do things a little differently. With a nod from the members, I explained that I didn't think that we should spend our time praying the problems but should use the occasion to pray the answers. I challenged each person to give me a biblical promise relating to the need rather than just stating the need. Rather than talking about someone's uncle with cancer, I insisted that we talk about the provision Christ had made for the uncle's condition. When I taught them to pray the answer, it changed the entire complexion of the prayer group. They moved from making announcements of bad news to proclamations of the Good News.

One of my responsibilities at the ministry came quite by accident. But I have to tell you a bit of the backstory. Remember from the previous chapter that I was involved in the Full Gospel Businessmen's Fellowship – an organization that was characterized by having item after item in their announcements and lots of other preliminaries before the main speaker was given the podium. In fact, there was a standing joke that everybody who went to one of those meetings deserved to get a miracle if he lived through all the announcements and preliminaries. I made the decision that if I ever had to make announcements, I was going to make them enjoyable, interesting, lively, and quick. Then came the day when Dr. Sumrall asked me to talk about one of his books. After I got up and advertised his book, he told me, "That's your job. You're going to do this from now on." He was impressed because I made what could have otherwise been a boring part of the service both entertaining and brief. After hearing me make announcements, one guest speaker whispered to me, "Brother, if they ever don't treat you right here, I've got a place of you." He was joking, of course, but all the guests at the church came to know me because I was the one who made announcements. It was a gift, and – as foolish as it seemed – getting up and making people laugh when you are trying to sell them a book is a gift that made a place for me and brought me before great men. All the renowned ministers who came through our church remembered me when they came back the next year because they were intrigued with my ability to make a fool out of myself while making announcements.

Of course, there was the one time that I was doing a live commercial during a television broadcast when I did literally make a fool of myself. The cameraman kept making a strange hand signal that I didn't recognize. I understood all the common sign language for "Stretch it out," "Wrap it up," and the like – but this hand motion was one I had never seen before. Eventually, I realized that he was trying to tell me that I was holding the book that I was advertising upside down. By the time that I caught on to his message, I was just ready to end the commercial; but I had just enough time to salvage the advertisement by closing with, "Of course, when we send you the book, we'll have it right-side-up!"

My responsibilities at the ministry included a lot more than just directing the Bible college and making announcements. I also had a lot of other hats to wear – including helping Bro. Sumrall do research for his sermons and books, editing his books, teaching his Sunday school and Bible college classes when he was away, and even occasionally hosting his television show. These ministry opportunities afforded me some wonderful experiences like the time when just as I was ready to receive the tithes and offerings in church one Sunday morning, a lady in the congregation stood up and spoke out in tongues. Since I was holding the microphone and was in the position to speak out the interpretation so that everyone could hear, I asked the Lord to give me the meaning of her message. After I had spoken what I felt were the words that the Holy Spirit inspired me to give, we went on with the offering and the rest of the service. It wasn't until the next morning in school that I came to understand the significance of the whole event. When one of my students asked me if I knew what had happened, I replied with, "It was a message in tongues and the interpretation. Of course, we all know how that works." His response to me was astounding, "But, you see, I'm from India, and my native language is Hindi. When the lady spoke, she was speaking in perfect Hindi. When you spoke, you gave the exact word-for-word translation of what she said!"

I had many other opportunities to develop the spiritual gifts in my day-to-day dealings in the ministry. "He's not a doctor. He's not a doctor," those words kept ringing inside my heart every time I would hear Dr. G_____ paged on the intercom system in our offices. He had first started working for the ministry as a volunteer

126

and, therefore, did not need a resume' or background check. Proving himself with the responsibilities he had been given, he was eventually asked to take a position with the organization. Since he had been around the operation for a while, the office manager assumed that we knew him well enough to simply accept his word about his background so no investigation was done on the entries he listed on his formal application for the position. It was a bit unusual that he requested that he be addressed as "doctor" when the position he held did not require that level of education, especially considering that I never asked to be addressed with my title even though the position of dean at the Bible college would have mandated a doctorate education. But every time he had to be paged to pick up a phone call or meet a visitor at the reception desk, the phone operator would page him as Dr. G____, and my spirit would respond immediately that this was not a true title. Eventually, he asked the principal of our Christian school if he could serve as the counselor for the young men in the school. He boasted that this area was the specific focus of his training in graduate school. As a member of the school board, I was made aware of his request. My immediate response was that the principal needed to check into his credentials before seriously considering his application. The background check revealed that, not only was he not a doctor, he hadn't even completed his bachelor's degree program. Much like Frank Abagnale, Jr., whose fake career as a doctor and airline pilot was popularized in the movie *Catch Me If You Can*, he had been able to slip through the cracks in the system time and time again. It was only by a word from the Holy Spirit that we were able to stop him. The real miracle is that we also learned that he had a record as a pedophile and wanted the position as the counselor in school for all the wrong reasons!

Another of my duties was to help coordinate the annual campmeeting that drew thousands of the ministry's friends and partners from across the country and around the world. In order to properly honor and host these out-of-town guests, we sponsored a reception after the evening service each night. It was a gala event with three hot menu entrees, fresh fruit, garden salad, hot vegetables, bread, peel-and-eat shrimp, crab salad, ice cream sundaes, homemade pies, cake, and a full line of hot and cold beverages. The feast was so extravagant that it took about twenty volunteers to serve the food and wait the tables. To say that arranging such a spread every night for a week was a lot of work would be a major understatement. We certainly didn't want to spoil such a significant effort by having more people show up than we had preparations for; so, we made the dinners by invitation only. Each evening during the service, we would discretely distribute the invitations to ensure that enough – but not too many – guests would be present. Since not everyone would get an invitation on any given evening, we also made available a pastors' hospitality suite so that anyone who did not receive an invitation to the dinner would have a place to go and fellowship after the service. This hospitality room was mainly just a place to meet and talk while munching on snacks and finger foods.

One evening after the service, I stopped by the hospitality suite only to discover that whoever was in charge that evening had failed to show up. There was no food out, but there were a couple people sitting patiently in the otherwise empty room. I immediately busied myself trying to serve these unfortunate guests. I found some cups and offered them a soft drink. Then I looked under the counter and found a tray of stale donuts that had been left out since that morning and a bowl of soggy potato chips remaining from the previous night. Embarrassed over what I had to offer, I joked with the couple, asking if they had ever noticed how two different things can react totally oppositely under the same conditions – chips get soggy; donuts get hard and dry when left uncovered. As we chatted for a minute, I noticed that the pastor was holding one of the invitations to the after-service dinner. Relieved that I could now offer them something better than the soggy potato chips and stale donuts, I explained that they were in the wrong room and offered to escort them to the right place. I wasn't prepared for the next thing that happened. As we stood to leave, the pastor's wife said, "I'll just take my potato chips with me." I actually had to talk her out of holding on to those soggy potato chips by reciting the menu awaiting her in the other room!

All the while, the question was running through my mind, "Do you really think that we would have gone to the trouble to make a printed and engraved invitation if we were only inviting you to eat stale donuts and soggy potato chips?" The couple's invitation clearly stated that an usher would meet them at the door to help them be seated; however, there was no usher at the door of the hospitality suite. This should have been a clue that they were in the wrong place; however, they took a seat rather than continuing to look around until they found the usher mentioned in the invitation. Their invitation also clearly stated that they were invited to join Bro. and Sis. Sumrall for a meal. Having come to the room and found that our pastor and his wife were not there and that the room was not even set up for a meal, it would have seemed that our unwary visitors would have decided that they were not in the right place. However, they took a seat and patiently waited for something that was not going to happen – at least, not where they were. The life lesson I came away with that evening was a similar question, "Do you think that God has gone to the trouble to give us a printed and engraved invitation just to eat soggy potato chips and stale donuts?"

One of the benefits of working closely with a man of the caliber of Lester Sumrall was the opportunity to glean from the wisdom he had developed from so many years in the ministry. I'll always remember his advice, "Another person's head is a very funny place to keep your happiness" – words that bring clarity to the situation when others try to challenge or discredit me. Nor will I ever forget the statement that he had written in the front of his Bible, "If I die rich, I die a traitor to the cause" – especially when I was with him on the last day before he fell ill with the sickness that soon took his life and witnessed him empty his wallet to send his secretary out on a shopping spree with the wife of a guest minister. Of course, I can't forget another note that he scribbled on the flyleaf of his Bible, "Nothing I have ever done or am doing is as great as what I am going to do" – a perspective that constantly drove him to greater and greater exploits of faith.

Occasionally, he would turn to me and offer me some unsolicited and unexpected off-the-cuff advice. One of the things that he said once was, "Always surround yourself with bright men." He didn't bother to explain himself; he just left me to figure it out. When I did, I understood that if I had bright people above me, they would pull me up to where they are because I'd always be challenged to understand what they know, what they are talking about, and the perspective they see things from. If I had bright people below me, they would push me higher by asking probing questions that keep me constantly pressing to stay sharp enough to give good answers. If I have bright people behind me, when I am tutoring and instructing them, they draw out the best in me. And if they are really bright, they are still standing there with their eyes open wanting more. And when I have given out everything that I have and they are still hungry, that means I have to draw deeper into the Spirit and deeper into the Word of God so that I have enough to continue to give. That makes me grow because I have somebody who is pulling out everything I have and still wanting more. When they want more, that means I have to get more. So, as I surround myself with bright people, it causes me to advance. If I surround myself with people who are satisfied with status quo, I can become satisfied and stuck in the mud, but if I surround myself with people who are progressing, the ones in front of me can pull me to where they are while the ones behind me push me beyond where I presently am. Someone has said that we are the sum total of our friends. Someone else added that we are the product of our environment. I don't know that this statement is necessarily totally true, but it does bear a certain amount of truth because when I am around bright people, I will become brighter.

But the most important lesson that I ever learned from Dr. Sumrall came from the opportunity of sharing early-morning prayers with him. Even though the prayer sessions were open to anyone who would like to come, it was often just the two of us. The thing that was so amazing about these prayer times was that even though Dr. Sumrall was constantly involved in the most extraordinary adventures of faith – like building a broadcast empire that included a dozen television stations, five shortwave stations, and satellite, operating a humanitarian organization that sent two cargo ships and a cargo plane around the world distributing food, medical supplies, and gospel literature, and a "zillion" other evangelic outreaches – I never heard him pray for ships, planes, television stations, or shortwaves. Instead, his constant and consistent prayer was, "Lord, I want to know You"! Much like St. Francis of Assisi who was known to spend whole nights praying that same prayer, Bro. Sumrall had learned the most important lesson of all, "The people that do know their God shall be strong, and do exploits." (Daniel 11:32) He knew that it was only out of his relationship with God Himself that he would be able to do those greater works that he had written about in his Bible, and – more importantly – he knew that it was only the things that were birthed out of such a relationship that were worth doing!

Speaking of exploits that were birthed from having a relationship with God, I could tell you story after story of challenges that everyone else thought would be impossible – yet Dr. Sumrall took them on and succeeded at them because he knew that he had the heart and mind of God on the situation. One was the construction of shortwave radio stations to reach the world with the gospel of Jesus Christ. Although he had a full network of television stations covering the US and a satellite service reaching the world, he was convinced that the majority of the people in third-world nations could never be reached by television. However, he was also convinced that he could get to them with shortwave radio. The only problem was that the US government had a regulation that prohibited private organizations from owning shortwave stations. Even though there were already organizations using shortwave to broadcast the gospel, none were operating from American soil because the government had restricted the use of this form of communication for government purposes only. But when the Lord spoke to Dr. Sumrall that he was to build shortwave stations in the US to blanket the world with the Good News, not even the US government could resist. Dr. Sumrall's response when he was told that he would not be permitted a license for a shortwave station was, "Well, bless God, I'll get one!" And, bless God, he did! Before long, there were five facilities broadcasting to every corner of the globe.

I must share one very personal story. I will always remember that day! There were just four of us in the private office that day – Dr. Lester Sumrall, a husband and wife missionary team, and myself. After a brief conversation, Dr. Sumrall slid a check across his desk to my missionary friends, who ran feeding centers in one of the impoverished nations of Asia. Along with the check came these gruff words, "God hasn't called me to feed the devil's children, and I don't believe in this sort of thing. When I go to the mission field, I don't see naked babies. But I'm giving you this for your work because I don't want the world to say that we don't try to help people." Yes, Dr. Lester Sumrall was a man of faith who traveled around the globe setting people free from the devil's power. Yes, he had built nation-changing churches in several countries, raised up a world-wide broadcasting network, and authored scores of life-changing books. Yes, he had been in the ministry for more than fifty years and had ministered in more than a hundred nations.

But, there was still one thing lacking in his ministry – compassion for humans' physical needs. However, all that was to change late one evening in Jerusalem. Shortly after retiring after a long day of touring and taping television programs followed by preaching and ministering to the tour members, he was suddenly awakened by the words, "It is not only ten minutes to midnight in Jerusalem; it is ten minutes to midnight prophetically!" For the next five hours, the Lord continued to talk with His servant concerning a new commission of establishing a global ministry to feed the hungry saints who lack their daily bread. At first, Dr. Sumrall retorted that he was seventy-five years old and that God should get a younger man to take on this job. Eventually, he understood that God had saved this job for him until this stage in life because he was now seasoned enough to take on a project of this immensity. From that moment until the day he drew his last breath, Lester Sumrall poured every ounce of energy he had into seeing that this vision would be fulfilled. Upon his return to the US a few days later, I again sat in the apostle's office and witnessed him slide a piece of paper across his desk. This time, it was a page from a yellow legal pad totally filled with the words the Lord had spoken to him that night in Jerusalem. The paper contained not just words, but also huge smears where warm tears had dissolved the ink – evidence of a heart in which a new level of pity and compassion had been birthed.

When this new element became operative in his ministry, Lester Sumrall stepped to a new level in his career as a man who made a difference in his world. Because of this new birth of pity, he was able to impact thousands on every continent of the world in the last few years of his life and bring influential change to whole nations and people groups. The words of the apostle Jude so adequately sum up the story of this chapter in Lester Sumrall's life and ministry, "Some have compassion, making a difference." (verse 22) As Dr. Sumrall began to share his vision with the pastors and Christian leaders in America, Europe, and Australia, something phenomenal began to happen. Individuals and churches that were struggling financially began to prosper, and ones that considered themselves to already be financially secure began to abound. It was as if Dr. Sumrall's vision had unlocked a new door of prosperity within the Body of Christ. And actually – it had. For the most part, the "Word and Faith Movement" churches in which Dr. Sumrall basically ministered previously had no humanitarian programs. But now that he had introduced the new Feed the Hungry program, their attention was redirected in a way that could best be described as, in the prayer of Bob Pierce, founder of World Vision, "Let my heart be broken with the things that break the heart of God." Certainly all these churches and believers were well-versed in the principle of sowing and reaping – but something new happened in their harvests the minute they stepped across this new threshold in their planting.

In the process of hearing from the Lord concerning the birth of this world-changing ministry, Dr. Sumrall heard one special word that he didn't know what it meant – Hercules. When he mentioned the word to one of the staff members who was a retired Air Force colonel, the colonel immediately responded, "That definitely is a word from God because a Hercules is a military cargo plane that would be perfect for delivering supplies to remote places around the world." With that assurance, Bro. Sumrall began the search for a Hercules C-130 aircraft – only to get the same response that he had encountered when he wanted to build the first shortwave station. When Bro. Sumrall was told that the C-130 was a classified military aircraft and the government prohibited civilians from owning them, his response was, "Well, bless God, I will!" And he did; the US government had to totally reverse their policies to grant him a permit!

My work with Lester Sumrall gave me the opportunity to travel with him to the Orient and to the Holy Land – and to eventually lead tours to Israel for the ministry. On one of those pilgrimages, a friend and I took a free day to try to find the people we had heard of who were preparing for the restoration of the temple in Jerusalem. For many years, I had heard of a group of Jews who were desirous of rebuilding the temple and, in fact, were making preparation for its construction. After much searching and questioning, we had finally made contact with them. My heart pounded and my mind whirled as I was ushered into their chambers to discuss their dreams – and their plans. First of all, they explained that there are three different and distinct groups who are part of a great scheme that has no human coordinator. Each group is basically aware of what the others are doing, but they have no direct link among themselves, nor do they work on any orchestrated program to bring their various activities into relationship with one another. One group feels that its role is to rebuild the temple structure. A second group feels that their destiny is to prepare and construct all the implements and utensils that will be used to resume the Levitical sacrifice and priesthood system in the temple. Yet a third group feels that their calling is to train the priests for their temple operations. When I asked how it would all fit together, I was told that when messiah appears, he will make everything gel. As my host took me into another room, I found myself surrounded by the treasures that will one day fill the temple in Jerusalem. My heart raced, my eyes bulged, my spirit leapt as I realized that I had been ushered into prophecy in the process of being fulfilled! After having the opportunity to actually hold in my own hands the lots that the high priest will someday cast to determine which goat will be sacrificed and which will be sent into the desert as the scapegoat bearing the sins of Israel, my friend and I made our way back to the hotel and shared our discovery with our Israeli tour guide. Today, the Treasury of the Temple is a standard stop on most tours of Jerusalem.

I also had several opportunities to represent the ministry as part of a Feed the Hungry team on the mission field. One such event was in the nation of Nicaragua where we were to deliver a shipload of food and building supplies after the coastal nation had been devastated by a hurricane. Mike (another team member) and I had to fly down because of other responsibilities that did not permit us the time to travel with the rest of the team on the cargo ship carrying the supplies. All the logistics had been coordinated so that the ship with the team and supplies was to arrive the same day that we were to land. The team was to begin immediately with a series of evangelistic outreaches where the relief supplies were to be distributed to the people. The only problem was that no one had anticipated the possibility of a storm at sea which might delay the voyage through the Caribbean – and, of course, this is exactly what happened. Mike and I arrived to find that we had back-to-back crusades scheduled with no relief supplies to distribute nor team members to assist with all the responsibilities! For the next four days, we carried out a schedule of responsibilities that had originally been planned to be shared among a team of more than a dozen workers.

When the team eventually did arrive, there were even more unexpected difficulties: the ship was too large to dock at the port and had to be anchored in the middle of the harbor. Small dinghies were needed to shuttle the people and supplies between the ship and the dock. Since the portal through which people had to exit was about two stories above the waterline, a rope ladder was dropped down for climbing in and out of the ship. Such an arrangement would have been fine for a team of Boy Scouts; however, the team faced a challenge that the average Boy Scout Jamboree never has to consider – all the ladies on the team were required to wear dresses any time they went ashore. Because of some of the modesty requirements imposed by the local culture, missionary women were not permitted to appear in public wearing pants. This meant that the team had to come up with a graceful way for the ladies to climb the rope ladder while a couple guys stood on the dinghy below securing the ladder for them – not an easy task, to say the least! Of course, the problem only compounded when a huge wave washed the dinghy away from the ship while one of the ladies dangled helplessly halfway through her descent. These complications were annoying but our difficulties were complicated by the fact that all this was taking place during the rainy season. This meant that the open-air crusades were often held in drenching rain and that the team would have to scurry to get all of the electronic sound equipment under cover every time a shower would begin. We often spent whole days in clothes that were soaked all the way through to the skin. Seeing all these difficulties and realizing that most of them could have been avoided by simply rescheduling the mission for a couple months later when the weather would have been more agreeable, I asked the local missionary if the people's situation was really that desperate that they had to have the relief aid right then. His response was that waiting the few weeks for the dry season would not have caused a problem at all. This trip certainly produced a lot of "missionary stories" – unfortunately, they were all self-induced!

On another mission for Feed the Hungry, I had the privilege to make my first of many visits to the country of the Dominican Republic. While in the city of Santo Domingo, the team and I were participating in a church service where there was a special seating section for the church leadership. As the people were dancing and rejoicing during the praise and worship time, I noticed one of the ladies from that reserved seating section dancing in a very erratic fashion – essentially out of her natural control. Soon, a group of people began to create a human chain around her – encircling her as if with a wall of protection to keep her from bumping into other people, the church pews, or other furniture. Disturbed by this manifestation, which certainly was not the Holy Spirit, I found it hard not to intervene. However, knowing that this lady was obviously part of the church leadership since she was privileged to sit in the special section and aware that this manifestation must be a common occurrence since everyone knew immediately what to do, I felt that it would be out of place for me to intervene since I was a guest in the service. Eventually, she collapsed to the floor and began to writhe about on the concrete. At that point, I could no longer contain myself. I jumped up from my seat, broke my way through the wall of people around her, and commanded the demon to come out of her. Once she was free, I asked her what had happened, and she replied that she had made a visit to the Haitian border a number of months before and that this sort of thing had been happening to her ever since the visit. She then thanked me for setting her free and praised God that He had sent someone to help her.

If you know anything about Lester Sumrall's ministry, I'm sure that you would know that he was recognized around the world as being an authority on the demonic realm and our authority over evil spirits. And as his "left-hand man," I had plenty of experience in dealing with demons. I dealt with individuals who pulled their hair, ripped their clothes off, burned themselves with cigarettes, and even cut themselves while under the demonic control; however, not one of them was ever able to touch me during a confrontation. Why? Because I knew that I don't have to be subject to these spirits. They respected my authority over them. They could only torment those who allowed them to. One young lady was miraculously delivered of a number of very powerful spirits yet still was addicted to smoking cigarettes. That seemingly insignificant fault had an unbreakable hold over her. As I prayed for her, a man's voice spoke through her lips, "I'm not coming out because she wants me here." Upon questioning the young lady, I found that she was actually a willing victim of the nicotine spirit. It did not come out until she decided that she really wanted it out.

I remember one Indian lady who came to my wife for deliverance. Even after she had spent several sessions ministering to the woman, nothing positive had happened. Finally, I stepped in on one of the sessions and asked if the woman really wanted to be free; when she could not answer positively, I advised my wife to let her alone because she was only creating her own problems. Jesus told a story that is recorded in Matthew chapter twelve and Luke chapter eleven in which He explained that, if a spirit is cast out of a person and that person allows it to come back, the end result for that individual will be much worse than his initial condition. I feared that this is what would happen to the woman if we were able to cast out the spirit, but she really didn't care about being free – it would come back to tempt her and she would allow it to come back in, worsening her condition. My wife and I have seen this sort of willing acceptance of demonic torment in a number of cases, especially when sexual pleasures are associated with the demonic influence. Another woman came to our church asking for special prayer but noted that she had already been to all the "big" evangelists and they couldn't do anything for her. Of course, we did everything we could to help her; but, of course, she left in just as bad a shape as when she came because she really wasn't wanting help – just another "notch on her gun" that she could use as proof when she bragged about how bad her case was.

When I rebuked the spirit in one man who came to my office for prayer, the demon threw him across the room, and he crashed into the wall. When he picked himself up, he began to hop around the room like a frog as his mouth began to spew out the vilest forms of blasphemy and profanity. Yet, at the name of Jesus, he was instantly free and stood to his feet a new man. When he came back for follow-up counseling the next day, he stopped at the receptionist's desk and asked to see me. The receptionist called me to inform me that a gentleman claiming to be the one who had been in the prior day was there for an appointment. She added, "But this isn't the same man; I've never seen this man before." He was so radically changed that it showed on his face.

One of the trophies that I keep in my bookcase is a large hunting knife that was presented to me by a young man in desperation. A spirit of murder had controlled him, tormenting him with the thought of killing his sister and dismembering her body. After the demonic control over his life was broken, he went home as a man finally at peace with himself. Yet that night, he awoke with the haunting nightmare that he was going through with the diabolic plan. It was only after he returned to my office the next morning and surrendered this weapon to me that he knew that he was free from the spirit of

140

murder. Any physical property that has been dedicated to the devil's purposes, (such as that knife) or any item of pagan worship or witchcraft (such as the occult books in the hotel in North Carolina) can become lodging places for demonic entities that can remain to torment those susceptible to their control.

On another occasion, I was invited to attend a church service to hear one of my students minister. As a special guest, I was also called to the front to help minister to the people during the altar service. Two young girls approached me for prayer to receive the baptism in the Holy Spirit. As I ministered to them, I could hear a commotion across the church. It soon became obvious that a demonic manifestation was out of control at the other end of the altar. Finally, the girls began to speak in other tongues, and I turned them over to one of the elders for further instruction. When the elder looked at the girls and warned them that a man was having demons cast out of him and that they should keep praying or the demons might go into them, I knew that the church was ignorant of the spiritual world. After reassuring the girls that they could not arbitrarily be taken over by unclean spirits, I went over to assist in the deliverance. I found the man sprawled out on the floor covered with open Bibles and even the big brass cross from the front of the church. They were trying every gimmick possible to make that spirit go out of the man. At least they were not beating him on the head as I have seen done in Nepal. However, the biblical way is that the name of Jesus be used in faith. When I did that, he was instantly set free. God's work done God's way produces God's results.

On another occasion, a guest minister at our church had "set some ground rules" concerning ministry during his crusade: no one other than his personal staff was to minister or lay hands on anyone during the services. Even though I was an associate minister at the church, I submitted to that authority and was, therefore, carefully avoiding any form of intervention in situations that arose during his campaign. However, when a woman began to manifest demonic control as she lay on the floor flipping back and forth, I was really disturbed that such a blatant display was going on unchecked. I simply spoke the name of Jesus and exerted my authority under my breath without ever leaving my seat. As soon as I whispered the command for her to stop, she suddenly became calm and restful.

I remember making the last round through the church one night after a very long day during a convention. It was now almost eleven o'clock and I had been there since before sun-up and would be back again before dawn the next day as well. However, I couldn't leave and lock the building until everyone was out. My problem was one elder who was frantically trying to cast a demon out of a man. When I walked up to the scene, I overheard the elder shout, "We'll stay here till 2 AM if that's what it takes to get you out!" At that point, I realized two things: first, that he certainly was not going to be with me at daybreak the next morning; and secondly, that he didn't understand spiritual authority. I promptly interrupted his deliverance session with a little teaching session by explaining that he had relinquished all authority he might have had prior to that time by setting a limit of two o'clock. I explained that the spirit recognized that the elder had granted a certain amount of authority to it and, therefore, it had settled in with no thought of budging right up through one fifty-nine. So, after instructing the elder about his comment, we cast the demon out right away and went home to bed.

Not all my adventures while living in Indiana had to do with my relationship with Dr. Sumrall. In a later chapter, I'll share about how God miraculously provided Peggy and me a beautiful home just across the street from the church, but at this point I'd like to tell you about

142

a miracle He did when we decided to move to a different home. The move was a step that stretched our faith because we had totally remodeled the old house and needed to recoup our investment by pricing the house a bit higher than the general market. It also happened that the same day we listed it, the headlines in our paper announced an increase in the mortgage interest rates! The next day I received my tape-of-the-month from Andrew Wommack Ministries in which he told the story about praying with a man concerning selling a house which had been on the market for two years; after the prayer, the house sold within two weeks. The key to the prayer was that Andrew prayed for the finances of the buyer because he felt that there was a buyer who wanted the house but couldn't get the money. When the house sold, the buyer said that he had been wanting to buy the house since the day it went on the market but had been tied up with a business deal that wouldn't close. However, the deal closed on the same day that Andrew had prayed with the man who was trying to sell the house.

I took the "coincidence" that I got that message at the exact time we were listing our house as a directive from the Lord that we should pray the same way over our house. What is even more dramatic is that two days later I received a phone call from one of the prayer counselors from Andrew Wommack's ministry asking if there was any concern about which she could agree with me in prayer. I had never called his prayer ministry, the ministry had never contacted me before that date, and the phone center has never called me since! I told the lady the story about the tape, and we prayed in agreement in accordance with the message Andrew had given. By this time, I knew that it was more than a coincidence! The house sat on the market for just over one hundred days, and we heard the same story from every couple who looked at it, "We can't get a loan."

Nevertheless, Peggy and I kept believing that the right couple was out there and that God was going to give them miracle finances to buy the house. Well, it happened, and it happened in grand style!

But before I tell that part of the story, I need to add just one thing. When the insurance policy came up for renewal, the company said that they would not renew the coverage since it was a vacant property. We finally negotiated a deal to rent the house so that it would be occupied in order to keep the insurance. When I called the realtor to tell her to drop the listing, she suggested that I let it stay on the market until Thanksgiving because the market is usually fairly active until then. Since that was only a matter of a month, I agreed. A couple days later, I made arrangements with a young man to move into the house; everything was set so that as soon as I could get the utilities turned back on, he could have the place. Within five minutes of the time that he walked out of my office, the phone rang; it was the realtor saying that she had just shown the house to a couple who were very interested. The next day they made an offer on the house, but it was really too low for us to accept. When we asked for more, we got a reply that the owner of the realty company had been this young man's mentor in the Big Brother program. The realtor had been working with the young man on the house purchase and had determined that he could not possibly afford more than the original offer. However – and this is a big "however" – the realtor would personally give the young man the extra money to match our request! The next day the mortgage company declined the young man's loan application. Now, here comes another one of those big "howevers" – the realtor decided to buy the house himself and resell it to the couple on a land contract! This was an exact answer to our prayers that God would provide miracle finances to our buyer!

144

I'm not Paul Harvey but I do have to tell you the rest of the story. When the inspections were done on the house, several items were noted as needing repair before the closing of the sale. A couple of the items were – in my mind, at least – unnecessary; so, I told the real estate agent that I simply wasn't willing to pay for them. The reply that came back was that the deal was off! But then God intervened again! I guess that the listing agent and the agent representing the buyer realized how much commission they were going to lose if the sale did not go through; so, they convinced the buyer to forgo one item and the two agents personally paid for the second one! We closed on the house the day before Thanksgiving. What a Thanksgiving we had celebrating the miracle finances which made our house sale possible! I can only imagine the Thanksgiving that the young couple must have had as they moved into their miracle home! Oh, by the way, it turned out that the couple were Spirit-filled believers and the wife used to be a secretary at our church!

God's miraculous care for us has often been manifest when we didn't exert faith in any specific way other than in our general dependence upon Him as our caring and loving Father. Just a few days before our summer vacation, my wife and I had gone out for our weekly date night. As we pulled out of our parking place at the restaurant, we felt a tremendous bump and heard a resounding thud as if we had just dropped our front wheel into a foot-deep pothole. Knowing that there were no such damages in the pavement and really puzzled as to why the car was sitting lopsided with the driver's side at least eight inches off level from the passenger's side, I climbed out to investigate. What I found was the car sitting directly on top of the wheel rather than being supported by the suspension system. Fortunately, we were only a few blocks away from our mechanic's shop and it was just a few minutes before his closing time. We limped the car to the shop and arrived just as he was locking the door. He helped us make arrangements to get home and checked the car in for repairs the following day. The miracle was in the timing. Had the suspension system snapped when we were on the freeway pushing the posted seventy-miles-an-hour speed limit, we could have caused a serious accident, possibly involving several cars and severe injuries if not deaths. Even if the breakdown had occurred without incident, it could have taken place hundreds of miles away from home, complicated matters in getting the car repaired and ruined our much-needed vacation.

Although this is not going to seem like a very "spiritual" story, I want to take a few sentences to share about being called up for jury duty while living in South Bend. Both cases had to do with loss of life. One was a rather cut-and-dried case of murder where a drug dealer bludgeoned a customer to death when he tried to run away without paying for the dope. The other seemed to me to be an equally open-and-closed case in which an intoxicated man, driving at eighty miles an hour in a thirty-five mile-an-hour zone missed a ninety-degree curve and plunged into the river. When the residents from the nearby houses rushed to the scene, they asked anyone else was in the car, and he responded that there was not. Unfortunately, the delay in searching the car that resulted from the drunk man's response was just long enough to allow his wife who was pinned in the car to drown. During the trial, the owner of a biker bar where the man had spent most of the evening testified that he had kicked the man out of his establishment because he was so drunk that he had begun to make a disturbance. In spite of all the evidence against the man, the jury deliberation went on for hours with the other jurors making statements like, "Well, I hate to convict this man because I've been known to drive with a couple beers under my belt." The simple reason that I chose to include

146

those stories is because most people immediately start looking for ways to get out of jury duty as soon as they receive their summons. However, I encourage you to see jury duty as a way to bring the wisdom of God into the judicial system rather than to leave these decisions in the hands of ungodly people who can't even tell the difference between a couple of beers and being so drunk that you get kicked out of a biker bar!

As I've already mentioned, we lived very close to Peggy's hometown. She had attended high school in South Bend, and I actually passed her old school on my way to and from work each day when we lived in the first house that we owned in the city. Being in such close proximity to her family gave us a great opportunity to develop some lasting memories with her parents. The most memorable have to do with leading both her father and mother to the Lord. Although they were outstanding leaders in the local community, exemplary role models, and very devoted Catholics (In fact, some of the top officials from the church and Notre Dame University attended her father's funeral), neither of them had been born again.

Her dad was at their winter home in Florida when he became very ill and was hospitalized. Realizing that this might be the last time we would see him alive, all of Peggy's family made arrangements to go visit him at the same time. By the time we arrived, the Catholic priest had already been there and administered last rites, assuming that he was not going to live. When the family gathered at the hospital, we decided that it would be too overwhelming for all of us to crowd into his room together, so we chose to go in by couples. Peggy and I were the first to spend time with him, and we found him totally alert when we went in for our visit. After a couple minutes of "small talk," Peggy turned to me in anticipation that I would initiate the conversation about his salvation. Wanting her to have the privilege of leading him to the

Lord, I insisted that she take the lead – which she did by saying, "We're here to get you ready to go to heaven." He was totally receptive and agreed to pray the sinner's prayer with us. When we began, his voice was very weak because of the cancer in his throat; however, with each phase of the prayer that he repeated, his voice grew stronger and stronger. When we came to the final "Amen," the power of God surged through his body and he physically jumped as if he had been jolted with electricity. Shocked at the physical manifestation, he looked at me and asked, "Did I get healed?" I responded, "You've received the greatest healing of all. Your soul has been healed!" At that point, he peacefully fell asleep. Actually, it turned out that he hadn't just fallen asleep; it was more like a coma – meaning that he was not awake during the time that any of Peggy's siblings were with him. Although we were sad that they did not get to spend time with him, we saw that it was the hand of God at work in that he was alert for our conversation and was not awake to hear any negative sentiment that the others might have brought.

After our time with her dad, Peggy and I walked out of the hospital to spend a few minutes in private reflection and prayer. As we strolled in the warm Florida evening, Peggy asked me, "Do you think that was real? It seemed all too easy!" Well, her answer came the next morning when we met her mom who had stayed by her husband's bedside throughout the night. She told us of an experience that had happened during her vigil – he had almost fallen out of the bed. When she asked what he was doing, his response was, "Don't you see Him?" Peggy's mom questioned, "See who?" and he responded, "Jesus! He's reaching out His hand for me to come to Him." Actually, this visitation from Jesus came three times during that night. But the clincher to this story is that before our prayer with her father, all the dreams and night visions that he had been experiencing were nightmares of spiders and bugs crawling on him!

Several years later, I awoke one morning with an awareness that this was the day we had to talk to my mother-in-law about her need for personal salvation. Before leaving for work that day, I told Peggy that she <u>had</u> to go visit her mom and share the gospel with her <u>that</u> day. When she questioned me if I thought that her mother was going to die, my only response was that I didn't know anything except that <u>that</u> day was <u>her</u> day. Peggy did drive over to visit her mother that day but it didn't seem as if there was any way to turn the conversation toward spiritual things, until her mom suddenly asked about Dr. Sumrall. Then Peggy reminded her that Bro. Sumrall had recently passed away. She then went on to remind her mother that she was the same age as Bro. Sumrall (In fact, their birthdays were only days apart). At that point, Peggy asked her mom where she thought that she would go when she died. When her answer came back that she was uncertain, Peggy told her the story of how her dad had been born again just days before he died. Then she asked her mother if she would also like to be sure that she would be ready to go with Jesus. After she prayed the sinner's prayer to accept the Lord, her mom – a chain smoker – asked, "Will I be able to smoke in heaven?" Peggy responded that it didn't really matter; all that counted was that she was sure that she would be there. Just a few weeks later, Peggy's mother began to show more and more signs of Alzheimer's disease, which soon led to her being admitted into a nursing home and eventually claimed her life. If Peggy had not shared the gospel with her mother on that particular day, she may never again have had the mental capacity to understand and accept the message. Now for the punch line to the whole story: at the funeral, the Catholic priest, referring to the socialite status that my mother-in-law had always enjoyed, made the really unexpected comment, "I can imagine her right now walking around heaven with a martini in one hand and a cigarette in the other."

I began working with Dr. Lester Sumrall when he was sixty-seven years old, at the time when most people are thinking of retirement. However, that word simply wasn't part of his vocabulary; he was determined to continue to minister until the day he dropped dead. And that is exactly what he did. He was still traveling all over the world right up until the last month of his life and he was preaching in his local church until the week leading up to his death at age eighty-three. That gave me the opportunity of working closely with him for sixteen years – a privilege that I actually considered to be a divine assignment. However, the desire to reach the nations for Jesus was burning in my heart the whole time and I always assumed that as soon as Dr. Sumrall passed away, God would release me to launch that missions endeavor. However, when Dr. Sumrall did go on to be with the Lord, I felt a strong direction from the Lord that I was not to resign from his ministry but that I should stay and help his son Steve through the ministry's transition. So, I stayed on in my position at the Bible college, but I was surprised that I was never really given any other responsibility through the transition that occurred within the ministry after Dr. Sumrall's death. Days turned to weeks, weeks to month, months to years – nine years to be exact! All the while I knew that I had heard God's direction but was totally puzzled that nothing had worked out as I had anticipated. Then came the day that Steve decided to move out of his father's ministry and start his own – and he asked me to work with him to make it happen. It was only then that I knew what the Lord's direction had been all about. After spending a year and a half helping Steve through that transition, I felt released to make my move to initiate our mission work. Since I had been so integrally associated with Dr. Sumrall's ministry, I knew that I had to move to a totally new location so that I could make a fresh start and have a ministry that would be recognized on its own merit rather than through any lingering association with Dr. Sumrall. And so, I moved on to the next chapter of my life – and the next chapter of this book.

Pikes Peak or Bust

Having made the decision to relocate from South Bend, Peggy and I were faced with the next big decision – where? We had received a prophetic word concerning "a place called 'there'" where God wanted us to be, but we had no clue where our "there" was to be. Since my dad was still alive, but was at the stage in life where it would be good for me to be in a reasonably close proximity to him, I considered places like Atlanta and Myrtle Beach. We also considered other cities as far away as San Francisco and made trips to several places to simply walk around in the city and listen to see if the Holy Spirit would speak to us. However, no matter where we went, He was always silent. Eventually, we began to think about the fact that Colorado Springs, Colorado, was essentially the epicenter for mission work around the world, with almost all the major mission organizations headquartered there. We realized that it would be the ideal place for networking with other missions-minded people. That, coupled with the facts that I really love the mountains and we had really enjoyed the scenery when we vacationed there one summer, made us begin to seriously consider that Colorado might just be our "place called 'there'" – especially, since there were two specific organizations that we had developed a real affinity towards. We had very strong connections with Every Home for Christ through working with their director in Nepal for many years. In addition, Peggy had used Dick Eastman's (the president of the organization) books on prayer as her textbooks for courses she taught in the Bible college in Indiana. In fact, we had even made a point to meet Dr. Eastman when he had visited Indiana to speak at a banquet several years before. The second organization was Andrew Wommack's Charis Bible College. We had actually been invited as guest lecturers at the school after having met Andrew Wommack through one of the graduates of Dr. Sumrall's Bible college in Indiana, who was then serving as an associate pastor in Colorado Springs. I remembered making the off-the-cuff comment that if I ever taught at another college it would be this one – even though I didn't have the slightest idea that such a statement might be prophetic.

Since we knew another graduate from the Bible college who was pastoring in the city and was also a close friend of Andrew's, we asked him to arrange for us to visit during our Thanksgiving break. Since we had not officially announced that we would be leaving our position at the school in Indiana, we were doing everything "under the radar." Our plan was to send the boys to the slopes for snow skiing while we stayed in town spying out the land and listening to see what the Lord might say. However, it turned out that we didn't have to wait until we got there to hear from God. He spoke to us "loud and clear" before we even left home.

Thirty minutes before I was to leave my office to pick up the family and head to the airport for our flight to Colorado, I received a telephone call from a good friend who pastors a large church in Nigeria. He said that he was reading one of my books when the Lord spoke to him to tell me Micah 2:10, "Arise and depart for the place where you are is not your place of rest." That passage hit me "like a ton of bricks." The only way I can describe what happened to me was like I was slain in the Spirit standing up. I was so in the Spirit that I could not relate to the natural things around me. I remember standing at my office door thinking, "How do I get this thing to open?" When I got to my car, I sat in the driver's seat with the keys in my hand thinking, "How do I make this thing work?" I have no idea how I drove home, but I somehow got to the airport safely and headed toward the next phase of my life. As we flew into the Colorado Springs airport, we all had that inner feeling as if we had come "home." During the whole time that we spent in the city, we were totally convinced that we had found "our place called "there.'"

Let's fast-forward to February when Peggy and I were in Atlanta where I had been invited to share the platform with Dr. Mills.   Remember him from the prophetic direction in Yosemite? When we bumped into one another in the hotel lobby as we were checking in, Dick immediately followed all the casual introductory small talk with, "From the moment I saw you, I've been hearing the word 'transition.'" I confirmed his inclination by explaining that I had made the decision to leave the position of dean at World Harvest Bible College and Indiana Christian University that I had held for a quarter century to pursue more missions work. I thought that was the end of the conversation, but God was not finished talking with us. That evening, Dick was ministering to a couple on the other side of the auditorium when he suddenly stopped right in the middle of what he was saying to the couple and pointed to Peggy and me and prophesied, "God says that He has a house waiting for you." He then went right back to ministering to the other couple.

Now, let's fast-forward again to April when we were seriously into our Colorado Springs house hunt – looking at internet listings and dealing long distance with an agent.   We had spelled out some specific requirements since we were giving up a lovely home in a wooded cul-de-sac that backed up to a nature preserve with hiking trails accessible from our backdoor and knew that God wanted to move us "up" when we obeyed His directions.   We wanted land so that we wouldn't be squeezed in next to neighbors and we wanted a view of Pikes Peak. Of course, these requirements priced all the qualifying properties far outside our price range. Suddenly, our agent called us to say that she had found something that she was sure we would like and that it was priced far below market value. She encouraged us to come out right away to see the house because she was certain it would not still be on the market in May when Peggy had planned to fly out to Colorado to do some house shopping. Reminded of the word from God, we decided that it would still be available if it really was the one God had for us. In the time between April and Peggy's visit to Colorado, the sellers turned down two offers. However, they accepted ours even though we offered less than the asking price! It was not until a number of months later that we learned a bit of the history of our house – it had originally been built by the gentleman who essentially pioneered the location of some of the major ministries in Colorado Springs. When we discovered that bit of information, we felt that it was essentially the "cherry on top" of God's blessing upon our move.

Not only did Dick Mills speak this incredibly accurate prophetic word into my own life, he also gave laser-beam accurate words for all my sons – even though he never met them. At that same conference in Atlanta, he asked me to write down my sons' names so he could take them to his hotel room and pray over them. That evening, he returned with a page for each of my sons that described them as accurately as if he had lived in our house with them!

I had the whole process of the transition logically and strategically planned out – we would put our house in Indiana on the market in April and make a bid on a house in Colorado in May. By the time that we would need the money for the Colorado house, we would have closed on the house in Indiana. The Colorado house would be ready for us to move into by the time we sold and cleared out of the Indiana house. However, things didn't work out that smoothly. The housing market in Indiana was in a serious slump – in fact, so serious that our realtor warned us that we might have to just walk away and leave the house abandoned. As the weeks went by with no seriously interested buyers, it looked as if his prediction might be true. On the day that we were moving out of the house – as we were hauling the furniture and boxes out of the house and packing them into the moving truck in the front drive, a couple came by and asked if they could look through the house. They placed an offer on the house and wound up being our buyers – on the last possible day!

Before I give you the punchline to that story, I have to back up a bit to lay the foundation. A couple months before our move to Colorado, Andrew Wommack was preaching at a church in Michigan which was exactly one hundred miles from our front doorstep. So Peggy and I called his office and asked to make an appointment to speak with him while he was in the area. We drove up and simply informed him that we had decided to move to Colorado and wanted him to know that we would be available if there was anything that we could do at the school. I told him that I wasn't applying for a job, but was willing to use the expertise that I had developed over the past twenty-five years as a college dean to assist him if he had any need. It turned out that he was also coming back to the area a few weeks later to minister in Chicago, so we asked if we could connect again at that time. The coincidence is that the Chicago date was the day after we had determined to move out of our house, so it would be the day that we were to begin our journey to Colorado. When we met with Andrew this time, he had his wife Jamie and his business manager with him – making Peggy and me feel that there was something up. And there was. Andrew told me that he was actually thinking of a couple positions within his organizations that he would like to consider me for and asked me to connect with him as soon as I arrived in Colorado Springs. On top of that, he offered for us to stay in his guest apartment while we waited for our furniture to arrive. Now, back to the house sale; Peggy and I were actually on our way to Chicago for that meeting with Andrew when the realtor called to tell us that the couple had made an offer on the house. We arranged for him to drive out and meet us at an intersection where we could stop long enough to sign the papers.

But the plot continued to thicken. When we arrived in Colorado, we were met with the news that the director of the Bible school – the gentleman who had been in that position since the day the school opened – had just resigned. It seemed as if "the planets were all in alignment"; I could have stepped seamlessly into the position. However, I knew that I couldn't accept the offer since I had just given up one full-time job for the freedom to do more international missionary work. Peggy and I did, however, accept part-time positions that allowed us to teach when we were not out ministering. My involvement in the college eventually grew to developing a missions department for the school and serving as the director of that department.

I mentioned that there were two ministries that I wanted to connect with in Colorado Springs, and I did get to connect with both of them. But before I share about that second ministry, I need to stop long enough to share some personal stories about how all three boys wound up joining us in Colorado. Jeremy, our youngest, was just transitioning into high school; so, he moved with us. In fact, making the move during the summer between junior and senior high was part of our deliberate strategy; we wanted to save him from having to make two adjustments – one from junior high to high school and a second one from Indiana to Colorado – by combining the move. Unfortunately, we had not factored one important element into the calculation – the fact that Jeremy would "blossom" at the exact time that we were going to move. Although he had always been well liked at school, he had never been exceptionally popular. But during his last year in junior high, he suddenly became one of the most popular kids on campus. And just when everyone was saying that they were going to vote for him to be the class president for the following year, we were totally uprooting him and tossing him into a totally foreign environment where absolutely no one would know him. It was as if we had "jerked the rug out from under him" and left him at the "bottom of the heap" as far as popularity was concerned. The trauma left him not only emotionally disturbed but even triggered physical symptoms. Fortunately, an evangelist friend of ours happened to be ministering in town and we were able to have her pray for him. Jeremy testifies that the power of God hit him like a football tackle and totally healed his body and emotions. I'm sure that you have already guessed the rest of the story – he went on to become one of the most popular kids in his class at the new school.

Christopher, our middle son was in college in Indiana; so, we decided that he should stay there for a year since we needed to be residents of Colorado for a full year before we qualified for in-state tuition rates. However, when he came to visit us over Christmas break, he essentially refused to go back to Indiana because he loved Colorado so much. Of course, we "bit the bullet" and paid out-of-state tuition for the next term so he could transfer to a college in town.

Jonathan, our oldest son, was working as a manager for Walmart at the time of our move and had just taken a position at a new store, requiring him to make to a twelve-month commitment to the new location. When he heard that we were moving, his immediate response was, "I want to live in Colorado too!" He finished his three-hundred-sixty-five-day commitment with the store in Indiana and contacted the company headquarters on the anniversary of the date that he had reported to duty at that store requesting a transfer to Colorado. Within forty-eight hours, he had been reassigned to Colorado Springs.

158

And now back to the story about my desire to be associated with Every Home for Christ. The whole thing came about in a most unusual way. It all began with a "bad hair day" that made us late for church one Sunday morning. As Peggy and I slipped into the sanctuary a bit tardy, our regular seats four rows in front of the sound booth in section one were already taken; so we wound up finding a spot in the back of the auditorium. A little later, two more latecomers took the empty seats on the row in front of us. These stragglers were Dick Eastman, the president of Every Home for Christ, and his wife Dee. Later in the service we had a chance to meet them, and we eventually asked them to join us for lunch. They graciously accepted our invitation and met us at a nearby restaurant where we shared about our connection with Every Home for Christ in Nepal. When Dick asked about our ministry, we told him about our call to go to developing nations and train the Christian leaders in some of the truths we had spent the last twenty-five years teaching in the Bible schools here in America. Immediately, he had his electronic organizer out of his pocket and was typing in our phone number and email address. Within a couple days, one of his top staff members contacted me and asked to set up a meeting. That meeting led to another and eventually to the request that I assist Every Home for Christ in a project that they were just initiating — a program for training Christian leaders in developing nations! We were late for church and not in our right seats, but we were in the right place at the right time to meet the right man just when he needed our help!

The outcome of this divine appointment was a worldwide platform for helping to develop and launch a discipleship curriculum. I became part of an international team who was developing a discipleship method that we decided to name "Be Fruitful and Multiply" because we genuinely believe that the focus on studying the Bible itself will produce fruit in the lives of the believers and the discovery process where the individual is allowed to find truths for himself rather than to have the principles handed to him by others will produce such excitement that the new convert can't help but share his revelations with others. A bad hair day led to the opportunity to use my ministry skills and training to affect Christian leaders around the world. It was an open door to the world that I never would have seen had I not been delayed in getting to church that morning. God is always in control — even when it doesn't look like it!

The work that I was able to do with the Be Fruitful and Multiply project turned out to be one of the most rewarding aspects of ministry that the Lord has ever directed me into in that I've seen it revolutionize so many lives all around the world. I was honored to be part of this team in developing this new cutting-edge ministry tool. We examined many existing discipleship programs and evaluated their strengths and weaknesses to determine which one would best serve the needs of the rapid growth that EHC was experiencing around the world. It needed to be simple, quickly translatable, and easily reproducible; a program to meet their specific needs. As a result, the team decided to tackle the task of developing a unique curriculum and method specifically adapted for Every Home for Christ. The team started out questioning, "What curriculum would be best to use in this discipleship process?" As one of the largest evangelical ministries in the world, they were seeing millions of new believers come into the kingdom each year and thousands of new discipleship groups birthed annually. The result was that they were faced with the challenge of finding an adequate and affordable curriculum, usable in the myriad of languages of the people they were reaching in ever-increasing numbers. We spent quite a lot of effort studying materials from a very wide variety of sources and eventually focused our attention on one specific approach. But, no matter how much the committee liked the materials, we were faced with an impossible task of making the materials fit the needs at hand. The sheer magnitude of the task before us disqualified this and all the other courses we examined. Our chosen curriculum consisted of material that filled eight volumes and cost about twenty-five dollars per set to print. In addition, it took almost two years to translate it into a new language. With six thousand five hundred twenty-eight languages in the world, it would take thirteen thousand years to accomplish the translation process and incalculable resources to print and distribute the necessary copies around the world. Although these roadblocks seemed insurmountable we knew that there had to be a simple solution. Eventually, we realized that every one of us was carrying the answer around with us without even realizing it – the Bible, God's original discipleship manual.

But now there was another question that we had to entertain — that of how people around the world could effectively use the Bible to disciple others without a set curriculum, an organized approach, or a training program. The answer again came from the example of Jesus Himself. Since He basically taught in parables, we realized that we would also need to focus on the use of parables in teaching and discipling the new believers across the planet. Since stories are easy to remember and retell, it seemed only logical that we should make the stories of the Bible the primary focus of the discipleship process. We realized that there is no need to simply disseminate facts and figures and label that "training" or "teaching." The true meaning of discipleship is to produce fruitful Christians who then go out and multiply through reproducing in others what God has done in them. Through this, we can disciple the nations — a task which is actually doable without an elaborate educational network or curriculum.

Once the program was developed, I had the privilege of traveling literally around the world to train the leaders in Asia, Africa, and Latin America in how to implement the program. One pastor commented, "This is really awesome. I am really excited about how this program will change the entire landscape of Christendom in my country." I witnessed people in every setting engaging the Bible in a new dimension that they had never done before. In fact, during the hands-on practice sessions, it was almost impossible to get the participants to come back to order because they were all so engaged in going through the lessons that they didn't want to stop their discussion groups in order to come back to the general assembly.

Eventually, I was invited to take a full-time ministry position with EHC. The offer was so tempting that "I could almost taste it" – a position that was very tempting to me because of the opportunity to work closely with some of the cutting-edge advances that are happening in the present-day arena of world evangelism. However wonderful the opportunity might have been, it would have required my full time and total commitment. That meant that I would have to surrender much of the mission work I was doing and the classes I was teaching at the Bible college. As I began to pray about the decision at hand, the Lord directed me to the reference to "gifts and calling" in Romans 11:29. Until that particular day, I had always assumed that gifts and calling were essentially the same; however, I suddenly realized that they are actually two different entities. Our gifts are our God-given abilities; whereas our calling is our divine appointment in life. The gifts are given to us as a means to an end; that end is our calling. In the particular situation I was facing, I was being asked to accept a position that would focus on the gift of administration and organization that God has given me. I could have done the job that was offered to me, and I could have done it very well because I have the

162

necessary gift for the position. However, I would have been neglecting the call upon my life – that of a teacher. Since the whole purpose for the gifting of God in our lives is to serve the calling upon our lives, I knew that I had to turn down the position in order to fulfill a higher purpose.

Far too many pages ago, I introduced the fact that the ninety-first psalm had played a significant role in my life, and now it is time to expound. However, we need to step into a time machine and go back in time a few years to when we lived in Indiana – right in "Tornado Alley." I was at the eye doctor's office in downtown South Bend when the tornado sirens began to blare. As required by the safety codes, I – along with everyone else in the building – was herded into a secure place in the interior of the building until the "all clear" signal was given. By that time, it had been determined that a tornado had touched down in the area of town where I lived. After fighting my way through the snarled traffic, I eventually found myself back in my neighborhood. Weaving a path around fire trucks and other first-responder vehicles, I could see that a huge tree had fallen on my neighbor's home. Prior to the storm, it was a split-level home; now, it was simply a split home. I could also see that another giant tree had landed on top of another neighbor's car. Although it had been a full-sized sedan, it was now a compact car. But when I got to my house, I could see that it had not suffered any damage. The extent of the damage to our house was a one-inch dent in one of the downspouts. We did lose several trees and a number of limbs out of the trees that weren't uprooted. In fact, the canopy was so altered that an entirely new ecosystem of vegetation sprang up the following season because of the additional light that reached the ground. Although there had been destruction on both sides, we had only observed it with our eyes and it had not come near our dwelling! (Psalm 91:7, 8, 10)

Now, we can re-enter our time machine and return to Colorado. Yes, we had left behind the terrible winters in Indiana and had escaped Tornado Alley, but we had failed to realize that we had moved into a wildfire-prone territory. But we were destined to find out soon enough. One summer Saturday in 2012, the whole family was enjoying a fun family outing when we received a reverse-911 call telling us that we had thirty minutes to evacuate our house because a forest fire had erupted just outside our back door. Well, we couldn't even get back to our home within thirty minutes; so, we resolved that our only option was to trust the Lord with everything we owned and finish the activities we had planned for the day. My biggest concern was that I had just received a new passport the day before and had left it on my desk rather than storing it in my fireproof safe – proof positive that I am a true missionary. As we drove back toward the city later that afternoon, we could see the gigantic smoke plume and tell that the flames were just over the ridge from our house. Since we had only the clothes on our back, we had to go to the store and get the essentials we would need to get us by during the evacuation and check into a hotel. There was constant coverage on the television since the fire was such a major threat to the city – to the point that Peggy and I eventually decided to rent a movie just to get our minds off the fire. Unfortunately, that plan didn't work out so well in that only a few minutes into the movie, there was knock at our door. When I opened the door, I was greeted by one of the hotel staff informing us that the fire had progressed to the point where our hotel was now in danger and an evacuation order had been issued. From that point, we had to spend the rest of our time on the sofa in our oldest son's basement.

About four days into the evacuation, the flames had crested the ridge and were being blown by a sixty-mile-an-hour wind directly toward our house. However, the Lord miraculously intervened and shifted the wind when the fire was only a mile or so from our house. Although I was really saddened by the loss of the three hundred forty-six homes and two lives when the inferno swept into the adjacent neighborhood, I could only attribute the preservation of our home to Psalm ninety-one! One last note is that when we were eventually allowed to return, there was not even the smell of smoke in our house!

Following the forest fire, I realized that I needed to add another verse to my repertoire – Isaiah 43:2, "When thou passest through the waters, I will be with thee; and through the rivers, they shall not overflow thee: when thou walkest through the fire, thou shalt not be burned; neither shall the flame kindle upon thee." Because the fire had destroyed all the trees and vegetation in the swath of land that it had burned, there was no ground cover to absorb the rain when the rains came the following summer. The result was that we experienced terrible flash floods every time it rained. Homes and businesses were flooded, cars were washed off the road, and the highways had to be closed. In fact, I came home from one mission trip to discover that Peggy had been staying in a hotel because the only road that leads into our neighborhood was closed. The blessing was that no matter how much destruction we saw around us, there was no damage to our property and although the creek near our home overflowed its banks and did a lot of damage in its path, it did not overflow on us.

Okay, so I've talked about Pikes Peak, but I've yet to mention "Bust"; so here goes. Remember the story I told about the mission trip to Nicaragua when so many things went wrong? I concluded that all our problems were self-inflicted. Well, the "bust" I experienced was also self-inflicted. I've always found a lot of satisfaction in being able to "have lots of irons in the fire" at the same time. Writing books, traveling all over the world, running the Bible college, serving in the church, and maintaining a family were certainly a lot of "balls to juggle" all the time, but I somehow managed to keep them all in the air. When people would ask me how I did it, I would always answer, "When you only sleep four or five hours a night, you have plenty of time to do other things." That is, until the night after two back-to-back mission trips when I woke up totally disoriented after only an hour of sleep. I knew that I was in my own bed rather than a hotel room somewhere, but I couldn't make sense of anything else. I couldn't lie down – only pace the floor. Eventually, I was able to get back to sleep by sitting up in a recliner chair. When the same thing happened again the second night, I finally agreed to go to the emergency room for tests. That evening, I developed such severe muscle constrictions that I had to make a second visit to the hospital.

A night in the sleep lab confirmed that the reason I was sleeping only a few hours each night was that I had sleep apnea. Decades of accumulated sleep deprivation – that probably started when I was in college – had finally caught up with me. What I had always considered to be my strength (the ability to work rather than sleep) was actually my weakness! I had a total collapse that blindsided me – no gradual build-up and no advance warning signs. The sleep specialist said that the only treatment was to get eight hours of sleep each night – a goal that I have been able to reach by using a simple dental appliance that pulls my lower jaw forward enough to keep my airways open so that I don't stop breathing and wake up during the night. Unfortunately, prior to discovering a dental appliance that would serve the purpose, he tried to fit me with a CPAP machine that blows air into the patient's nose to keep the airways open. I reacted with such extreme claustrophobia from the five-minute test run that I couldn't calm down for over two hours. Those effects lingered on for weeks so severely that I couldn't sit in a meeting unless I had an aisle seat and I panicked when putting on a snorkel mask on our Caribbean vacation that summer. It was only after Peggy laid hands on me and broke the residual effects of the trauma that I was healed.

The bust was that this whole episode occurred just days before I was scheduled to fly to Nepal to dedicate the churches and houses that we had rebuilt after the earthquake that you'll read about in a future chapter. The self-inflicted element was that I had simply over-programmed myself to the point that my body simply shut down rather than submitting to my over-demanding schedule. The lesson to be learned is that even though Jesus said that we were to go into all the world, He also promised He would be with us and that His Spirit would empower us. These promises mean that we can restfully pace ourselves and still accomplish all that He expects of us!

Life on a Shoestring

Several chapters ago, I shared the story of how I made the choice to accept a scholarship into the Pulp and Paper Science and Technology program at North Carolina State University rather than to follow my long-time dream of studying at Furman University. However, I didn't realize at the time that this decision had actually set me on the path for a very lucrative future. It was only after I graduated and began to receive the school's alumni publications that I realized that the Pulp and Paper graduates were the highest paid of all the graduates from any of the different programs of the university. Coupling that fact with the fact that I was always number two in my class (The student in the number one spot was a middle-aged gentleman who had years of experience in the industry), I was on track for a very financially secure life. In another place, I shared how I gave up my position as a graduate student on a research team to enroll in seminary. Not only did I give up a scholarship and a monthly stipend, I also stepped out of consideration for a career in the innovative research that would have placed me not only in the best paid career field from my university but also into an elite position within that industry. Instead, I accepted a position earning fifty dollars per month and free room and board in the Full Gospel Student Fellowship house – the house that I described previously as being on the edge of the shady side of town, next to the mental institution, and home to a houseful of college students. But the truth is that I have never had a second thought about those decisions.

Yes, I've had to live on a shoestring budget during much of my life but that shoelace has never come untied! I remember being challenged once by a relative who wanted to know why I had not pursued the top salary. I could only respond by mentioning some of the lives that I

168

had had the opportunity to touch and concluding that there are things in life that are worth much more than money. Had I stayed in the pollution-control career that my graduate program was preparing me for, I would have spent my life making dirty water clean; instead, I have had the joy of making dirty souls clean!

I have always seen God provide every need and every desire in my life. I am certain that it is because I have yielded my life to Him, and thus He has guaranteed to see that I have everything I need to fulfill the commitment I have made to Him.

I related earlier in this book that, after watching a missionary's grainy black-and-white slides of destitute people in India while I was still in Sunday school, I pledged to give fifty cents out of my regular one-dollar allowance to missions. That was a seed planted into my future, although I didn't know it then. In the same way, anything I've given up for Him, whether it was money or even my lucrative future in pollution control, also became blessed by the Lord.

Paul made it clear that a transformation occurs in the seed between the time it is planted and the time of its resurrection, "So also is the resurrection of the dead. It is sown in corruption; it is raised in incorruption: It is sown in dishonour; it is raised in glory: it is sown in weakness; it is raised in power: It is sown a natural body; it is raised a spiritual body. There is a natural body, and there is a spiritual body." (I Corinthians 15:42-44) But there is one interesting thing about the parallel between the process of death and resurrection and the principle of sowing and reaping; even though the resurrected body is radically different from the physical body, it is still a body. We see this displayed repeatedly in the resurrection of Jesus. Those who encountered Him had difficulty recognizing that it was Jesus (Luke 24:13-32; John 20:14-17, 20:26-28, 21:4-7); however, they all immediately recognized that the individual they encountered was a man.

Likewise, the harvests that we reap from our sowing will come back with a resemblance of the seed that we planted even though the real substance of the harvest is of a significantly different nature. This is a biological principle that Jesus used to illustrate the spiritual kingdom to us.

So is the kingdom of God, as if a man should cast seed into the ground; And should sleep, and rise night and day, and the seed should spring and grow up, he knoweth not how. For the earth bringeth forth fruit of herself; first the blade, then the ear, after that the full corn in the ear. But when the fruit is brought forth, immediately he putteth in the sickle, because the harvest is come. (Mark 4:26-29)

This illustration showcases the fact that the rebirth of the seed is radically different from the kernel that is placed in the ground. Blades and ears look nothing like seeds; however, the eventual harvest is filled with corn that is identical to the kernel that was originally planted. The message here is that even though we sow seeds that bring forth harvests of a different nature, there is still the element of the original seed in the new harvest. Since we have already seen that Jesus often likened the harvest to gathering the souls of men, let's explore the connection of sowing monetary offerings that produce a missionary harvest and at the same time produce a financial return.

As a college student, I lived on a very limited budget and helped organize my funds by taking my monthly check and dividing my spending money into four envelopes – one for each week. One night at a special missions rally, I felt impressed to empty my wallet for the offering. This left me a full week behind on my finances, but when I opened my envelope for the next week – much to my surprise – there was twice as much as I had put there! Another experience while I was in college was the night that I felt directed to empty my wallet in a missionary offering one Friday evening. I knew that that meant I would be penniless until the next weekend, but I also knew that my God would somehow take care of me. When I got back to the dorm that night, there was a note on my door directing me to call one of the college professors that night – no matter how late it was that I got in. Even though I hated to call at a rather late hour, I knew that there was an urgency behind the professor's message; so, I returned his call. He greeted me with the offer to work for him the next day. He had received an opportunity to do some side work and needed an assistant – work that I knew how to help him with. Of course, I agreed and met him early the next morning for a full day's work. At the end of the day, he paid me in cash – more than I had put in the offering the night before. That missionary seed brought me an immediate harvest! Not only that – the business opportunity continued for the professor, and he employed me week after week for a number of months, greatly multiplying the seed I had sown. But even more importantly than that was the fact that the money I dropped in the offering plate that Friday night somehow touched a life in some distant corner of the world and produced a changed life that I will never know about in this life but will certainly see the harvest in the next one!

When I began to make annual trips to Nepal, I witnessed how God used some really unusual ways to bring about harvests from the missionary seeds I had been planting from my childhood. On one occasion, the people from my church asked me to "stick my neck out for missions" by growing a beard and auctioning off the opportunity for the church members to shave it off with a straight razor. This happened to be the only time in my life that I ever grew a beard other than the time that I went without shaving for several days before taking an elephant-back safari into the jungles of Nepal – I figured that if I were to have an Indiana-Jones-type adventure, I should look the part! When the shave raised over three hundred dollars, I had no complaint about the decision. On another occasion, a Sunday school class put on a big barbeque and bake sale, the musicians from several churches arranged a big gospel concert, and five young children spent a whole weekend making and selling candy to help send my wife and me to Nepal. I knew that all this help and hard work – especially the support from the little children – was nothing more than proof that God had honored my fifty-cent pledge I had made back in Sunday school.

One of my favorite stories on the topic of sowing for missions occurred while I was dean of the Bible college in Indiana. In the backyard of our home stood a giant walnut tree whose upper limbs brushed the very heavens. It was the home of a multitude of gray squirrels that scampered up and down its trunk and ducked into its hollow knotholes only to reappear ten feet further down the trunk on the other side of the tree. This disappearance and reappearance of the furry little creatures became a little discomforting to us since it meant that the tree must be hollow for some major section of its trunk. Since the tree leaned across the roof of our home, we began to feel that it endangered our home and our lives if it were to be blown over. Several severe storms took their toll of limbs from other trees in our yard; yet the giant walnut remained intact even though it rocked and creaked with the violent winds. I talked to several companies about removing the tree, but each one offered bids that were far beyond my price range. One friend of mine who did tree removal as a sideline volunteered to take it down for us as a favor. But, after climbing the tree and surveying how much actually reached over the house, he descended and rescinded his offer. He told me that since the tree leaned over the house the only way to remove it would be to hire a "cherry picker" crane. The eight hundred dollars that it would cost was beyond my budget; so, I delayed on removing the tree.

But when a violent windstorm raged through our area bringing down one of the trees in our yard, my wife insisted that we act immediately before the next storm felled the walnut which, in turn, would crush our home. So, I agreed to call in the cherry picker, but I asked for just one week's grace. Since the next week was our annual campmeeting, I knew that I would be busy morning, noon and night, and would not have time to deal with the tree removal – even if I had the money. In one of the sessions at the campmeeting, Dr. Sumrall took a special offering for missions, and I responded by making a five-hundred-dollar donation on my credit card. Now, this was a real step of faith because I knew that I would have to pay eight hundred dollars to get the tree removed the following week; now I was adding an additional obligation of five hundred more dollars. Where would I get an extra thirteen hundred dollars before the end of the month? I had no idea. I only knew that I had to obey the Lord on the missions offering and my wife on the tree removal.

During the lunch break after the service in which I had made the missions pledge, I walked to my home – which was just across the street from the church — and found a stranger standing in my backyard. I went to find out what he wanted and he told me he wanted to buy the walnut lumber from the tree. He had been in the area for some other wood procurement and had spotted this tree towering on the skyline. It seemed ideal for his veneer business and he was willing to pay five hundred dollars for it. I quickly settled the deal and arranged for free removal – saving me the eight hundred dollars that it would have cost me to have a tree removal company take it down. I also pocketed the five-hundred-dollar check and used it to pay off my missions pledge. I'm still amazed how that the man was driving in my neighborhood and showed up in my backyard on the very day that I planted a missionary seed by faith. Not only that – he offered me the exact amount that I had given in the offering!

That's what I call a manifestation of one of the Hebrew names of God, Jehovah Jireh – the God who supplies all our needs according to His riches in glory through Christ Jesus. There are a number of great redemptive names for God in the Hebrew language. Each portrays one of God's great qualities. However, there is another name for God that was coined by one of the graduates of the Bible college where I used to teach – Jehovah Nick. This name demonstrates that He is the God who always comes through in the "nick of time." I suppose that He does things that way so that we can know that it really is God who is in charge. It must be His way of keeping our eyes on Him and Him alone. When God is all you have, you'll find that God is all you need. Allow me to recount just a few of the stories that emphasize the point that God may seem slow by our time tables, but He is always right on schedule with His. One of my favorite verses in the Bible is Hebrews 11:11, "Through faith also Sara herself received strength to conceive seed, and was delivered of a child when she was past age, because she judged him faithful who had promised." Here we learn the secret of a woman who had to wait years to get the answer to her request yet counted God faithful. She knew that if He said that He would do it, He was going to do it – period. That settles it! If you know what God's promises are, you can be assured that you will have them in due time – and right on time – if you don't give up your trust in Him. One hamburger chain advertised that you can have it, "Your way. Right away." Not so with God; it's His way and in His time to assure us that it's His plan.

On one of my trips to India, I knew how much money I needed and had been praying and believing for

174

the total amount; yet, the day to depart arrived and I was still a few dollars short of that amount. On the way to the airport, the friend who was driving me there, handed me some money which brought me to the exact total with twenty-five cents to spare! But then there was a very humorous thing that happened after I arrived in India. Rather than converting all my dollars to rupees at once, I portioned my money carefully for each segment of the trip – making the conversions in each city. However, as I traveled by train into some remote parts of the country, I found myself in one place where I could not get the money converted. Therefore, I ran out of Indian rupees even though I had US money in my pocket. Fortunately, I had a prepaid train ticket to the next city where I could get the money exchanged; so, I purchased a simple rice meal with the last coins I had and headed to the train station to wait for the next train. While I was sitting on the platform, a beggar came up to me and – putting his fingers to his mouth – motioned that he needed money for food. I responded by reaching into my front pockets and pulling them out to show him that I had nothing. He then sat down beside me and continued to beg from all the passengers as they came across the platform. The friend who was traveling with me snapped a photo and labeled it, "Two beggars in India." Of course, I wasn't a beggar – just a person waiting for Jehovah Nick to pass my way!

When my wife and I felt directed to go to Scandinavia and Russia, we had almost decided to cancel the trip because the tickets were far beyond our budget. Every time we talked to the travel agent, we walked away discouraged because nothing seemed to fit – until one airline representative asked, "Do you have to fly on these particular days?" When I responded that we could go a few days sooner if necessary, he answered, "Great, we have a promotion that ends today for flights a couple of weeks earlier than what you're looking at." By rearranging our travel dates, we bought tickets about a fourth the price that we thought we were going to have to pay! When we changed the air travel dates, it opened up another window of opportunity on the international travel because we happened to be able to meet a ship going into Russia and were able to arrange passage and lodging on board at a fraction of the overland travel package we had been considering. God knew what He was doing, even when we didn't and He allowed us to stumble upon the promotional on the last day that it was available to prove that He was in control, not the travel agent.

On my first two missions into Nepal, the Lord provided exactly the needed funds – to the penny. While we were on our first trip to Nepal, I had to pay some of the hotel bills with a charge card but found that additional funds had arrived after we had left the States that totally covered the credit card expenses. On the second trip, I had determined to take my wife to minister to the women of Nepal. That really put a strain on my faith since we had to raise money for two tickets plus the costs of the crusade and teaching conferences. Yet, I knew that God would supply since it was His will for her to come along. Having settled that issue, the Lord really began to stretch my faith when He spoke to me that if I wanted my children to grow up understanding my heart for missions and the ministry, I needed to start taking them with me on these trips. About that time, my mother, who had planned to keep the children while we were away, became ill and said that we would have to make other arrangements. My insides were churning with the question, "Did I really have enough faith for even more tickets and expenses?"

About two o'clock one morning, I woke up with a question ringing in my mind, "If God can show you where your tripod is, will you believe Him for the total expenses to take your wife and children?" The tripod for my video camera had been missing for several weeks. I had looked everywhere I could imagine – in every closet, under every bed, in every corner, in my office at the college, plus I had asked every person who might possibly have borrowed it. After weeks of futile searching, I was convinced that if it turned up, it would be a sign of God's direction; so I answered, "Yes," and dozed back to sleep. A few hours later, the alarm rang and I stumbled out of bed and toward the shower. After dressing, I stopped in the laundry room to deposit my dirty items. As I flicked on the light, my eyes caught a glimpse of something in the corner. Was it? Yes, it was the tripod I had so diligently sought. How could it be that it had evaded being seen the other dozens of times I had been into that laundry room? God only knows how He kept it hidden and then revealed it on the specific day I needed a confirmation. Likewise, only God knows how He provided all the money for the mission, but He did. The amount that was received toward the trip was almost to the penny of the necessary budget. A couple of the team members fell short of raising their total support, but extra came in through other gifts to cover their deficit. The crusade expenses exceeded the projected budget; but again, the Lord provided through last-minute donations that were sufficient to cover them. In addition, we had been believing God to supply extra finances to help fly our interpreter to the US to record shortwave radio programs – and exactly the amount we had been believing for was left in the budget when all other expenses were covered!

In a previous chapter, I shared about how Dr. Sumrall was miraculously granted permission to build shortwave stations in the US – one of which was aimed directly toward Nepal. When the Lord spoke to me that via shortwave I could be there fifty-two weeks a year rather than the one to two weeks I was able to travel there each year, I was ready to jump at the chance –

even though the airtime bill would be half my annual salary. I remember feeling like a fool because I could barely get the words out between my sobs when I stood up at the inauguration of the station and made a commitment to the Nepali broadcast. Those tears watered the soil that produced such an abundant harvest that the emerging church in Nepal became known in the following year as the fastest growing segment in the world-wide Body of Christ! The Lord supplied marvelously for the radio time, the interpreter, and a follow-up ministry in Nepal. The program style was a teaching format that began with the very basic questions of life such as, "Is there a God?" and progressed through all the issues of how to know which god was the true one and how to know Him.

As we went through the sessions, my interpreter would occasionally turn to me and exclaim, "We need this teaching to be made available to all our people. We have nothing that explains the Christian message so clearly in our language." Finally, we decided that these messages should be transcribed from the tapes and be printed in book form for distribution throughout the nation. But that would cost money and I had just committed myself to thousands of dollars to pay for the shortwave radio time. Where would I find money for printing? I concluded that it would come from the same source as everything else – *Jehovah Jireh* (or Jehovah Nick). We sent the tapes back to Nepal with the instructions that local Christians start working toward a publication date in the following spring. The books were then to be ready by my next visit. They began the laborious task of transcribing and editing the material.

Finally, as the project neared the production stage, it required a transfer of funds to cover expenses with the printer. Just after New Year's, I was contacted and asked to please wire the funds. I agreed that money would be transferred the next day – but from where? The following morning, at the office, a friend stopped in to wish me a belated "Merry Christmas." She had been sick with the flu over the holidays and had missed making rounds to distribute Christmas gifts. She visited a while – and left an envelope with a dinner gift certificate for my wife and me. After she left, I went about some errands and returned to my office about ten minutes later and met my friend as she stepped out of the ladies' room next to my office. Somewhat nervously, she thrust a second envelope in my hand explaining, "The first gift was from my husband and me. This one is from the Lord." She confessed that she had been in the restroom trying to convince herself to do it because she felt awkward giving a monetary gift to me even though she knew that the Lord had specifically directed her to do so. When I opened the envelope, I found, in cash, the exact amount that I had promised to send to Nepal! Our God knows how to have the exact amount at the exact place at the exact time!

Not only does our Lord care about getting His people on the mission field, He cares about our everyday needs in life. And He takes care of all of them. Many times, He appears as Jehovah Nick, but He always makes it to the scene on time. As newlyweds, my wife and I often struggled through on a shoestring budget. I remember one time when one of the officers of the Full Gospel Businessmen's Fellowship invited me to lunch, but I had no money and was afraid that he might not be intending to pay the bill; so, I insisted that we just stop at my house and share a can of soup.

At one point, we were down to only five dollars in our checking account and no cash in our wallets. We sat in our living room one evening calculating how we would make it through to the next payday. It was the time of month for the newspaper boy to come and collect his five-dollar charge and we knew that he would probably be arriving soon to ask for that last bit out of our checking account. When the doorbell rang, my wife whispered, "Don't answer it; it's probably the paper boy." I responded, "No, if we owe him and we have it, I'm going to pay him." To our surprise and relief, it was not the paperboy coming to drain our account; instead, it was a neighbor with tears in his eyes proclaiming, "Here, God spoke to me to bring you this!" As he handed us a thirty-dollar check, he explained that he had been reluctant to bring us the money. Even though he felt in his heart that the impression had come from the Lord, his mind reasoned that I had a good position at the college and didn't need any outside help. He then put out a fleece that if I didn't open the door, he would assume that the impression to bring a gift was not from God. Had I obeyed my wife's suggestion to ignore the doorbell, not only would we have missed the much-needed blessing, he would have also missed the confirmation that he really could hear from God. We all rejoiced because he had no way of knowing about our personal need except that it had been revealed to him supernaturally.

Even though our budget was really tight, Peggy and I were determined to own our own home rather than renting. We just couldn't see the purpose in giving money away without anything permanent to show for it. So, after renting a small house for just long enough to find the house we wanted, we purchased our first home. It was a real fixer-upper; so, I spent every weekend and every free night fixing and repairing until I finally got the house livable. Much to my surprise, the same weekend that I announced that I had finally completed the "to do" list, Peggy announced that she had found another house and wanted to move. Since it was across the street from the school and church, I agreed to consider it even though I was just ready to settle in and actually enjoy living in our little starter house. Since the house was in such close proximity to the church, the owner had made arrangements with the ministry's business manager that she would sell it directly to anyone on staff without going through a realtor. That little incentive was certainly a help, but the real incentive came when I tried to negotiate the price with her. As I bargained down and she countered we finally came to within two thousand dollars. At that point, she gave me two options: I pay the price that I was offering and take a personal loan from her for the extra two thousand dollars or we just settle at my offer. Of course, I chose option B.

The only problem that we faced at that point was selling our old house. Since I had put so much work into fixing it up, I had actually outpriced it for the neighborhood. There was no way that I was going to reclaim all my investment, even if I discounted my "sweat equity." When it didn't sell, we began to ask, "Why?" The answer seemed to come back that we should keep it to help bless other Christians in need. We decided to rent it out to Christians at a below-market rate in order to help believers have nicer housing than they could otherwise afford. That meant that there was only a marginal profit to be made each month after the mortgage payment was sent in. Therefore, if we ever missed a month of having a renter in the property, we would be faced with a mortgage payment and no resources to cover it. To make it an even greater faith commitment, we increased our missions giving based on the margin of profit from the rental income. Then we left the home in the Lord's hands to serve as our rental agent. He has always proven Himself.

Once as I was leaving for Israel, we received a notice from our tenant that she was being transferred and would be leaving within thirty days. What a challenge – only a few days to rent the house and most of the time I was to be out of town! On top of all that, it was the dead of winter, when there is little or no activity in the housing market in our far northern location. Yet, we knew that it was God's house and that He knew who the next tenant was to be. Quite out of normal routine, my wife happened to be in the college library one afternoon while I was away on the Holy Land tour. During her visit, she mentioned to the librarian that our house was coming open. In the next aisle, stood one of the church members who had stopped by the library for some reason even though she was not a college student herself. Overhearing the conversation, she introduced herself and became the next occupant of our – rather, the Lord's – rental house. The house didn't stand vacant for even one day.

The next time that our house was to come vacant was even at a more inopportune time – it was graduation time, and I was up to my neck in preparation for the graduation: final exams to grade, grades to average, grade reports and transcripts to complete, diplomas to issue, graduation ceremonies to arrange, the graduation banquet to plan – plus officiate, and then an immediate departure to the mission field of the Himalayas. How in the world could I manage to get a new tenant into the house? Again, my wife just happened to be talking with a lady who was babysitting for us. It turned out that she and her husband were looking for a temporary place since they had to move out of their present location, but they had not located a permanent home. They moved in the day our other renters moved out and stayed long enough for us to get through the rush of graduation, the mission trip, and get back to normal before finding the next person to lease the house. Jehovah Nick was at work again!

When our church was planning a mission trip to the Philippines, I felt a real desire to be part of the team, but there was no way I could afford it. We had no extra cash and what extra money I could collect needed to go to pay back a loan that I had taken from my father-in-law when we had bought our second house. One of the elders at the church knew of my desire to be part of the team and volunteered to pray with me about it. His prayer was that God would open the windows of heaven and make a way for me to go through the door of opportunity that stood before me. To be honest, I didn't anticipate much and went on with my life, with one of my primary objectives being to settle my debts. When I collected enough money to pay back the loan my father-in-law had extended to me I took the cash to my mother-in-law because my father-in-law had recently passed. To my amazement, she responded, "That was between you and him, not between us. You don't need to pay me." The debt was canceled, and I was left with the exact amount of cash necessary to pay for my ticket for the mission.

Can you bear just one more story? Early one year, I began to have a deep sensation that I should plan to join our ministry's Holy Land tour that year. Since the trip wasn't until November, I knew that I had plenty of time to make the arrangements, but there was one major hurdle in my path — the money. At that particular time in my life, our family budget was stretched to the max, and there was no way I could ever expect to add in the cost of a trip to Israel. As each day went by, I was more and more stirred in my spirit that I was supposed to be on that trip. I somehow felt that it was a divine appointment. But as each day passed, it was also more and more evident that I could not afford to go. I couldn't see any way to squeeze any more outgo into the budget without a new source of income. Then came the call from a pastor friend of mine asking me if I could fill his pulpit one Sunday while he was going to be out of town. Immediately, I thought of my need for some extra income and thought that this must be God's way of providing it. If I went out as a guest speaker in a few churches during the year, I could likely get enough honorariums to cover the cost of the trip to Israel. Since I had my own responsibilities at my home church, I told my friend that

I'd call him back once I checked with my pastor. To my chagrin, Dr. Sumrall's answer was, "No, I need you here!" All I was scheduled to do was to make announcements — a job that certainly didn't seem to warrant preempting my opportunity to go out to preach. However, I submissively called my friend and told him that I would have to decline his offer. Well, the weeks passed; and as time for the tour drew closer, I was sure that the plane would be taking off without me. That is until the day I was called into the office of the tour director. The lady who was scheduled to host the tour was pregnant, and her doctor had insisted that she not fly due to some complications that were developing. An alternative host had to be selected, and my name was on the short list. Since I was a Bible college teacher, I was certainly qualified to answer any questions the tour members would have. Plus, I had been to Israel as part of my seminary training, so I was at least a bit familiar with the sites that we would be visiting. As you might well guess, it only took a nanosecond for me to accept the offer. Apparently, I did a pretty good job because I was invited back as the tour host for the next several years and given opportunities to visit Rome and Egypt, as well as make numerous trips to the Holy Land.

When Dr. Lester Sumrall was alive, he did not receive a salary from the church, TV station, or any other aspect of his ministry. The only income he received was from two offerings each year – one at his birthday and one at Christmas. It was during his birthday offering one year that I felt the Lord directing me to give a hundred-dollar gift. Unfortunately, money was very tight at that particular time, and all I could afford without having to go into debt was a ten-dollar bill. I dropped the bill in the plate and figured that this was the end of the matter. However, in the service the next week, Dr. Sumrall took time to thank the congregation for his offering of $5,910 – a generous offering back in those days. He then made a comment about the fact that it was ninety dollars short of six thousand and mused that someone with the extra money must have been absent that day. Well, that person wasn't absent; he was right there in the service, but he was just lacking in the faith it took to obey the direction of God. I learned a valuable lesson that day about trusting God when He speaks to you. Too often, we simply assume that our disobedience doesn't make a big difference in the long run. We somehow think that God has a back-up plan with someone else to take over the responsibility He gave us. The birthday offering that day disproved that assumption. The amount I held back was the exact amount that the offering lacked. If this principle is true in offerings, I'm sure that it applies to every area of obedience.

From that day forward, I've always tried to follow those little promptings from the Lord in detail – no matter if the necessary resources weren't readily available. One example was the request that I received from a pastor friend in Uganda, stating that he needed a new computer. The request came a couple days before one of my students was to leave for the country; so, I had to make a quick decision to get the computer to her before she left the States. I found a lot of used and refurbished laptops at affordable prices; however, I knew that I needed to get a new one since it would be a waste if there were problems with it in Africa. Thinking of the Golden Rule, I decided to buy the one that I would want for myself – a thirteen-hundred-dollar machine. Fortunately, I could get it for a little over eight hundred dollars online. The next day, a lady that I had never known before came up to me at a meeting and handed me a check for a thousand dollars. That surprise gift covered the cost of the laptop plus some extra! The African pastor was so excited with the new machine that he could hardly find words to express himself for the provision of the necessary equipment to make his work faster, easier, and more enjoyable.

Even though I've shared a lot of scraping-the-bottom-of-the-barrel sort of stories, I don't want to leave you with the impression that we have ever lacked. If you have been calculating how much all the adventures and missions that I've described in the book so far – and there are still more to come – must have cost, I'm sure that you have realized that much more money has passed through my hands than I could have ever made in the paper industry. Yes, God has always provided – both supernaturally and through giving me wisdom in making investments that have provided for my family. Dr. Sumrall had often suggested to me that the best investment was real estate, saying "Land is the only thing we can't make more of." But it wasn't until my first son went away to college that I began to take his advice seriously. After paying rent for his apartment every month that he was in school, I calculated that I could have come pretty close to buying the place; so, I decided to take action when my next two wound up going to college at the same time. I bought a house near the campus, moved the two boys into the house and rented out the other rooms to their classmates. Rather than paying rent each month, I was collecting rent from others – a simple investment that turned into a full business model. This sort of divinely inspired wisdom has allowed me to support myself and supply for my family while using one hundred percent of the money that I raise from ministry honorariums, donations, and book sales for our mission and charitable work.

Allow me to close this chapter by sharing just one more story in each of these two categories: God's miraculous provision and His supernatural wisdom in investing. When Peggy and I had made the decision to get married, I had been able to save up a few hundred dollars that would have bought an engagement ring with an almost microscopic diamond, but she loved me enough that a ring wasn't about to stop her – in spite of the fact that she really had a desire for a nice diamond. The same month that we announced our plans to be married, her mother found a very valuable diamond necklace that she had lost years before. It was God's exquisite timing. If she had found the necklace before that exact time, she would not have thought of giving it to us for the engagement and had she found it after I had ordered that tiny diamond I could afford, she would not have interfered in our lives by offering us the stone. As it was, it came at the exact right moment and I had enough money to have it set into a beautiful engagement ring.

My next story also has a small link to Peggy's mother in that it happened on the way to visit her. After Peggy's father passed away, we made a practice of visiting her mom on a regular basis, and part of the ritual was that we would stop by a popular hamburger joint to pick up two milkshakes – one for Peggy's mom and one that Peggy and I would share. Even though I love chocolate itself, I really don't care for chocolate ice cream or milkshakes; therefore, the one that Peggy and I would split was always vanilla. On the day after we got our first big return from an investment we had made, we were at the burger place ordering our two shakes when Peggy said, "Would you consider ordering a chocolate for us today?" At that point, I replied, "Actually, we can afford three shakes now. I'll get you your own chocolate and a vanilla one for me!"

Mission to the Rooftop of the World

One question that I'm often asked about my life as a missionary is, "What is your favorite country?" I often respond with, "The one I'm going to next," but I guess the real answer would have to be, "Nepal." It's not much more that a small blob of color splashed between the great nations of China and India. Yet, this tiny kingdom contains the highest point on planet Earth, Mt. Everest – literally the rooftop of the world! But more importantly, Nepal is millions of souls held captive by pagan darkness. The words, "Kathmandu, Nepal," are almost musical to my ears. They have somewhat of a lilting, melodious ring. They conjure up the most vivid and intriguing images: thousands of cute, little, bright-eyed, brown children, majestic snow-capped mountains, bustling public plazas, ancient Buddhist stupas, massive Hindu temples, and sharing my bus ride with goats and chickens inside and sheep tied on top. And, of course, these words also remind me of the Oriental Revenge – a serious travelers' dysentery that one time forced me to bring four of my team home in wheelchairs and run a little infirmary in the back section of the airplane. It is like stepping back in time – traveling over rugged paths and bumpy, unpaved dusty roads, merchants crying out, selling vegetables, spices, and multicolored fabrics, pilgrims praying aloud at small shrines, autorickshaws honking their horns, and sacred cows wandering serenely through the streets. Everywhere you turn, fascinating scenes of life hardly changed over centuries are played out right before your eyes.

I have spent more time in this Himalayan nation than in any other country that I've been privileged to minister in – traveling there at least once every year for over a quarter century. In fact, the passport agent at the

Kathmandu airport, after thumbing through my passport and seeing so many Nepal visa stamps, looked up at me and asked, "Why don't you get residency in Nepal?" On my seventeenth visit to Nepal, I was using a newly issued passport without any visa stamps from previous visits, so I was really surprised when the officer asked me, "Is this the first time you have been in Nepal this year?" I assume that they had become so accustomed to admitting me to the country that they were expecting me to show up all the time. Additionally, I've been able to build a fruitful relationship with the nation by beginning my work there early, when the government first granted religious freedom and allowed the Christian community to come out from underground. Through repeated visits, the various teams that I brought were able to help lay foundations of faith for the emerging church and build layer upon layer of solid biblical teaching. In addition to these spiritual contributions we were also able to make tangible ones by building a home for the national leader, a Bible college, and by reconstructing several churches and homes after a devastating earthquake. I can't overlook the fact that I was privileged to do all this with first-generation believers who express a freshness and zeal that is rarely found among those who have grown up in Christian nations. Of course, there is also the joy of doing all this in some of the most picturesque settings in the world and with the friendliest and most gracious people on the planet.

The small nation of Nepal is still basically Hindu; however, Christianity is growing at a phenomenal rate and during much of the time that I spent in Nepal it was estimated that the church was growing faster there than in any other nation in the world. I know people in the country who remember when they could count all the believers in the country on their fingers, but today that number has risen to more than a million. One Parliament member with whom I became friends told me that if growth patterns continued, he anticipated that half of his constituency would be Christian within the next few years!

The first believer in Nepal was expelled by the royal decree in 1914, "There is no room for Christians in Nepal." Some forty years later, his grandson, Rajendra Rongong (our personal friend), was among the first group of Darjeeling Nepali Christians to return to Kathmandu. It was at that point that Christianity really began to take root in the country under the leadership of our dear friend Rev. Robert Karthak. Other close friends of ours who came into Nepal at this same time to do social work and to spread their faith included Eileen Lodge who gave more than fifty years of service to the lepers of Nepal and Elizabeth Mendies who cared for the country's orphans for the same amount of time. When Every Home for Christ began its outreach into Nepal in 1982, it was illegal for Christians to share the gospel, but their former director (the gentleman who became my closest ally in the country) began working with a handful of courageous believers with the vision of visiting every home in the country to share their faith.

Though there is a tremendous revival spirit throughout the country, not all is peaceful. Nepali Christians have faced all kinds of abuse and isolation in recent years. Many have even paid the ultimate price for their faith. Just after one of my visits to Nepal, a bomb was detonated inside one of the churches I had preached in while in the country, killing two believers and injuring fourteen others. Miraculously, the kingpin behind the bombing plot was arrested and placed in a prison where there is a very active Christian Bible study and fellowship. He began attending their fellowship meetings and repented for his deeds and has extended an official apology to the church and asked for their forgiveness. In addition to the religious hostilities the believers have experienced, the country as a whole suffered greatly under the Maoist insurgency that cost the country thousands of lives and untold difficulties through strikes that have totally shut down the government and economy of the country. The people experienced extreme shortage of daily supplies, and the prices of daily essentials increased unexpectedly. At one point, the insurgents implemented a policy of extortion of Christian leaders in which demands for large sums of money were accompanied by threats of kidnappings or burning of homes if the funds were not delivered. Very close personal friends and co-workers of ours in Nepal were targeted in these extortion plots; however, they were protected through God's grace and the prayers of the saints.

My involvement in Nepal began in 1986 when I met Charles, a Nepali believer who shared about the persecution of the Christians in this Hindu land; he told of imprisonment for simply owning a Bible, of beatings for sharing the love of Jesus, and of death sentences for baptizing converts. Then he humbly asked that we pray for his suppressed people, living in a land of pagan darkness where the king was not only a human monarch but was also worshipped as a Hindu god. From that day, I began to intercede daily for the precious people of this isolated nation nestled in the lofty heights of the Himalayas. I claimed the biblical promise that the heart of the king is in the hand of the Lord and I asked that the Lord turn his heart! (Proverbs 21:1) Since Nepal was ruled by a king at the time, I felt that this was a tailor-made verse for the situation. Four years later, I heard that Charles was imprisoned because he was caught bringing Bibles into the country. I reminded the Lord of the Psalm that said that I could ask Him for the nations as my inheritance, and I asked for Nepal as mine. I emphasized the wording in Ephesians chapter six that tells us of our spiritual battle against evil spirits in high places, reminding God of the demon powers that control this rooftop of the world.

Then, suddenly, the whole world changed overnight in the spring of 1990 when His Royal Majesty Birendra Bir Bikram Shah Dev declared religious freedom for his subjects! Four years of prayer ministry had prevailed over hundreds of years of religious persecution! By the way, Charles – along with a number of other Christians – was released from prison as soon as the new constitution was signed. My prayers for Nepal continued until one day, the Lord spoke to my heart, "Now it's time for you to go see what you have been praying for." Now that God had granted my prayer request for freedom in the country, I began to pray about what my next step should be. The answer came that I should begin going into Nepal to train leaders for this emerging church. Amazingly, the Lord began to make things fall into place for me to get into the country. I received a letter from a believer in the country inquiring about applying to the college I was serving at the time. Even though it turned out that this connection really didn't prove significant when I actually went into the country, it seemed to be a sign that God was beginning to open the doors.

During the four years that I had been praying for Nepal, I had collected every scrap of information about the country and the conditions of the Body of Christ there that I could get my hands on. One of the sources that I found was the newsletter of World Literature Crusade (later to be known as Every Home for Christ). Although their outreach was done "under the radar," they did publish occasional comments in their publications. Every precaution was taken to protect the identity of their workers in the country so there were no photos or names in any of the updates. However, once the new constitution was in place, I thought that it might be possible to get the contact information for their director in

Nepal. When I wrote to the headquarters, I received a personal reply from Dick Eastman, the president of the ministry. He supplied me with the name, postal address, and fax number for Solon Karthak, their national director in Kathmandu. Years later, when I became directly involved with EHC, I mentioned the incident and was met with shock and the reply that such a disclosure was totally against all the organization's policies and protocol – proof to me that God had definitely been in charge of getting me into the country. Solon became not only our interpreter and the coordinator of all we did in Nepal but he was actually the one key person in the nation who seemed to cross all lines and hold together everything that was happening in Nepal. The next thing I needed was literature in the Nepali language, no small hurdle since no one was working in the country; all ministry there had been strictly forbidden. I contacted organization after organization asking for literature and was met with one dead end after another. In all my searching, I found one tract that had been published by the Foursquare Gospel denomination, but then – to my surprise – I discovered that World Missionary Press, a gospel publishing company that was essentially in my own backyard – about thirty miles away – and with whom I had a very close friendship, was producing Nepali-language scripture portions "by the ton."

Armed with several cases of literature from World Missionary Press, a group of six of us set out for Kathmandu. At the customs counter in the airport I was questioned about the cases we were transporting into the country. I explained that they were filled with literature that we intended to distribute free-of-charge to the people of the country. I then ripped open one of the boxes and started handing samples to all the customs officers. I've always wondered if these might have been the same men who arrested Charles for having Bibles in his suitcase before the new constitution was implemented.

Once we got into the country, we found high-traffic places and began handing out the tracts. One scene that I will always remember was being caught in the middle of a huge mob of close to fifty cute little brown school children begging and grabbing for "one." Dubar Square, the temple plaza and city center of Kathmandu, echoed with the chatter of these children as they all reached for our gospel tracts! In a nation where two years ago I would have been arrested for even owning gospel literature, I was allowed to freely distribute the little Nepali versions of the gospel pamphlet *Help From Above.* Before long, I saw a policeman approaching. When he asked what I was doing, I explained that I was just giving away free literature. His response was to ask for the box, which I surrendered. To my amazement – rather than arresting me as he would have done a few months before – he began to assist me in handing out the pamphlets. He explained that the crowd of people who had gathered was blocking traffic and he wanted to help disperse the people so that the traffic flow could continue freely. The people eagerly reached out to receive the tracts! Their eyes and hands demonstrated a sincere hunger and a humble appreciation for our witness. Our team distributed over five thousand of these tracts during our visit. We could have easily handed out ten times that quantity had they been available. We saw only two or three of the pamphlets discarded. Usually the people would stop and begin to carefully read the literature as soon as they received it. Buddhist monks, Hindu sadhus, Hari Krishna devotees, the guards at the king's palace, and even a few Americans who were in Kathmandu to study Eastern religions received our witness. As we moved throughout the city and the remote villages, we could sense a real spirit of freedom and revival in the land. We considered it prophetic; the gospel of the kingdom of God was being preached in Nepal, fulfilling the Lord's words that it would reach every nation before the end of this age. (Matthew 24:14) Our team preached in churches, testified in home groups, shared the gospel with a professionals group, ministered at a leprosy hospital, and freely witnessed on the streets, in the shops, and at the hotel. In every sector we found a genuine desire to hear the gospel message. Many could understand English well enough to talk personally with us and then be led in the sinner's prayer.

Another focus of that first visit to Nepal was to connect with Mommie Mendes – Charles' mother – who ran an orphanage in Kathmandu. Since the students from the Bible college in Indiana had been sponsoring one of her orphans for the past four years, I was excited to get to meet Kaji in person.

Earlier, I mentioned that I had received an application from a potential student in Nepal. It turned out that by the time we arrived in the country, he had become the pastor of a church and was actually having the dedication of his new church building during the time we were in Kathmandu. He, of course, invited our team to participate in the festivities. Since it is customary to remove your shoes before entering a building in Nepal, we all took off our shoes and left them at the door of the church. At the end of the service, it was impossible for me to find my shoes in the massive pile that had accumulated as the church filled up. Even though I had to walk back to the hotel barefooted that night, someone from the church showed up the following morning with the one pair of shoes that was remaining when the building cleared out the previous night.

The Lord gave us a wide open door into the hearts and lives of the people of Nepal. As revival surged through the land, the one thing that the thousands of new converts needed was clear, simple Bible teaching. One local Christian leader stated it plainly, "Tell them what 'Hallelujah' means." We all know the Lord's statement that the harvest is plenteous but the laborers are few.

However, I would like to suggest a little different consideration of the situation; the harvest is plenteous but the laborers are untrained. At the time I began to work in Nepal, seventy to eighty percent of pastors in Nepal were semiliterate and, therefore, could't read their Bibles. Since our commission from the Lord is to go into all nations and teach the Christian leaders so that they have an adequate foundation from which they can then train their people, I began laying foundations – building block upon block with each return trip.

In churches, home groups, and special pastors' conferences, we began to teach and to explain the gospel. We began at the very beginning with simple questions and progressed right through the basic foundations of the Christian faith to cover all the truths of healing, the baptism in the Holy Spirit, the gifts of the Holy Spirit, and deliverance from demonic power. The people were so hungry for truth that it was overwhelming.

We had scheduled one free night for some shopping, the pastors found out what store we had gone to and followed us there. They began to almost beg for more and more instruction and we wound up sitting on top of a pile of Tibetan carpets explaining the gifts of the Spirit rather than looking for souvenirs to take home; there was no better treasure to bring home than the memory of the light in their eyes as these pastors caught the revelation of the power of God for their ministries! The next morning as we were packing for the trip home, the pastors showed up at the hotel pleading with us to give them just a little more time to help them understand the moving of the Spirit. They had so many questions I thought that I was going to have to leave all my baggage and rush to the plane with just the clothes on my back! Again, it would have been worth the trade – my luggage for the joy of knowing that I had helped establish one more truth in the hearts of the leaders of this exciting move of God.

In divine timing – at exactly the same time that I made my first trip to Nepal and met Solon – LeSEA Broadcasting was building its new shortwave radio station in the Hawaiian Islands, beaming a twenty-four-hour-per-day gospel message right into Nepal! The message for Nepal continued to bubble inside of me and I realized that this was nothing short of a God-ordained coincidence. I had to know that I was speaking into the lives of these beautiful saints every day so I began to raise funds to cover the airtime and to bring Solon to the States where we could record programs for the half-hour daily Nepali broadcast, "The Voice of Joy," to be broadcast on the new gospel giant reaching across the Pacific Ocean, over the Himalayas, and into the hearts of those humble people. Since so many Nepali were eager to learn English, we knew that even people who weren't interested in the gospel would tune in because the Nepali/English format would help them with their language skills. Not only did we broadcast the lessons, we also developed a correspondence follow-up program for all who responded. When the Christian leaders in Nepal began to hear the truths in the broadcast lessons, they expressed concern that the people who really needed to know these truths might never hear them because they don't own shortwave radios or because they wouldn't know when to listen even if they had radios. "Put this teaching into a book," they pleaded. So we did. And then another. And then another.

It was also during that first visit that Solon introduced me to two men who became very significant in our work in the country. Pastor Robert should actually be considered the apostle of the nation. When Billy Graham sponsored his worldwide satellite crusade, he called on Pastor Robert to be his representative for Nepal. Pastor Robert is the individual who was invited by President Clinton to represent the Nepali Christians at the Presidential Prayer Breakfast. Solon also introduced me to Ravi – an executive with the largest tour company in the country. Since tourism is a major facet of the economy of the country, it is often joked that there are three religions in Nepal: Hinduism, Buddhism, and tourism. Therefore, being an executive for the largest company in the most lucrative industry put Ravi in an influential position in the country. At first, our relationship was basically a business partnership. Since I had planned to bring teams to Nepal every year, I needed someone to make all the hotel and travel arrangements – something that Ravi could do with top quality expertise. At first, he basically stood outside during our services but then he began to come in and sit in the back to listen. Gradually, he began to participate. Eventually, he began to interpret for me. Finally, he became my disciple. In the process of our relationship, I prophesied that he was to give up his important position and open his own company to help Christian ministries organize mission trips to the country. Of course, this was a big step of faith, but he felt that it was the Lord's direction; so, he stepped out and founded Agape Himalaya Adventures and became a leader in the discipleship movement in the country and a pioneer church planter.

When I asked the church leaders about the biggest need in the Nepali church, they responded without hesitation, "Training for our women." In a third-world country such as Nepal, the women are second-class citizens, which could almost be considered to be winding up in sixth place! But to Jesus, every person is in first place. I promised to bring Peggy with me on the next trip so she could begin to raise up women who could serve as role models within their churches. This special emphasis on a forgotten and neglected element of society has produced tremendous fruit both in the individual lives of the women and in the strengthening of the church in Nepal, particularly since in their churches there are more women than men.

The following year my wife and several other team members joined me on the second mission to this once-forbidden Hindu kingdom. I planned two leadership conferences: one in Kathmandu for the Christian women and one in Pokhara – the second largest city in the country – for pastors and Christian workers. In conjunction with these conferences, we distributed tracts in the surrounding area, ministered in home groups and churches, and held evangelistic crusades. One notable incident marked the evangelistic meetings in Pokhara. A tall, stately gentleman, who made you sense that he was someone important just by looking at him, responded to the altar call. It turned out that he was someone important. He was the head of the Pokhara Buddhist Religious Association – but there he stood at the front of the City Hall Auditorium before more than eight hundred local residents, all of whom recognized him and knew his position in the community. Boldly, in full view of his followers, he prayed the sinner's prayer to receive Jesus Christ as his Lord and Master.

But his was just one of the many testimonies that came out of our gospel crusade and Christian leaders' conference in Pokhara. The evening area-wide gospel rallies drew hundreds into the beautiful auditorium for evangelistic messages and special music by Christian groups. During the daytime teaching sessions, nearly two hundred selected Christian leaders came for lessons on how to wage spiritual warfare to free themselves, their families, and their nation from demonic control. At the close of each service, the altars were packed with those seeking the laying on of hands as our entire team prayed for them for salvation, healing, and deliverance. We distributed over seven thousand Nepali gospel tracts to eager hands in the markets, on street comers, in school yards, in villages, and along the highway as we traveled across the country. Even a breakdown of our van served as an added opportunity to distribute literature. National

Christian leaders were so motivated by the openness of the people to receive the gospel literature that they planned follow-up distributions. Preaching and ministry services were arranged in every area of our itinerary. Even a "pit stop" along the highway to Pokhara turned into an open-air crusade as one of our team members caught the attention of the villagers and began to share his testimony. In personal counseling sessions with pastors, we helped encourage and instruct them in matters of moving in the Spirit in their ministries. The women's conference in Kathmandu drew capacity crowds from the capital area. Everyone present reported a life-changing encounter as Peggy and the ladies of our group ministered to them. Several received Christ, many were healed of various diseases, at least one blind eye was opened, a number were delivered from demonic oppression, and all were motivated to become prayer warriors and soul winners. But as miraculous as these stories might be, there is one more testimony from this trip that causes them all to pale in comparison. I'll let Peggy share in her own words:

I had just begun to participate in the Great Commission as a short-term missionary but as I lay in my bed in Pokhara, growing closer and closer to unconsciousness, shaking uncontrollably with chills while burning up with a fever, I wondered if this was how my life was to end.

I had finally begun to see the power in II Corinthians 4:3-4, "And even if our gospel is veiled, it is veiled to those who are perishing, in whose case the god of this world has blinded the minds of the unbelieving so that they might not see the light of the gospel of the glory of Christ, who is the image of God." (NAS)

When I spoke the truth of the Word of God, the blinders came off the non-believers and the truth of the Good News was setting people free. The Buddhists and Hindus were just waiting to hear the news about Jesus

Christ. They were eager to respond when they heard that He was what they had been searching for. What joy and excitement I experienced when I saw God reveal Himself to these lost souls! I was thrilled to witness their happiness when they became new converts.

My husband and I, along with our mission team, had been preaching for several days in Nepal, a primarily Hindu nation which had recently opened its doors to the gospel. Before this time, we could have been imprisoned for preaching in Jesus' name. Now we carefully began holding meetings and watched in amazement as God saved, healed, delivered, and did the miraculous. I was just beginning to relax and realize that it was His hand upon mine and His anointing on my words that made these things possible. The Lord had brought me such a long way from when I was first saved. Back then the thought of doing mission work had never entered my mind; I was still uncomfortable witnessing and laying hands on the sick in my own town, much less going to the ends of the earth to share my faith! But then Romans 10:13-14 jumped off the page at me, "For whosoever shall call upon the name of the Lord shall be saved. How then shall they call on him in whom they have not believed? And how shall they believe in him of whom they have not heard? and how shall they hear without a preacher?"

The challenge of these words had finally compelled me to become a woman for the harvest. But now here I lay in what I thought could be my deathbed. Why had He brought me so far only for my ministry to end so abruptly?

My husband and the rest of the team had gone on to hold a meeting, not realizing how sick I was. Mustering all my energy, in a whisper, I asked Angie, the one team member who stayed back with me, what the awful stench was that was coming into our room. She looked out the window and became upset as she reported that our room was directly above a statue of King Cobra, one of the gods the Hindus worship. The odor was coming from the incense they were offering to this statue. She went on to say that the devotees were offering food and ringing bells, inviting demonic spirits. Just what I needed to hear! I asked her to please start singing "Oh, the Blood of Jesus" and to believe God for a miracle. I felt like I was dying. Depressing and desperate imaginations, such as the thoughts that I would never see my children and husband again, raced through my mind. "Lord," I cried, "did you send me here to die? I have too much work to do for you, and my kids will not have a mother."

As my friend paced the floor singing and praying, we heard a knock on the door. Who could it possibly be? All the people we knew were at the meeting. Again another knock. Little did we know that on the other side of the door was one of God's messengers. When Angie opened the door, she was greeted by a polite Nepali man with a doctor's bag. As he gently entered the room, he spoke to us in perfect English and told me that I was a very sick woman. He then added that I would soon be just fine. I kept thinking to myself, "How did he find me? Who sent him?" There was only one doctor for every twenty-five thousand people in Nepal. When we passed by health clinics, we would see long lines of people waiting and were told how they had to wait for hours to see a doctor. But now here was a kind doctor who actually came to me! He checked me over, gave my friend some instructions, left some medicine, and seemed to leave as quickly as he had come. How relieved I felt! The Lord had heard our prayers. My companion kept saying, "Soon you will be fine, Peggy. You will be fine just as the doctor had told you." We prayed and thanked the Lord, and shortly after I was asleep. When I woke up, I was soaking wet with no sign of fever. Though I was still very weak, I knew that the

202

worst was over and that my healing was surely starting to manifest.

At long last, my husband came back from the service and was shocked to see my condition. I told him what had happened and how thankful I was that he had somehow arranged for a doctor to visit me. Perplexed, he responded, "Peggy, we did not send a doctor. We did not know how sick you were. Besides that, there are no doctors around here." I remembered telling Angie that our visitor must have been an angel; but I really thought that it had been my fever speaking to say such a thing. But now I was beginning to wonder if my musing might have really been the truth! We checked with our Nepali team leader and the hotel manager, but no one knew a thing about sending for a doctor. God knew my need and – through His mercy, love, and faithfulness – sent just what I needed. He could have healed me without sending a doctor, but it was even more exciting and awesome for me to see how God sent an angel from nowhere to bring my healing. The next day my sickness was over. Though tired and weak, I was able to finish our trip and was soon totally restored, healed, and back to the work God had for me to do.

The following year, we went back to Nepal with another team to lead more training conferences and evangelistic meetings when something humorous happened. "Dr. Shur Lee, Dr. Dell Run," the people in the meetings all politely requested as they came to me one by one to describe their ailments and diseases. Then – as I followed Jesus' directions to lay hands on the sick – they were all healed. It wasn't until the second day of the conference that I realized that these humble Nepali people were coming to me thinking that I was a medical doctor. Actually, they were surprised that I was treating them with prayer rather than medicine. At the next meeting, I explained that the healings were coming not because I was a medical doctor, nor because I was an

American, and not even because I was a preacher. I explained that any believer could see the same signs follow his faith. This was the kind of supernatural manifestation that accompanied our ministry in the city of Tansen in western Nepal.

Perhaps the confusion that the people were experiencing was because of the location we had secured for the meetings – a medical clinic and the campus of a nursing college. In this venue, that literally hangs off the ledges of the majestic Himalayan Mountains, over two hundred and fifty hand-picked Christian leaders had gathered for three and a half days of intensive training on the power of the Holy Spirit to renew and energize their ministries. Many came from great distances, many traveling two or three days in rickety buses over treacherous mountain roads to attend this historic conference. Never before had such a training session been held in this part of the country. We believed that this meeting would serve as a catalyst to stir the Christians to more aggressive and anointed ministry. After all, this is exactly the report that had been received from the Pokhara area after the previous year's conference. The principal of the nursing college welcomed us and commented that she felt that God had personally arranged for the conference to be in their facility – we were the first outside group to be granted use of their property in its twenty-year history. All the local brothers who had helped organize the meeting agreed – every other facility they had tried to arrange – including erecting a tent – ended in a closed door.

During the three sessions each day, the appointed delegates hungrily latched on to every word as we taught on the baptism, gifts, fruit, and anointing of the Holy Spirit. In the evening meetings, the crowds swelled beyond the conference hall's capacity as local Christians poured in for training, inspiration, and anointing. My team members said that they felt like Peter and John on their mission to Samaria to impart the Holy Spirit to the believers there (Acts 8:14-17) as they saw countless Nepali Christian leaders receive the baptism of the Holy Spirit and begin to operate in the gifts of the Spirit. A number of the leaders were also slain in the Spirit, something that they had never experienced before. As we moved from Tansen back to the capital city of Kathmandu, we found that the same outpouring of the Holy Spirit had occurred at the women's conference which Peggy, and her team of ladies were holding while we were in the western mountains. Healings, deliverances, and miracles had been daily occurrences. The same anointing followed us to the Holy Spirit conference that we conducted for the Kathmandu Valley churches. A thousand or more eager believers packed the hall to be trained and anointed – and they were not disappointed. Again, we witnessed a mighty outpouring of God's Spirit as the conference delegates responded in faith to the promises of God.

In addition to the three conferences, our team also split up each Saturday to minister in the local congregations. In Nepal, Sunday is a regular workday; so, the churches meet on the official weekly holiday, Saturday. Again, each team member returned with overwhelming reports of God's blessing. At one youth meeting, over one hundred of the kids received the baptism in the Holy Spirit! On the streets and in the markets, we distributed thousands of gospel tracts to eager hands begging for the bread of life. Some people even offered to pay us for the precious gospel we shared with them. An added blessing was the personal ministry we were able to share with the leadership in Nepal. One pastor had encountered such difficulties that he was ready to quit, but our prayers and encouragement rekindled his fire for the Lord. His face physically showed the difference that was now in this heart.

Another "chance encounter" occurred when my wife and I spotted an American missionary wearing a wig as she tried to slip through a hotel lobby. When we followed her to a private area in the hotel and asked what was happening, she shared that she was under surveillance because of her ministry work in the country and was considering leaving Nepal. After our prayers, she regained her confidence and continued with her bold proclamation of the gospel throughout the nation.

One of our missions on this trip was to deliver a load of toys that we had collected for the children at the Mendies Haven orphanage. One item that I had felt led to buy was a volley ball set which caused me real problems in trying to pack the poles; they just don't make suitcases to fit volleyball poles. But I felt that it was necessary that we get that particular equipment there regardless of the difficulties. When we arrived at the orphanage, we were greeted with the news that only a couple of hours before they had finalized the purchase of a small plot of land which they would use as a playground and were thinking that they would like to have a volleyball court on it!

Just before we returned to the US, Solon showed me a piece of ground that he had been able to purchase in one of the more progressive parts of town, where there is actually electricity, phone service, and running water. He explained that with the new freedom in the country, there were more and more international businessmen moving into Kathmandu with their foreign currency and that the local people were being more and more abused by their landlords. Homes with running water, electric power, and telephones were at a premium, and the landlords had no reservations about evicting the tenants in order to get renters who could afford to pay more.

For the ministry to operate effectively, its offices needed to be located in a facility with electricity to run the office equipment and telephone service to connect with the outside world. It also needed to be in a stable, long-term location where the workers could confidently go about their business without having to worry about packing up and moving every few months! Solon laid out his vision to build a three-story facility with a large meeting room on the ground level, offices that would serve as the nerve center for reaching the whole nation on the second floor and his home on the third floor. The surprise came when he said that he only needed fifteen thousand dollars to put up such a simple but totally functional facility. I was astounded at the idea that such a small investment could bring such a big return. Additionally, once he was in the new building, he would never have to raise money for the home base needs. From then on, every cent (or rupee) could go directly to the work of spreading the gospel.

As soon as I got home, I contacted all the graduates from the Bible college and asked them to help me fund the project, and they did. In fact, one pastor who received my letter asking for help came into my office a couple days later and thanked me, saying that she had been feeling for a while that there was more that their church should be doing for missions. On the morning before my letter arrived she had been in the church office and looked up at the bulletin board, noticing the report letter that I had sent out after my previous trip. She went back to her house with a real awareness that the church was supposed to do something for Nepal. When she got home, my letter was waiting in the mailbox! Additional funds came from the sale of my new book *The Will of God at Your Fingertips*. With this excellent teamwork, we were able to make Solon's dream come true. He was able to move into the new facility just a week prior to our next visit, at which time we had the privilege of dedicating the building!

We were back in Nepal with more tracts when one little lad chased us down the street grabbing all the tracts before the others had a chance to take them. Finally, we asked our driver to have the boy stop. Unfortunately – or actually, fortunately – our little Nepali chauffeur did not understand and he interpreted our request as a wish to turn around. Now we had two problems: the young lad was still trailing us and now we were headed the wrong way — or at least what seemed to us to be the wrong way! Soon, our evangelistic venture was beset with what would seem to be a third problem — my sister who was sharing the rickshaw with me was beginning to have leg cramps from sitting in the tiny seat which perfectly fit two Nepali customers but not two Americans! We tapped the driver on the shoulder and got him to stop so that she could get out and walk a bit to ease her leg. That is when it happened! That is when we suddenly understood why all the unusual events were beleaguering our literature distribution. When my sister offered a copy of *Help from Above* to a young man standing at the bus stop where we had gotten off the rickshaw, out of his lips came the most amazing response – not "Thank you," not, "Oh, I'm a Christian," not, "I've seen this before" – but "I know Delron Shirley." Nothing on the tract gave my name: the only association was that it was the same material that we distribute every year on our missions to Nepal. You can never imagine the surprise when the next person who walked up on the conversation was the other passenger from the rickshaw – me.

It was at that minute that we realized the impact that our mission was having on the hungry souls of the nation of Nepal. This young man had received a tract four years before as we were distributing literature on the streets of Kathmandu. As a young believer from Chitwan State, he had come to the capital city for a training conference and had just happened down the street as we were handing out the gospel tracts. He then followed me back to the hotel where I gave him a box of tracts to take back and share with the people in his region. Now here we were – four years later and a couple of hundred miles away from Kathmandu – when he again just happened to be where we were distributing the little gospel portions! Now he was the associate pastor in a little church with fifty-eight converts! After all those years and all those miles, he not only remembered the tract but the name of the man who shared it with him. It is moments like that that make you know that it is worth all the effort, all the money, all the time, all the prayer, and all the trouble to get the gospel to the hungry souls of Nepal. To these people, the little gospel portions are not just pieces of paper; they are their lifeline to Heaven! After that, my sister began to address me with a line from a song that she felt had been written just for me since I grew up in the Carolinas and was actively ministering in Nepal, "He's known in Carolina and in Kathmandu. It's amazing how one man gets around."

When I first started doing missionary work in Nepal, I decided to learn a little of the language. So I bought a Nepali-English dictionary, picked out a list of what I considered useful words, made flashcards with the English word on one side and the Nepali word on the reverse. After spending almost a full year learning a new word every day or so, I was ready to impress the people when I returned for my annual visit. Unfortunately, when I began to pray for people at the first church service, one of the elders came to me and politely asked that I not pray over the people in Nepali. Apparently, the phrase that I thought meant, "I bless you," actually meant, "I'm in love with you." When we went out to a restaurant after the service, I again put my foot in my mouth when ordering lunch. Instead of asking for beef, I had told the waiter that I wanted to eat a holy cow.

One of the most memorable events was the conference held at a remote location on a mountaintop in Chitwan. About two hundred fifty men and women crowded into a wooden building with the women sitting on the floor on one side and the men on the other side. After the meetings, the women and children bedded down for the night inside the church while the men slept outside. Most of the delegates were from other villages – some having traveled days or even a week to attend the meeting – so, I asked how they managed to direct everyone to this remote venue. The answer was that the leaders had told the people to come to the town and ask, "Where is the place where they sing?" What a testimony! It was easy to locate the believers because their lives were characterized by joyful praise and worship.

I've already mentioned that the country is dominated by the Hindu and Buddhist religions, but I need to emphasize that much of the practices of these faiths actually involve demonic power. One morning we rose early and rode to a popular Hindu temple to watch the people bring their offerings to the idol. When we arrived, the line of devotees stretched outside the shrine, around the side, across a bridge, and back around again. My guide estimated that there were possibly seven thousand worshippers in line waiting to bring their live goats and chickens to slaughter before their pagan idols. In this land, demonic possession is commonplace. It was rare if any of our services would go by without the wonderful experience of seeing captives freed from tormenting spirits.

One such experience had to do with a woman who was essentially a nameless face in the crowd – and what a crowd it was. We had rented the civic auditorium, the largest meeting place in the whole district and it was filled beyond capacity with people sitting on the floor down the aisles and peering in through the doorways. But back to the nameless face – even without a name, her face itself spoke volumes. Tattoo markings covered almost every exposed inch of flesh and jewelry piercings left puncture marks in her nose as well as ears. Her skin was rough and wrinkled far beyond her natural years. These signs told the story of her life and status in the tribal culture of the Chitwan jungle district of Nepal. It was a sad story of hard labor, poverty, abuse and – worst of all – witchcraft. But the most dramatic part of the story was told by the eyes – not her eyes, but another set of eyes that lurked behind them and controlled this helpless woman's life. They were the eyes of a demon that had invaded this poor soul as she followed her traditional role of servitude to the Hindu gods and local animistic jungle spirits. Now seated in our gospel crusade, this tormented woman heard the message of hope for healing and deliverance, and she joined the mass of humans who thronged the stage seeking prayer. As soon as hands were laid upon her, she began to shake violently and to bounce up and down. The eyes behind her eyes tried to hide from the anointing by cementing her eyelids together. But, praise God, through effectual, fervent, persistent, and insistent prayer – the spirit left and her eyes were normal again. No, not normal – this time there was a ray of hope and a sparkle of joy that had not been there before!

"I can't come out. I can't come out." In perfect English intonation, without even a hint of a Nepali accent, these words tumbled out of the mouth of a young man who otherwise couldn't speak a word of English. The victim of this demonic manifestation had come for prayer, reporting that he had some sort of sickness. Before his interpreter could begin to explain what the young man's problem was, the evil spirit that controlled him began to cause his whole body to launch into convulsions. With arms thrashing, legs jerking violently, and head lashing from side to side, the poor subject of this demonic torment fell to the floor in the most vicious demonstration of fiendish control we had ever witnessed. As we commanded the demon to go out of the boy, his lips became the instruments of the spirit telling us that he could not come out. Rejoicing in the fact that the devil is a liar, we knew that this was nothing more than an announcement that he was ready to yield to our command. Within minutes, the boy was again on his feet and calmly speaking to us in his native Nepali language.

The devil not only torments his subjects spiritually, he also determines to destroy them physically. But we came to Nepal with a message of deliverance for the total man – body, soul, and spirit. In the same crusade where the woman was set free from the demonic powers that controlled her, we also prayed for a little paralyzed boy and his precious mother and believed until his limbs began to straighten and his joints began to bend. Many others received miracles in their backs, stomachs, ears, and eyes.

After the evangelistic meetings, we held a retreat for the local pastors at a mountain resort. Even though the location was only a two-hour bus ride from Kathmandu, most of the pastors had never been able to afford the luxury of visiting the place – and most of them had never been on a luxury bus that didn't also carry goats and chickens along with the passengers. Since we had rented the entire facility and there were no other guests for the workers to attend to, I told the hotel staff that they were free to sit in on the meetings when they were not actually serving us. After the retreat was over, my team and I stayed over for an additional night to rest before heading on to our next activity. With no new guests arriving that evening, I asked the hotel employees to gather for a short meeting so we could share with them. After asking how they felt about all that they had seen and heard over the past couple days, I gave them an opportunity to pray with the team members if they wanted to receive Christ. The result was that each member of staff of the hotel prayed the sinner's prayer and received a Nepali Bible to study.

I was privileged to take my entire family with me to Nepal. It was a real answer to prayer for us to be able to take all the boys and allow them to understand what it means to see a land held in the clutches of paganism and to see the delivering power of the gospel as it wrenches the souls free from the bondage of the devil. That year, we invited the wives of all the leading pastors to join us at the National Pastors' Conference that we sponsored. This was a real "first," since women in Nepal are regularly left out of all such activities. At the pastors' conference, we heard pastors quoting some of the teachings we had given them the previous year – proof that the seeds we planted had taken root! We also received what is possibly the greatest compliment that can be given when the delegates asked for another teaching session in the late evening after all the scheduled activities of the day had been completed!!

The eagerness of the people to receive Christian literature never ceased to amaze us. At one hotel, the manager asked for a supply of the literature to distribute to his guests. During a rain shower, we took refuge under the front awning of a store, but continued to distribute tracts to the others who had joined us in this little dry enclave. When the owner of the store noticed us outside, he came and asked us for enough tracts to hand out to the people huddled inside his little shop. Our total time was so booked up with ministry at conferences, churches, Bible schools, and literature distribution that it was almost impossible to find time to take the team to see some of the tourist sights of Nepal. However, we did slip in a half-day jungle visit where we rode elephant-back to see the rhinos in their natural habitat. Also, the Lord was very gracious in allowing the weather pattern to change on the last day of our visit so that the air pollution and clouds were blown out of the Kathmandu Valley, revealing an awe-inspiring view of the snow-capped Himalayas. One highlight that will live forever in the hearts of our team members was our visit to the strongholds of the Hinduism and Buddhism in Nepal.

After once seeing the captivity of the souls bowing to, praying to, and sacrificing to the demonic idols of paganism, we knew that no Christian should ever take lightly the command to see that the light of the gospel of Jesus Christ is spread to all who live in darkness. An even more indelible mark was made the afternoon we spent with some of the persecuted saints of Nepal. One elderly gentleman shared the story of his spiritual quest some fifty years ago when there were no Christians at all in the country. Knowing that there was a spiritual reality he had not found, he searched even beyond the borders of his homeland until he found some people in India who offered him an open door to a new faith – Christianity. Returning to his native land, he was confronted with a stern resistance to his newfound faith. Over the next forty years, he suffered interrogations, beatings, and imprisonment for sharing this "alien" religion and gathering a few followers. Even at the age of seventy-four, he was jailed and mercilessly beaten, resulting in permanent damage to his head and back. It was only the miraculous move of the hand of God through the 1990 declaration of religious tolerance that freed him to practice his faith and build his church.

Because emotions run very high during elections in developing nations, there is always a concern that violence may erupt. In Nepal, the government takes precaution by banning all motor vehicles, other than emergency vehicles with Red Cross flags, from being on the roads. They feel that if the people are restricted from any movement other than walking to the polling place, hostilities can be held at bay. Thus, this national election shut down the whole nation – except the Mission to the Rooftop of the World! We had managed to gain the use of an ambulance from a Christian hospital so we were the only ones on the road, able to travel to three different Bible colleges and training centers to teach the students whose regular teachers weren't even able to get to the classes! We left Nepal the day after the election for a three-day training conference for pastors from the Himalayan region of India. Well, let us say that we <u>tried</u> to leave Nepal; we were detained at the border because one of our jeeps had been involved in a hit-and-run accident with a sacred Hindu cow just before picking us up. The car and driver were held by police for a lengthy interrogation. When we were finally allowed to leave, we were so far behind schedule that, even after the all-day trip in the sweltering heat and dusty conditions, I had to rush right into the pulpit without taking a shower or even changing clothes. The pastors were so eager for the Word that they had waited for almost an hour for us to arrive.

Our millennium year trip in 2000 was actually two missions in one. Peggy and I split up as I led a group directly into Nepal to participate in a nationwide conference and Easter celebration and a special service commemorating ten years of religious freedom in the Kingdom of Nepal while Peggy led a group that visited the nation of Myanmar to host a national Christian women's conference and Easter celebration before joining the rest of the team in Nepal. Again this time, we invaded the Himalayan region of India as well as Nepal. In addition, we ministered in a Bhutanese refugee camp in Nepal.   On previous missions, I had conducted national leadership training conferences in the capital city of Kathmandu and regional conferences in many of the districts of the country. However, this was the first time we were able to hold a conference on a scale massive enough to encompass every district of the nation. The conference brought in seven hundred delegates from all over Nepal and other Himalayan regions that were still closed to the gospel. Another highlight of that year's mission was the dedication of a piece of ground which the Lord had helped us buy for the construction of a Bible college in the city of Pokhara (To date, that school has trained over one thousand pastors and Christian workers from Nepal and neighboring Nepali-speaking regions.) where the next generation of national leaders can be trained – a dramatic leap forward for both our ministry and the work of God in the nation. The property already had a building, which we were able to renovate for the college use. We were also able to help purchase a vehicle for the director of the ministry – an all-terrain vehicle to be used to take the gospel from one end of Nepal to the other, across the streams, over the mountains, and through the jungles!

Although the kingdom of God was advancing greatly in Nepal there was also an escalation of political turmoil in the Kingdom of Nepal. During the entire time we had been ministering in the Himalayan kingdom, we had seen the ebb and flow of the various forces that tried to dominate Nepal's delicate political landscape. Over a period of almost a quarter century, the Maoists had continued to flex their muscles through violence and threats. These hostilities, added to the already constant instability between Nepal's monarchy and the democratic parties, had greatly intensified Nepal's already sensitive balance of power. One year, I had to be escorted between the airport and the hotel by six armed military patrols. We had to cancel some of our conferences due to the Maoist-mandated strike that kept everyone off the public roads and away from any form of mass assembly. On another occasion, we had just left the country when the entire royal family was massacred – except for one survivor, who was immediately seated as king. The new king then ousted the democratically-elected government and took full authority within the country with the aim of crushing the Maoist insurgence, in which over thirteen thousand people had died. Of course, there were retaliations from the Maoists as well as the general populace. The conditions became so touchy that the

216

United States and most European countries recalled their diplomats from the country.

The following year Nepal suffered severe conflict, political deadlock, and the loss of hundreds of lives. Many felt that it was one of the worst years in the country's history. One of our good friends in Nepal summed up the situation, "Killing of men and women has become like killings of birds and animals. Only prayer can change the situation in our country." In addition to the tragic loss of lives, there was direct suffering and oppression of the people due to the violence. The nation also suffered economically from the many strikes and curfews which caused extensive disruptions of transportation, communications, and business. There was a major downturn in tourism, one of the country's main sources of income. The upheaval in the country also prompted cutbacks in international aid – which was financing about a quarter of Nepal's budget – leaving the country on the brink of a humanitarian crisis. A negotiated ceasefire between the government and the Maoists failed after four months, with the Maoists claiming that the king had failed to keep his side. In the election that was to reestablish the democratic government, two hundred candidates dropped off the ballots after threats from the Maoists.

Out of the political turmoil came religious persecution as well. The democratic government that ensured religious freedom was no longer in power. Thus, in many areas of Nepal, choosing to follow Christ would again lead to ostracism, rejection, or even death. After confessing Jesus as Lord, the new believers were expelled from their Hindu families, cut off from support, and considered unclean. In fact, when a believer visited the house of a strict Hindu, the home would be ritually purified after he or she left. In villages, Christians were often forbidden from using public wells and were forced to walk miles to find other water sources. The physical

217

and psychological toll this rejection took on new believers was great, and many Nepalese – seeing this harsh treatment of Christians – were afraid to follow Christ even if they were convinced He was the truth.

Our contacts inside the country and our friends in the deposed government all advised us that the situation was very unstable and that it was uncertain as to whether we would be able to hold any public meetings when we came back into the country. Therefore, we decided to replace our 2005 visit to Nepal with a mission to the tsunami-affected areas of India and Sri Lanka. We had no concern or fear that any harm would have come to us when we were inside the country. Our concern was one of stewardship of mission funds and time. We did not want to spend the Lord's money and our time only to be quarantined in our hotel due to travel restrictions. In fact, even before we received the news of the developments in Nepal, we had already been praying about the possibility of rearranging the schedule to allow us time to stop in India and Sri Lanka to visit some of the ministries we were supporting in their tsunami relief efforts. As soon as we had received the news of the tragedy, we contacted ministries we had worked with in Myanmar, India, and Sri Lanka to ensure that they were safe. We immediately sent funds to help in their efforts in responding to the disaster. We were also blessed to be able to pay the shipping for a full container of food to be shipped to the tsunami victims in Indonesia. When I walked into the office of the director of Feed the Hungry to ask him how much it would cost to ship a container of food, he was awestruck. He had just received the donation of a full container of beans and had just gotten off the phone with the shipping company, establishing the transportation charges. When I walked in he had been at his desk asking the Lord where the funds would come from to pay the freight! A few days later, I was able to see the container loaded and the precious life-giving cargo sent on its way.

Peggy and I also had the privilege of actually going to Sri Lanka and India to do relief work after the tsunami. What we found there was too overwhelming to describe. We have all had some experience with floods, but my understanding of flooding was limited to a flooded basement resulting from a broken pipe or news coverage of natural disasters in faraway places. However, we saw a totally different picture as we drove for hours, covering hundreds of miles. There was no relief from the devastation. No matter how far we drove there was seemingly endless destruction and rubble. Heaps of debris and splintered remains marked what had once been the homes of people whose lives had come to tragic ends in a split second. We were on the battlefield of nature versus mankind, and from all we could see the brutality of nature had triumphed. Even though the help we were able to provide was essentially only a "drop in the bucket," we were blessed to be able to be the Lord's heart and hands in the lives of the few people we were able to bless.

By the following year, stability had been restored in Nepal, and we were right back in the country for a large pastors' conference at the new Bible college in Pokhara. We launched our visit by hosting a banquet for the local pastors. In addition to a great meal, they received a challenging message from I Thessalonians concerning the five foundations of a successful ministry (the Word, the power of God, being led by the Holy Spirit, assurance, and a godly lifestyle). For the next two days, the campus became a conference center. The auditorium and two overflow tents were packed to capacity with approximately seven hundred pastors and leaders from the surrounding region. We hired buses to make rounds throughout Pokhara and the neighboring cities to bring the delegates to the meetings. Following seven different routes, the buses picked up the delegates from congregations within a two-hour drive of the campus. Some of the buses were so packed that delegates scrambled to the roof of the vehicles to ride in typical Nepali style. A special highlight of our visit was seeing the new building that we had helped erect on the campus. We were also delighted to see that many general improvements had been made to the campus grounds and the facilities. We were also able to present the school with a gift from a church in South Carolina: a tape duplicator. They put the duplicator to immediate use by offering pastors the tapes from the conference.

We ministered to the Bible students on the day before the conference began and each evening after the delegates boarded the buses for home. The concluding days of this mission were spent in Kathmandu where we ministered in six different churches. In one church we needed three services to accommodate the growing congregation. A highlight of our visit was a banquet with about a hundred and thirty-five of the nation's top Christian leaders. Not only were we able to input into their lives, the local ministries could network together and build relationships. We also held a two-day leadership conference with leaders from ministries that reached throughout the whole nation and surrounding Himalayan region. Peggy was the featured speaker at a full-day Women's Aglow seminar in Pokhara and another two-day Aglow conference in Kathmandu. Not wanting to waste a moment of our time in Nepal, we even stopped at a local Bible college and spoke in their chapel service while we were on our way to the airport to head home.

The theme of the pastors' seminars was based on the letters in Revelation chapters two and three to the seven churches. We especially emphasized the pure heart which the Lord searched for in the churches and the open door He had especially set before the Philadelphian church. We encouraged the pastors that they, too, have an open door set before them – a door that is getting wider and wider each day. We drew examples from the initiation of the new Tibetan church and the news of the recently opened door to Bhutan, as the king had decided to yield the throne to his son who pledged to establish a democratic government within the next couple years. Another open door came from the Nepali government recently giving the Nepal Prison Fellowship permission to build a chapel inside the federal prison. Top leaders within Nepal asked that the conference messages be transcribed and released as a book in Nepali. Because of the scarcity of biblical teaching materials in Nepali, the available materials are treasured and shared widely among the leaders.

In celebration of ten years of ministry in Nepal, we did a national tour to – as Paul and Barnabas described the purpose of their second mission trip – "go again and visit our brethren in every city where we have preached the word of the Lord, and see how they do." (Acts 15:36) Counting the day we landed and the day we flew out – we were on the ground twenty days, yet I personally taught thirty-one sessions. My traveling companion ministered in one session each day to give me a couple hours break before the evening rallies. Including his ministry, we had a total of forty-two preaching and teaching sessions. It was a tiring schedule but the people's hunger for the Word of God made our fatigue and exhaustion pale in comparison. In addition to our itinerary, Peggy held an additional eighteen women's meetings – bringing the total number for our team to sixty meetings. That was an exhausting schedule; we traveled to nine different cities in three countries during those twenty days!

I have seen some remarkable changes over the years that I have been visiting the country. In fact, I had a front-row seat when the government entered negotiations with the Maoist leaders to end their hostilities and grant them recognition as an approved political party, able to hold elected political office. The negotiations were held in the same hotel where I was staying – just two doors from my room. I have always felt that this was God's way of showing me that He was honoring my faithfulness in the country. I have seen environmental issues addressed with the removal of the heavily-polluting auto-rickshaws, which were once the mainstay of transportation in Kathmandu. I have observed the economic advancement of the people from year to year, evidenced in the changes in the way they are able to dress. We have watched a younger, more educated generation move into leadership, obvious from the greater percentage of folks who can communicate in English and the fact that almost everyone takes notes in the teaching sessions – something that was unheard of when we first began our missions in their country. We have seen the church prosper and flourish with large, beautiful, new buildings – most of them with sound systems and other modern equipment. I also witnessed official recognition of Christmas as a legal holiday in this nation.

May 2008 marked the twenty-fifth anniversary of Every Home Concern – the local name for Every Home for Christ in the nation of Nepal. Because of the close relationship between Teach All Nations and EHC, I had a real desire to be able to participate in the celebration. However, since I had just been in Nepal in November of 2007 to take part in the fiftieth anniversary celebration of the presence of Christianity in Nepal and because Peggy was to be in the country for a large women's conference in September of the same year, I had not planned on going to Nepal at all in 2008. But as we all know, the Lord promises to give us more than we can think or ask (Ephesians 3:20), and He did exactly that! I wound up going to Nepal twice that year because of my work with the international office of Every Home for Christ – once to attend a conference for the South Asia leaders (India, Sri Lanka, Nepal, Sri Lanka, Pakistan, and Bangladesh) in March, and then for a follow-up meeting that was scheduled to coincide with the silver anniversary celebration in Kathmandu. By this time, I had already received a number of emails from Solon, asking me to be there for the anniversary. Each time I had responded that I didn't think that it would be possible. Finally, Solon replied that he was believing for a miracle. I, of course, acknowledged that it would take a miracle for me to be able to come again. Well, only two days later I received the invitation from EHC to join them for the follow-up conference and the Silver Anniversary Celebration!

On my twentieth visit to Nepal, I learned that some delegates from the remote areas of the country had traveled for as many as four days — three days of walking and then another day of bus travel — to be present. It was a very humbling experience to stand before such dedicated believers who had given so much in order to be trained and equipped. Upon arrival at the church, I was given a program for the conference with the explanation that the other scheduled speaker had been selected as a delegate to the Lausanne World Evangelism Conference in South Africa, so I was to have the privilege of speaking in all the sessions for the full three days of the program. What a blessing it was when the coordinator of the conference came to me and shared that his twelve-year-old son had been able to explain to him all the major points of the teaching. He was certain that if this young man had understood the message it must have been clear and relevant. The elders from the church summed up the conference in an appreciation email saying, "We all have received a new direction to develop our spiritual life. It was truly a revival conference."

Once the Kathmandu conference came to a close, I was off to the city of Pokhara to minister at the Bible college and in a one-day conference for the local pastors and leaders. Many of the approximately one hundred sixty delegates shared with me how the word that I had ministered was exactly what they had needed at exactly this time in their ministries. I concluded the meeting with a challenge for them to recognize the strategic significance of the Bible college for the Body of Christ in Nepal and to begin to aggressively support it.

One of the blessings of our time in the country was the opportunity to reconnect with many of the friends we have made over the years. Since Peggy had been in Nepal that spring and her new book had been released in the Nepali language, many women would come up to me with messages to bring back to her about how much they had been blessed through reading her book. I was also greatly moved by the number of men who came up to tell me about how they had been trained in previous leadership conferences and were now pastors or leaders within other ministries. One pastor told me that he was at a retreat that we had sponsored for the Kathmandu Valley pastors in the early 1990s. He stated that that opportunity for the pastors from the various ministries to get together for fellowship and direction had been a breakthrough that brought unity among the pastors and revival to the churches.

Over the years of ministry in Nepal, I've traveled to almost every corner of the nation, including one exciting trip to Mustang on the Tibetan border. After waking up in my hotel room in Bangkok, Thailand, at what would be 2:30 AM in Kathmandu, Nepal, I headed to the airport for the first flight out to New Delhi, India, and onward to Nepal. Although I had scheduled the earliest possible flight out of Bangkok and the quickest connection in Delhi, I still arrived in Kathmandu too late to catch the last plane of the day to Pokhara. I did not have the convenience of being able to wait the night in Kathmandu and fly out the next morning because Pokhara was only a transit point on my way to the city of Jamsom in the Mustang district of Nepal on the Tibetan border. The flights to Jamsom must always be scheduled in the early morning hours while the air is still calm in the pass that the planes traverse between the mountains. Even getting the earliest plane out of Kathmandu the next morning, I would not be able to make it to Pokhara in time to catch a flight that day, thus delaying me a second night.

Therefore, I jumped immediately into a friend's jeep and settled in for a seven-hour drive across the mountains. We had to make two separate stops for dinner on the journey because Nepali culture, in a holdover from the caste system, prevented our driver from eating with us. In spite of my insistence that he join us for dinner, he waited in the car while we had our meal. Then we waited for him to eat at another roadside teashop further down the road. Even when I was able to get him to eat in the same restaurant with us later in the trip, he still insisted upon sitting at a different table. When we arrived at our destination for the evening, Ravi and I commented that the totally clear sky was a good sign that we wouldn't have any weather delays the next morning. With that assurance, I crawled into bed for the four hours of sleep I would enjoy before my cold shower and the drive to the airport for the first flight to Jamsom. We had purposely scheduled the earliest flight so that we would have priority in case there were weather delays and some flights had to be canceled. Unfortunately, when I walked out the front door of the hotel, I discovered that there had been a total change in the weather. Instead of the clear sky from the night before, it was pouring rain. Hopeful that the weather might clear, we checked in for the flight and waited, and waited, and waited – five hours, to be exact. Even though the skies did eventually clear up in Pokhara, the weather pattern simply shifted to the mountain pass, blocking our way to Jamsom. Now, our only options were to wait the day in

Pokhara in hopes that the planes would be able to fly the next day or to drive to Mustang. Since we had a two-day conference scheduled in Jamsom and were going to miss one day of it already because of the canceled flight, we knew that we couldn't afford to gamble on another delay the following day. Therefore, we chose Plan B – the drive. Our choice was based not only on our own logic but also on the fact that I had bumped into an old friend while we were waiting in the airport. She told me that she had been scheduled to fly to Jamsom to speak at a three-day seminar and that she had been stranded in Pokhara for the entire time, hoping each morning to be able to catch a flight. The road trip for the day was to take us through two restricted areas for which I had to have special travel permits and the vehicles had to be registered in order to travel the road. The result was that we wound up using three different vehicles in order to make the journey – the one in which we had left from Kathmandu, one to get us through the first restricted area, and another one to transit the second restricted area. Our nine-hour drive took us through the second-deepest valley in the world on roads – some of which pretended to be paved – requiring an off-road vehicle. We stopped at a little roadside hotel for dinner, a short night's sleep, and another cold shower. When I walked out of the hotel the next morning, I discovered that I was surrounded by a breathtaking panorama of the beautiful Himalayan Mountains. But there was little time to take in the sight since we still had another two-hour journey ahead of us.

When we finally arrived at the church in Jamsom, I discovered that it was on a hill overlooking the airport, essentially within walking distance of the terminal – and that the runway was busy with planes taking off and taxiing in from their flights to Pokhara. Had we waited, we could have arrived by plane at the same time we did by car. But we knew that the gamble would not have been worth the risk. Now we had to make a decision about gambling on the flight back the next morning.

Even though we knew that we could have won the bet on the trip to Jamsom, we now had to determine if we wanted to take the risk on a return flight. After some careful calculations, we opted to redo the torturous journey. That meant that we'd have to leave immediately after teaching all day in the conference, drive as far as possible that evening, stop for a short night's sleep and another cold shower, and press our way over the rugged terrain in order to make the early afternoon flight to Kathmandu where we would be picked up for the five-hour mountain drive to the next conference in the eastern mountains of Nepal near Mount Everest. In addition to all the factors we figured into the calculation, we had even more unknowns such as a broken suspension rod on our vehicle in the Mustang plateau and an overheated radiator in our jeep on the road to the Mount Everest region – all this on a road where the service station consisted of a teenage girl sitting on the side of the road with a five-gallon jug of gasoline and a funnel. When we arrived in Pokhara we discovered that we had made the right choice. All fights from Jamsom that day had been grounded. In case you're wondering why I'm talking so much about the travel and saying nothing about the ministry. "Were all those transportation troubles worth it?" The answer is, "Definitely, absolutely, positively, unquestionably, and unequivocally yes!"

Even though we missed a full day of teaching at the conference in Jamsom and I only had from 9 AM until 3 PM for teaching on the day that I did have with the delegates, the training was pivotal for these fairly new believers in this area where the gospel was just beginning to get a foothold. The theme of the conference was on becoming disciple makers. This has always been the most effective way to penetrate an area with the Good News. As each believer develops a vital relationship with Jesus and purposefully shares that living faith with other individuals so that they can also pass this new abundant life to others, the Body of Christ grows exponentially and essentially effortlessly. The principle is from II Timothy 2:2, "And the things that thou hast heard of me among many witnesses, the same commit thou to faithful men, who shall be able to teach others also."

The delegates from Jamsom and also the surrounding towns and villages listened intently as I taught, eagerly interacted during the question-and-answer session, and gladly received the Nepali versions of my books. They were enthusiastic about taking the message to heart and putting it into practice.

Straight from one end of the country, we headed to the opposite end where our east Nepal conference drew the pastors and leaders from eleven churches in three districts in the region. These handpicked delegates were the men and women from their area who had shown determination to take positions of influence and become agents of change. As I looked around the room during the praise and worship before the opening session of the conference and observed the intensity in each delegate's eyes, the Lord spoke the words of the Apostle Paul into my heart, "I will very gladly spend and be spent for you." (II Corinthians 12:15) Almost all the delegates were energetic, well-educated young professionals, bubbling over with zeal for the Lord. Recognizing their potential, I immediately knew that the huge financial investment that we had made in this mission and the days of grueling travel that I had endured to get to them were well worth it. The first day I taught from my book *Interface*, encouraging and challenging them to step into places of authority and decisive change in their society.

It was only that evening that I learned that this particular area of the nation is quickly developing as one of the most strategic centers of economic power in Nepal and is anticipated to become the center of the nation's wealth. When that significance is realized, there will be a core group of leaders with a biblical worldview and scriptural ethic guiding the region's newfound power. The second day was dedicated to training the delegates on discipleship techniques and Bible-study methods, providing them with tools to truly impact their world with the gospel of Jesus Christ. Before leaving the country, I preached in the main church in Kathmandu where many church members came to me after the service to express their appreciation for the encouragement and challenge of the message. One particular young man, a medical doctor, said that he had come to the service crying out for the answer to issues that had been challenging and perplexing him all week. He pulled out the notes he had been taking during the sermon and pointed to one specific line, proclaiming, "I got my answer!"

I had known for years that it wasn't a matter of "if" but "when" Kathmandu and the surrounding cities and villages were to be met with a significant earthquake since Nepal ranks eleventh among the list of most quake-prone countries. In fact, I had even written about this impending doom as I'd encouraged the believers to take seriously the mandate to share the gospel with as many of their fellow Nepali as possible. You can certainly imagine how heartbroken I was when on April 25, 2015, I received word, while I was in the South American country of Colombia, that a 7.8 magnitude earthquake had shattered the nation. Ironically, I was in the middle of writing emails to my coworkers in Nepal concerning my upcoming visit when the Internet notification of the earthquake came through. Immediately, my email inbox was flooded with messages from all over the world, asking if we were in Nepal and if we were safe. One particular message really touched me deeply, "I know that both you and Peggy are in a very stressful situation, torn between your responsibilities in Columbia and wishing to be right there in Nepal doing whatever you can. Think about how so many hundreds, maybe thousands, who have come to know Christ due to your obedience in daily prayer for Nepal starting way back in the 80s."

In the earliest reports, the estimation of the causality count was just over one hundred, but each news broadcast brought more and more detail and the death toll continued to rise. As the extent of the tragedy began to unfold, I realized how God's hand had orchestrated my upcoming visit. Due to other pressing items in my schedule, I had cut the one-week visit back to two days – just long enough to be there for the board meeting of the Bible college and then head on to other assignments in India. When it became apparent that the whole nation was in chaos because of the earthquake, I knew that it would have been impossible for me to have proceeded with the scheduled teaching conferences. Knowing how the buildings were constructed with stone or brick, without proper earthquake resistance, I could only imagine how devastating the massive quake must have been. However, my imagination still fell far short of the magnitude of the reality. My short visit would allow me to assess how Teach All Nations could best assist with the disaster relief effort.

Jeremy (my youngest son) and I had the opportunity to survey the devastation in both Kathmandu and some outlying villages and to meet with a couple pastors whose churches had been destroyed. As I traveled around the country, I discovered a very simple brickmaking process that was perfect for the reconstruction effort since the old bricks from the fallen structures could be ground up and mixed with cement to make much stronger bricks that are formed in a way to allow reinforcing rods to pass through the bricks so that the structures built with them could be earthquake resistant. The technique was a hand-operated procedure so it could be operated by the same people whose houses are being rebuilt. I also met with one of the young men who received scholarship funding for his college education from Teach All Nations and was surprised to learn that he is associated with a company that is producing prefab homes in Nepal – another excellent option for the rebuilding project.

Through the generous support of the partners of our ministry, we were able to complete eight different projects – three church buildings and five homes for the pastors. We had to either purchase land or make long-term leases for property for some of the projects since most of the churches and homes that we rebuilt had actually been in rented facilities before the earthquake. Now, they have permanent facilities. Since most churches in Nepal are simple one-room sanctuaries, our projects included some "extras" that might be considered commonplace in the American church but are actually innovative additions there. For example, we built in two toilets and a shower at one church and in another church we constructed three extra rooms that are being used for classes and children's ministry. We also put up greenhouses so the people could grow their own food to help them recover from the loss of livelihood due to the devastation. My plans were to revisit the country in April of 2016 to dedicate the new buildings on the anniversary of the loss. Unfortunately, I experienced "the bust" just before the departure date. However, an associate – who had traveled with me to Nepal and was familiar with the country and people there – was able to take my place and minister at all the meetings and dedication services.

Into All the World

Jon Krakauer wrote two really exciting true-life adventure stories and gave them both titles highlighting the word "into": *Into Thin Air*, the account of his 1996 deadly expedition on Mt. Everest, and *Into the Wild*, the reconstruction of Christopher McCandless's travels across North America, his experiences, and his eventual death in the Alaskan wilderness. Inspired by these two great adventure sagas and because the true-life adventures that I share in this chapter are the result of my being sent into all the world, I want to introduce this next section of my life with the word, "Into"; therefore, the title "Into All the World." Even though you can see from the previous chapter that I have spent much of my time overseas in Nepal, I actually got my start in mission work first in Japan, then India and Sri Lanka.

Because of the burning desire in my heart to help develop solid leadership for the churches in nations of the world where it was difficult to obtain a good Christian education, I began to work tirelessly recruiting students from third-world countries to attend the Bible college in America where I taught and also served as dean. Soon, the school blossomed into an international campus with foreign students outnumbering the Americans. Unfortunately, there was a serious downside – many of these young African and Asian ministers became accustomed to living in American houses, driving American cars, and eating American food. Some even married American wives. And they weren't willing to give up these "luxuries" to go back home and minister in their own nations. As I faced disappointment after disappointment, I realized that the only solution was to train these developing leaders in their home environments, avoiding the American distractions and allurements that so easily deterred, detained, detoured, and derailed them.

It was then that I understood the significance of the first word in the Great Commission — "Go." If I was to accomplish what God had on His heart and had placed into my heart, it was wrong to expect the students to come to me. I realized that the dreams, visions, and prophecies of ministering to the nations meant more than simply training a few students from each nation and expecting them to go back to their homes and impact their countries with what they learned in Bible school. Those visions, dreams, and prophetic words had to be taken literally; that I was to go personally and bring the gospel to them. With that revelation, I began to organize my life for the transition. Knowing that I would have to leave my full-time position at the Bible college, I began to get my finances and family arrangements in line for the "move" — one that I assumed would be a logical transition to the *Jungle Book* mission field of Nepal.

You may remember my fascination with the geography and cultures of the whole world, suggesting that God had a bigger mission in mind for me than just the one nation of Nepal. However, since we had built a Bible school in Nepal to train the upcoming leadership, it seemed only natural that my next step in fulfilling the destiny to which God had called me would be to move to Nepal to oversee the school. With so many years' experience in teaching in and directing a Bible school, it seemed like a natural next step both for me and for the college in Nepal. However, God is not interested in natural next steps; He is always working in the supernatural rather than the natural and He often makes quantum leaps rather than next steps. Every time I would pray about making my move, the Lord would direct me to read Matthew 28:19, "Go ye therefore, and teach all nations..." I would respond, "Yes, Lord I'm ready to go to Nepal and teach. You just show me when." He would then respond, "You haven't read Matthew 28:19." I would argue back that I had read it and that I was ready to go to Nepal as soon as He would release me to go. Again, the Lord would challenge me that I hadn't read the passage, and, again, I would argue. Finally, one day I saw it — the passage said "all nations," not "Nepal." At that point, I remembered the one common thread that ran through all the dreams, visions, and prophecies I had received over the years – I had to go to the nations all around the globe! I've already shared the story of the man from Wrightsville Beach who lifted me off the floor and whirled me around in the air, telling me that God was going to send me around the world. I've also told you about the television engineer who prophesied to me about making the decision to enroll in seminary. However, I haven't shared the rest of that story; he gave essentially the same prophecy as the man at Wrightsville Beach. And then there were two dream-visions that I had received during my college days. In one dream, I saw the words "John 1:23" as if they were written in neon lights. When I got up and found the scripture, I discovered that it spoke of being a voice crying in the wilderness. Even though that experience came years before my involvement with the country of Nepal, I felt comfortable applying it to the Himalayan nation since much of that primitive region is genuine wilderness. However, I did have to be honest enough to recognize that "wilderness" would certainly apply to almost anywhere I found myself around the world. In the other dream, I saw myself preaching to a large crowd of brown faces – making me think of regions of the world like Nepal where the people are dark complexioned. But as the dream continued, the faces miraculously turned from brown to black – suggesting Africa. Then the faces took on an Oriental appearance. At any rate, I was certain that the Lord's plan was much more far-reaching than I could ever accomplish in a Bible school in Nepal. I knew that the vision was becoming a reality on the day that the US passport control officer was looking through the visa

234

pages in my passport to find a spot to stamp my reentry imprint and looked up at me to ask, "Are you trying to visit every nation in the world?"

It was in the early 1990s that God began to really speak the word "Africa" into my heart. It came repeatedly into my spirit with no further explanation – just the word "Africa." At that time, the closest I had ever been to Africa was Busch Garden's Dark Continent theme park in Tampa, Florida. As I kept encountering this single word over and over with no explanation as to what it could possibly mean to me, I began to have more and more interaction with Africans. In fact, at one point there were more Africans than American students. Within just a few months a new area of international ministry developed through Indiana Christian University, and I was sent on three trips abroad – one in Nigeria, one in England, and one in Canada. My first mission was to Nigeria to speak in the matriculation service of a Bible college that was affiliating with Indiana Christian University. The miracle of God was that the very day we arrived, the Nigerian Department of Education shut down almost forty Bible colleges because they were not properly aligned with recognized educational institutions – but they didn't touch the school where we were ministering because we had all the proper documents.

Not long after I returned from my first trip to Kenya, Sister Bobbie Jean Merck, a woman who is greatly used in the ministry of the prophet, spoke a word to me that the Holy Spirit had shown her. She said that the thing that had been in my heart for several years was ready to dawn; that its full day had finally come. She said that the desire I had to minister in the nations of the world was to become a reality. In fact, she continued to say that there were at least fifteen nations waiting for me in which to publish the good news and that when the invitations started to come in, I would have to organize the schedule in order to go to all the places that would be begging me to come. A month later, Elf Eckman from Sweden grabbed hold of me and said that he felt the Lord saying that it was now time for my faithfulness in the kingdom to be rewarded and that what God had in store for me was going to be even bigger than I had ever imagined.

These messages were indeed prophetic. Before long, Peggy and I headed out to Africa to answer some of those calls to nations begging for the gospel. It was true; I really had to organize my schedule to fit in all the places we needed to visit! We were originally scheduled to minister in Kenya and Zimbabwe. Then the itinerary expanded to include Rwanda, in answer to a desperate call begging me to speak at a conference in their capital city. When we first started making plans to go, Peggy and I were faced with some serious scheduling problems. There were no tickets available for the dates we needed to travel, and the only ones which could be confirmed would make us stay almost a week longer than we could possibly arrange to be away. It looked like a great time to let the Lord prove that it was really His desire for us to go, so we "set out a fleece" that the arrangements would work out if it was really God's will. The next morning, we received a call from the travel agent saying that tickets were available on the exact dates we wanted to fly. The next hurdle was, of course, money to pay for the trip. As we have always experienced, the Lord proved again that if it is His will, it will also be His bill. Just one example of how He provided came on the day that I had to pay the travel agent for my ticket. One dear little eighty-something-year-old lady called me and said that she wanted to bring me some money rather than mailing it. She arrived with just the exact amount that I needed to give to the booking agent.

One of the African countries where I minister regularly is Nigeria – often with my good friend, Dr. Tunde Bakare, at one of the nation's leading churches,

Latter Rain Assembly. I often find that the Lord perfectly orchestrates my visit and ministry there. For example, months prior to one of my trips, I had prayed about the messages I was to bring for the conference and had felt directed to prepare a series of teachings on the letters to the seven churches in Revelation with an emphasis on the closing statement in each of the letters, "He that hath an ear, let him hear what the Spirit sayeth to the churches." Due to a flight cancelation from Niger, where I had been ministering before going to Nigeria, I arrived at the conference two days late. When I asked what Dr. Bakare had been teaching during the two days I had missed, the response was that he had given three lessons on hearing the voice of God – the exact focus of the messages that I had in my heart! How thrilling it was to know that even though we had not collaborated on what we were going to teach, we were bringing the same word – confirming that the Lord had a definite message He wanted communicated to the Christian leadership in Nigeria.

Among those who shared that the ministry had impacted their lives was one couple who testified that their daughter had been run over by an automobile just days after one of my previous visits. Both the mom and dad confirmed that the lessons they had learned in the meetings had been their sustaining force during the ordeal. On another occasion, Pastor Bakare stepped into the pulpit for the morning service and began by reading a text message from one of the men in the congregation. The text was a request for an appointment to discuss some issues and questions the parishioner had. The pastor then went on to say that he hadn't answered the message; he was so busy that he hadn't found a slot in his calendar to accommodate the appointment. Dr. Bakare then went on to read a follow-up text that had come from the same gentleman just minutes before the service had begun, "Don't worry about trying to arrange an appointment time for me. Dr. Shirley's lesson in the Bible class this morning answered all my questions!"

The next scene was in Rwanda, a nation that had recently experienced a horrible genocide in which almost a million souls were brutally taken in ethnic violence. The people were not only emotionally careworn but spiritually thirsty. We had just given the invitation at the end of one of the meetings, "No, no...I don't think that they understood. Maybe the interpretation wasn't clear. We weren't asking everyone to stand – just the ones who are responding to the altar invitation. Please ask the rest of the people to return to their seats so we can pray with the specific ones who need ministry." But even after the translator emphasized that we were not asking everyone to stand, no one was seated. Essentially everyone in the whole room was responding to the message that the Lord gave me to deliver from II Corinthians chapter six where Paul listed what one translation calls "a godly man's arsenal." Different from what we usually think of when discussing spiritual warfare, this list includes such weapons as purity, long-suffering, kindness, and sincere love – qualities that bring victory through healing and restoration. The people's response was overwhelming, and the pastor confided that it was one of the most enlightening teachings he had ever received.

The nation was still in the process of trying to heal the emotional wounds and scars of the great genocide. As we had been sitting, waiting to be called to the podium to address the capacity assembly in the massive sanctuary, the Lord quickened a scripture to my heart – a passage which promised a time when we would no longer remember the things of the past. I mentioned it to the pastor. It was a verse that the pastor knew must be somewhere among the prophetic writings, but he had no idea where. When he opened his Bible, the first passage his eyes fell upon was Isaiah 43:18-21:

238

Remember ye not the former things, neither consider the things of old. Behold, I will do a new thing; now it shall spring forth; shall ye not know it? I will even make a way in the wilderness, and rivers in the desert...I give waters in the wilderness, and rivers in the desert, to give drink to my people, my chosen. This people have I formed for myself; they shall shew forth my praise.

His miraculously turning to the passage was a confirmation that God wanted to speak a message of hope and restoration to the wounded spirits of the nation! A thunderous roar of praise erupted from the people as he read the passage to them. Again, God had reconfirmed the theme of the conference: Africa was ready to arise from her ashes and shine with the glory of God!

Our next teaching was to the pastors and leaders who had gathered from at least six nations (Rwanda, Burundi, Congo, Tanzania, Kenya, and Uganda) for the training at the conference. In the opening session with these men and women of God, I felt directed to encourage and refresh them rather than to start off directly with training and teaching. As I concluded the session, I invited those ministers battling discouragement to come for prayer. Again, almost the entire assembly began to press their way forward. Again, I asked the interpreter to reiterate that this was not a general call for prayer but a specific invitation for those who were especially discouraged in their work for the Lord. Again, no one returned to his seat. Again, I knew that I was on target with the message for Africa. A following message drew as enthusiastic a response as could ever be expected, though maybe not as gracious as we might have hoped for. After noting that only a handful of the delegates at the pastors' and leaders' seminar were ladies, I felt led that it would benefit the ministries represented to be encouraged and challenged to begin to invite women into active roles in their ministries and even into church leadership. I deliberately ended the session early to allow for questions. And did I ever have questions:

"If God wanted women in church leadership, why didn't He call a woman into the original twelve apostles?"

"If you place a woman as the pastor of a church, what will she do when it is time to baptize new believers and there are big men who need to be baptized?"

"Who said that women don't have to wear head coverings?"

"This year you are telling us to ordain women. Will you be telling us next year to ordain homosexuals?"

This wasn't just opening the proverbial can of worms – I had opened the whole barrel! As each question was dealt with honestly and with scriptural reference, the delegates began to see that I was not there to preach an American ideology but a biblical truth. The fact that Jesus and the apostles wanted to abstain from the very appearance of evil as they traveled and lived together in close quarters would not allow them to call a woman into their company. Just because the pastor is a woman doesn't mean that she has to be the one to personally baptize the converts. In I Corinthians 11:16, the Apostle Paul himself said that, although it was a custom for women to wear head coverings, it wasn't a requirement. Whereas the Bible specifically condemns homosexuality, it was God Himself who said that it was not good for men to be without women – a principle which extends beyond the home into the ministry. After reviewing the robust discussion engendered by the session, the director of the convention guaranteed my wife and me, "You'll see a difference when you come back next year. The sessions will be full of women ministers and pastors. These men heard what you said, and they want their churches to grow so they will put your advice into practice."

When I was invited to preach in one of the churches, I immediately felt impressed to share about David and Goliath. And when I stepped to the extra high pulpit, built specifically to accommodate the pastor's extra tall stature, I joked that it made me feel like tiny David facing the giant. After the service, the pastor shared with me that the message was especially appropriate for his people who – even though most of them are physically tall – feel spiritually small.

A mission to the Democratic Republic of the Congo had been in my heart for several years. However, it seemed that the opportunity to go was always delayed. When I finally made the decision to go one year, I began to run into one obstacle after another. When I contacted the visa agency, they informed me that we had a fifty-fifty chance of getting a visa and that if the visa was denied that there would be no explanation – simply a rejection letter. Furthermore, I was told that the process could take between seven to nine weeks since the Congolese embassy in the US no longer had the power to grant visas. The applications actually have to go to the Congo itself for review. This bit of news left me in a real predicament since I didn't have that amount of time to be without my passport because I had already scheduled essentially back-to-back trips to Colombia, Mexico, Sri Lanka, and the Philippines. Additionally, there was some concern as to when to apply for the visa since the visas are good for only three months – twelve weeks. This meant that the visas could expire before the trip if, for some reason, they were issued shortly after we submitted them. On the other hand, we might have difficulty making the airline arrangements if we waited until fairly close to the travel dates to make the application and the visas were not granted until the last minute. Of course, we also knew that it was not a good idea to book the tickets until after the visas were approved. Most of the members of a team that had planned to go the previous year had their visa applications rejected and the one member who was approved received her visa after the scheduled departure date. After doing a little research, I discovered that I was eligible to be issued a second passport so that I could have one to travel with while the second one was in the hands of the Congolese embassy. The process did require a trip to the passport office in Denver, but the application was approved on the spot and the new passport arrived in the overnight mail a couple days later.

In addition to all the concerns over the visa, other questions about the trip began to surface with news reports of increasing violence in the Congo. There had been more than four hundred deaths, including an attack on the police force resulting in the decapitation of forty-two officers. Two hundred thousand citizens had been displaced. These hostilities, coupled with reports of an Ebola outbreak, raised serious concerns among some of the team members. However, I had a special promise to fall back upon. When I was in Colombia, a gentleman came up to me with a handwritten note in Spanish. I was able to make out a few of the words, but asked a friend to translate it so I could be sure that I understood. The message was that the gentleman had received a prophetic word from the Lord concerning me, and one of the four points was that I was supposed to go to Africa! With that confirmation of what I already felt in my heart, we had pressed forward with the plans for the trip. The visas were approved in time to make the necessary travel arrangements, and we actually found better flight schedules and prices than were available before we sent off our visa applications.

The pastor of the church where the conference was to be held asked me to be part of an ordination service for two of his men who had started branch

242

churches. When I was first invited to speak as part of the program, I had planned to preach "David's Stick"; however, as the day went on, I decided to just get up and greet the people and sit down. Then the most unusual thing happened; they presented the new pastors with a walking stick as part of the ordination ceremony. At that point, I knew that I had the right message but not the time. So I did stand up and make a comment or two about the spiritual significance of the stick and sat down after about three minutes. When the service finally ended, they had a reception. A few people speak a very limited amount of English, but the ones who do all said that they wished that I had preached a full sermon.

When we arrived at the local church where I was to preach, the building was packed to capacity with four hundred fifty villagers. The pastor later told me that his normal attendance was about two hundred eighty. I preached on the story of the demoniac of Gadara, making the point that there were four powers at play in the story: the power of the devil, the power of the presence of God that made Legion fall down and worship Jesus without even having heard Him preach, the power of the spoken word that cast out the legion of demons, and the power of Legion's testimony that changed the atmosphere of Decapolis from running Jesus out of town to welcoming Him with more than four thousand on His return. I also paralleled Legion's symptoms with the ways that the devil affects our lives: living in the tombs and the isolation and hostility we express within families, tribes, and nations; crying with the emotional distress that can be so severe that we can't even express it; and his cutting himself with stones with the self-destructiveness that can lead to physical cutting or injury and even to suicide but may also manifest itself in a negative self-image.

One highlight of the trip was the release of my book *Finally, My Brethren* in Swahili. We gave each pastor a copy of the new translation along with a few copies in French and English. We also introduced the new Swahili translation of *So, You Wanna Be A Preacher*, which was not be officially released until the next time we returned. On my return to the Congo the following year, I was greeted at the airport with shouts of "Duboo! Duboo!" Since I illustrated one of my messages by telling the story of an encounter with one of the bears that live in our neighborhood and often invade our backyard and had learned the Swahili word for "bear" to use when I told the story, everyone remembered both my illustration and me – resulting in my nickname, "Duboo."

In Kenya, we hosted the pastors' conference in a church a couple hours' drive outside of Nairobi. Everyone is very attentive and so appreciative that we have come to them because other ministries always hold their conferences in the city and do not include the rural ministers. After the first session, the wife of the bishop commented, "I learned so much even in the first few minutes." The bishop then followed up with, "This kind of teaching is what we need," and then added that he wished we could come back annually.

One other African country that had been on my heart for many years was the nation of Liberia. When I was working with Dr. Lester Sumrall, the Feed the Hungry program had sent a boatload of food to sustain the people during a tragic civil war. After hearing reports of how that one act of humanitarian aid had impacted the nation, I had carried a strong desire to actually visit the country to see the country firsthand. After becoming involved with Every Home for Christ, I had the opportunity to become acquainted with the national director for Liberia and eventually was able to arrange to visit the country and hold a series of pastors' conferences. After arriving in Liberia, I shared with my host the story of how I had first become engaged with his nation. It was at that point that I received the shock of my life – my host turned out to be the very person who had been in charge of the distribution of all the food that had arrived on the Feed the Hungry ship!

The first three days of our visit were plagued with torrential rains, which hindered the attendance at the conference in the capital city of Monrovia. Since Liberia is a seriously underdeveloped nation, the people who live off the main road get stranded in severe storms because the dirt roads to their houses become impassable. Additionally, many of the homes even get flooded. And of course, the people who don't have their own cars can't get out and walk or ride their motorbikes or bicycles in such bad conditions. However, many delegates braved the drenching rains and made their way to the meetings, eager to be trained and blessed. We concluded our two-week stay in Liberia by preaching in the capital city. When I handed the pastor at one of the churches where I ministered a copy of my book, *Living for the End Times*, his wife immediately grabbed it and exclaimed, "The Lord just spoke to our women's group that we needed to learn how to live for the end times!"

My parting messages were ones of hope and victory, encouraging the people to believe God for miracles in the face of seemingly impossible situations. These were timely words, not only because of the nation's desperate economic condition, but also because the country was facing a horrifying Ebola epidemic that has left many people petrified with fear. In fact, one gentleman even refused to shake hands with my traveling companion, afraid that he might be carrying the virus. I shared a long conversation with a doctor who works at the hospital where the Ebola patients are quarantined, and she shared with us stories of how a pastor and a Christian sister had died after laying hands on a sick person who was later discovered to be infected with Ebola and how a doctor and nurse had also died after treating a patient who was later diagnosed with the virus. It wasn't until I was back home that I began to realize the full impact of why the Lord arranged for me to be in Liberia at this exact time. My host wrote to me about the significance of our ministry in their nation. He said that he felt my visit had been in God's divine timing to strengthen and prepare the church to lead the nation during the time of crisis. He added that the church leaders were treating the Ebola epidemic as spiritual warfare and were positioned to win because of the training they had received in the conferences. His wife – who is a medical doctor working in the top hospital that was dealing with the Ebola crisis – added that she wished that thousands of pastors and church leaders had been able to receive the teaching but that she was thankful to God for the hundreds who were able to be trained, prepared, and equipped.

Before moving to another topic, I must share one last African story. Just prior to landing in Nigeria, the stewardess on the airplane came through the plane to distribute the landing forms that we had to fill out for the customs officers in the terminal. Since there are two different forms – one for Nigerian citizens and one for foreign visitors – she wanted to make sure that each passenger received the proper document. Stopping next to my seat, she asked, "Are you a Nigerian?" Pausing a moment to look at the white skin on my hand and then pointing to my chest, I replied, "Not out here; only in there."

In the Great Commission, the Lord asks us to make ourselves available for three distinct aspects of His plan to reach the world: witnessing (Luke 24:48, Acts 1:8), evangelism (Mark 16:15), and disciple-making (Matthew 28:19). While witnessing is a simple testimony of what we have seen and experienced, evangelism is a presentation of the gospel message with the intent of bringing the hearer to a point of making the decision to place his faith in Christ, and disciple-making is the process of helping nurture the new converts into fully mature believers. Even though my main calling in life and ministry is to disciple through Bible teaching, I have always incorporated the other two elements of the Great Commission in my travels around the world.

Witnessing is the most basic element of the Great Commission and opportunities can present themselves in unexpected situations. In fact, for my first ministry experience in Mexico it was totally unintentional. I had taken my family to a beach resort on a fishing trip. The day we had reservations for the deep-sea fishing boat, we woke up to very poor weather conditions and very choppy seas – just perfect for seasickness, which we all got! I spent most of my time throwing up. I wasn't a very good fisherman, but we did a fairly good job of fishing for men. I was wearing a T-shirt from Nicaragua that said, "Jesus is my best friend," in Spanish. While I was hanging over the gunwales of the boat throwing up into the sea, the captain read my shirt and asked if I knew what it said. When I told him that I did, he replied that he didn't think that Jesus was his best friend. He said that he didn't want to go back to the Catholic Church because of all that was happening with the Catholic priests. He wondered if he should go to the Mormon Church. I, of course, told him, "No," to that idea. Between bouts of throwing up over the edge of the boat, we talked a lot the rest of the day. He prayed the sinner's prayer and asked me to write it down so he could pray it again later and also share it with his family. I got him to give me his address so I could send him some literature to read. Later the next day, I stopped in a drug store for sunburn lotion because our son had gotten a really bad burn on the boat. Noticing an open Bible on the pharmacist's counter, I asked the girl if she were reading it. When I discovered that she was a Spirit-filled Christian, I got the address of a church to send to the boat captain so that he didn't have to try the Mormon Church!

But that was not – as the British would describe it – a "one off" experience. On another family vacation in Mexico, Peggy and I decided to attend a couple of timeshare presentations so we could see other resorts that we might be interested in visiting on future vacations. Both encounters turned out to be "times to share" more than timeshares.   When we were approached by the representative to go to the first presentation, Peggy was reluctant – well, let's be honest – she was downright resistant. Even though we wanted to get the inside view of the resort, she didn't want to go through the "high pressure" sales pitch and waste a lot of our vacation time. Eventually she decided to accept the gentleman's offer, and we headed to the resort. Our salesman was a young Mexican gentleman who started with the usual "chatting us up" routine by asking about our family and telling us a little about his. Somewhere in the conversation, Reuben mentioned that he had been forced to walk out on a presentation he was giving the previous day because he had a sudden physical attack brought on by a high blood pressure condition. He said that he actually had to go to the hospital for treatment after the episode. At that point, he shared a little about what the doctors had told him he would have to do in order to keep the condition under control. At that point, I suggested that we knew a better way than drugs for treating his high blood pressure. Reuben's response was to start talking about diet, exercise, and alternative medicine.   I then replied that we were talking about prayer and shared the story of how we had prayed for a friend with cancer who was totally healed.   Peggy followed up by sharing her own testimony of the healing she had received when she was first born again. The salesman was immediately receptive; so, we began to ask him about his relationship with the Lord. He told us how that he – like almost everyone in Mexico – had grown up as a Catholic. He went on to tell us about how his mother had recently invited him to go with her to a new church where "you can feel the Spirit during the mass." Even though he was still using the Catholic terminology, we understood that he had truly been born again at this Spirit-filled non-denominational church. After we finished our introductory conversation, we headed to the model unit in the timeshare complex for the tour. When we were in the privacy of the model, he said, "Okay, this is the place," and we knew that he was ready for prayer. When we laid hands on him he was overwhelmed by the power of the Holy Spirit, and I had to help him sit down on the edge of the bed before he fell on the floor. During the rest of our time together, Reuben was glowing with the joy of the Lord and kept telling us how much better he felt. He was certain that he had been completely restored to normal health. When we were offered an opportunity to visit another vacation property the next day, I was surprised that Peggy accepted the invitation without any argument.

When we were introduced to the young American salesman who was to show us around, he apologized for asking us to ride to the next building even though it was only a short walk away. He explained that he had suffered a knee injury while playing tennis a few weeks previously and found it too painful to walk between the buildings. Our ears perked up, suspecting that this might be another divine assignment. Certainly enough, as we sat together, there was a perfect spot in the conversation for Peggy to interject a few words about the possibility of divine healing for his knee. When Mark seemed receptive to the idea that God was interested in his need, Peggy asked him if he had a personal relationship with Jesus. He responded with an adamant, "Yes, I do," and proceeded to share the whole story about how he had realized that he had a huge void in his life that he had tried in vain to fill with drugs, money, and all the other worldly things that elude so many. He then told us how that a client had shared with him that only Jesus could fill that emptiness and how that he had found the true fulfillment that he was seeking when he turned his life over to the Lord. Mark then pulled out his smart phone and showed us how he logged his daily prayer and Bible study right on his ever-present phone. We then told him the story of how Reuben had been healed just the day before and asked if he wanted us to pray for him like we had for Reuben. He responded with an enthusiastic, "Yes." When we got to the model unit, we asked if it would be a good place for the prayer. I started to close the door, but Mark volunteered that he didn't care if anybody came in and saw him getting prayer. At that point, we knew that he was genuinely serious! Just like in the case with Reuben the previous day, Mark began to sway under the anointing as we prayed for him and he too, wound up sitting on the edge of the bed. He said that he could feel his knee moving during the prayer, and afterwards he could walk without any "catches" or "clicks" in his knee. During the rest of our time together he kept walking back and forth around the room, commenting on how he could walk without any pain or problems in his knee.

Another excellent example of how just being present as a witness is important occurred during another family vacation in Australia. While visiting Sydney, we spent some time with the Australian Every Home for Christ national director who, knowing of our work in Nepal, mentioned that he would like for us to meet a young Nepali man he had befriended. When we met Deepla, he shared that he had been having some serious problems with depression, fear, sleeplessness, and terrifying dreams. He had tried Hindu prayers, Buddhist amulets, medication, and even a stay in a psychiatric hospital – but was no better. Realizing that his problem was demonic, Peggy and I began to question him about his relationship with Nepali religions and with Christ. He

250

told us that his sister was a baptized Christian and that she had shared a lot with him and that he read his Bible every night even though he didn't understand a lot. Eventually, Deepla began to accept our message that Jesus is the only true God and that he needed to renounce all other religions to receive Christ as his personal savior. After praying the salvation prayer with him, we began to address the spirit tormenting him. Our new friend then fell over under the power of the Holy Spirit and was "out" for at least an hour. When he eventually came to, he said that he had never experienced anything like that before and that he knew that he was free from the demonic control that had been working in him! In fact, he was still so "drunk in the Spirit" that we had to walk him to the door when we took him back to his apartment at the end of the night.

When we saw the EHC director several months later, he shared with us that Deepla was growing strong in the Lord and that he was attending a church near his apartment. He also commented that when he talked with Deepla about Bible questions — even from Old Testament passages — he remembered and understood what he had read. This is a great breakthrough considering that, prior to our prayer, he was never able to understand anything he read. When the EHC director was to give a report at the annual meeting of the international board of the ministry, instead of talking about the accomplishments of his ministry, he told the story of Deepla in full detail and then concluded with, "I'm used to seeing people get born again the Billy Graham way, but here we were with this young Nepali boy sprawled out on our living room floor!" Actually, I was in another meeting where the EHC director told Deepla's story instead of giving his ministry report – not because he had nothing exciting to talk about but because the young man's story was so unusual. Deepla went on to attend Bible college and seminary, pioneered a couple churches in Sydney and joined the staff of the Australia Every Home for Christ office.

One of my favorite jokes is to comment about how James 1:2 is my favorite verse, "My brethren, count it all joy when ye fall into divers temptations." In my typical corny sense of humor, I love to add, "Just tempt me to go to diving in the Bahamas and see how much joy I will count." The truth of the matter is that I don't dive. In fact, I quit my SCUBA lessons in the middle of the second class when they told me that I had to take my mask off under water! But I do snorkel and enjoy a good boat ride if I can make it through without getting seasick. On the other hand, I consider that I do have sort of a seasickness ministry (Remember the Mexico story.) Well, our ministry in the Bahamas was, indeed, part of my "seasick mission." Peggy and I had gone out for a day on a pleasure boat when I began to feel the anointing for this special ministry. I wound up spending much of the day on the bridge with the captain; this gave me the opportunity to have plenty of time to share with him one-on-one. The captain confided in me that he had some serious problems that he was embarrassed to confess to anyone locally because the community was so small and he was sure that anyone he talked to would soon spread it through the whole neighborhood. Between my bouts of queasiness, I was able to counsel him and share God's answers to all his problems.

Peggy, on the other hand, also has a unique ministry that could be called her "shopping mission." As she meanders through the tourist trinket shops, she seems to always pick out the shopkeepers who have some need of prayer. You would never be able to imagine how many times she's taken the sales clerk into a back corner for prayer, prayed for a fellow guest in the hotel elevator, or laid hands on the hotel front desk clerk right in the hotel lobby. She has even prayed for people and seen them slain in the Spirit right on the public beach!

While traveling between Zambia and Uganda, we had a very long layover in Kenya. Rather than just sit in the airport, Peggy and I decided to hire a cab to drive us into town for dinner. As we were leaving the airport property, we were amazed to suddenly be in the presence of giraffes and zebras. Since Nairobi National Park actually borders the airport grounds, these animals frequently migrate right up to boundary lines. Peggy said that she figured that the animals were just being polite by coming as a special welcoming committee to greet them. As I jumped out of the car to photograph the animals, Peggy took the time to share the gospel with the cab driver.

When ministering in the South American country of Colombia, I took the team for a treat at a local ice cream parlor, where we wound up leading the waitress to salvation and the baptism in the Holy Spirit. When we saw tears of joy well up in her eyes because we had given her a generous tip, one of our team members realized that there was an open door to witness to her. Within a few minutes, the whole team was on their feet, hugging and praying for the young lady as tears rolled down her cheeks.

After traveling all day to reach Ecuador and not getting into our hotel rooms until four o'clock in the morning, we scheduled our first day to be a slow-paced day of leisure. Our plan was to spend the day at a tropical botanical garden where we could enjoy a time in the pool and some relaxation in a beautiful natural setting; however, the Lord had His own agenda for the day. It turned out that another group was also retreating at the park for the day. When our group gathered at the open-air plaza for lunch, the senior citizens group was also at the plaza enjoying dancing to some traditional local music. When we began to mingle with the group and ask to learn some of the dance steps, they gladly welcomed us. Soon, we offered to give them an impromptu presentation of one of the skits we had prepared for the trip. After the presentation, the president of the seniors group thanked us and explained that they, too, were a Christian group and that they were blessed to have met us in the park. At that point, a couple of the students shared their testimonies, and we offered to pray for those who needed prayer. Before long, the day of leisure in the park was transformed into a revival meeting with almost everyone from the seniors group receiving prayer. We saw many healings among the group with at least two men receiving restoration of their hearing.

When the owner of the hotel where the group stayed in Ecuador learned that our group was a mission team, he asked if we would like to hold a church service in the hotel while we were there. Since our schedule was already very full, we declined his offer. However, he asked if we could have a special meeting just for him and his family. Although no one in the family was a believer, they all listened very intently as we shared the gospel message and some testimonies. The hotel owner and his wife shared about an experience that had driven them away from church. One Sunday, both of them witnessed the appearance of a demonic apparition in the church. When they turned to one another and asked if the other one had seen it, they were surprised that it had not been a figment of their imaginations but a real manifestation that was visible to both of them. At that point, they left the building and determined never to return. However, difficulties in their family and business had brought them to the point to ask for help from the visiting missionaries in their hotel. The conclusion of our little private session was that the father, the mother, the two sons, the daughter, and her husband all six prayed to receive salvation and asked for the laying on of hands for God's blessings on their lives.

When I was leading a team of students on a mission in India, we took some free time to attend a cultural event in the city on Saturday morning. As they were standing on the street corner waiting for the parade to pass by, a man stopped and asked if he could take a picture with me. After getting over the surprise of the fact that a random stranger would just walk up and ask for photo (or snap, as he said in the Indian culture) I realized that this must be a divine appointment and asked him a little about himself. It turned out that the gentleman was from about two hundred fifty miles away and was in town to have surgery at the major hospital there. The mission team, of course, prayed for him for healing and shared the plan of salvation with him. Another time, we were scheduled to have a children's crusade since it was a national holiday dedicated to the Hindu deity Shiva and the children would be out of school. However, we received a call that morning telling us that there were some issues. When the local authorities saw the local Christians setting everything up for the meetings, they confronted the Christians as to why they thought that they could have a special event on a Hindu holy day. Eventually, permission was given for the event to go ahead as long as everything was held indoors. Of course, the venue grew very hot and stuffy with all the windows and doors closed, but we had a wonderful time with the children – playing games, singing and dancing, doing skits, sharing testimonies, and ministering the Word of God. At the prayer time, we saw a genuine move of the Sprit as many of the children were touched by God and fell out in the Spirit. The evening evangelistic meeting was equally as anointed.

But the really exciting events of the day took place after the scheduled meeting was over. The local official who had originally challenged the pastor about having the meeting called him just as the evening service was closing. At first, we were concerned that we had caused some trouble and would have to face some consequences. Instead, the official said that she was glad that we had gone ahead with our plans and would like to have a couple of the members of the American team visit her home. When the delegates arrived at her house, the local official greeted them by explaining that she had a lot of pressure on her because of her administrative duties and civic responsibilities. She wanted prayer for peace. After the students ministered to her and prayed for her, she replied that she felt much better. Even though she was not interested in accepting Jesus, she was very open to prayers in His name. After her prayer, the official directed the students to her husband and said that he was having some physical problems. He didn't want to say anything specific about his issue, but he was receptive to prayers in Jesus' name. When one of the team members began to pray, she felt directed to pray for a blockage that was hindering the natural flow of his body.   After the prayer, the gentleman confirmed that his problem was some sort of blockage that was hindering him from urinating! The second divine appointment of the evening was back at the rented hall where the meeting was held. The venue was a large room that a local family had added to their home to rent out for extra income. Even though the local church was one of the regular tenants, the lady who actually owned the property was not a Christian. When a couple of our team members stopped in at her home to chat with her, she was receptive to the gospel and prayed to receive the Lord into her life!

On the flight home from that same mission to India, I was editing some of the photos from the trip on my laptop when the young lady in the next seat who appeared to be an Indian asked if I had been to India. Since this was the flight between Seattle and Denver, she was not expecting to meet anyone who was traveling from India. I told her a little about our trip and asked what part of India she was from. She replied that she lived in Colorado but had come from India when she was a college student. Her trip to Seattle was to attend the funeral of one of her Indian friends. At that point, I asked if she were a Christian or a Hindu. When she replied that she was a Hindu, we launched into a discussion about the differences between the Hindu and Christian views on life, death, and the afterlife – a talk that occupied the entire rest of the flight. Although she didn't seem to want to accept Jesus at the moment, she seemed very open and was very appreciative that I had taken the time to share with her and to comfort her during this time of extreme sadness. When I gave her one of my books, she was happy to receive it and promised to read it.

I had a real surprise at the hotel Livingstone, Zambia, one morning when I was greeted by the manager who had been at the hotel in Lusaka, when I was there on a previous trip to Zambia. She had asked me and the friend who was traveling with me at the time to pray for her because of some real problems she was encountering in her job. It just so happened that the hotel chain had sent her to Livingstone to fill in temporarily for the manager there who was going on vacation. On this trip, she was thrilled to be able to share that there had been a marked difference in the situation after that prayer. I praised God for the blessing of being able to see the fruit of the previous ministry!

Coming home from Zimbabwe, I had what I label as an "almost adventure." On Saturday afternoon before I was scheduled to fly to Nairobi on Sunday, my host thought that it might be good to double-check the reservations. When he did, he was told that I had been canceled off the flight. The pastor and I rushed to the airport to try to get the problem straightened out. It took about an hour to get reinstated on the flight, but we also learned that my flight was now scheduled for 11 AM rather than 1:30 PM. That meant that I would miss preaching in the Sunday morning service, but at least I wouldn't miss getting to Kenya in time to meet Peggy to fly back to the US. It was only after the plane was ready to depart that I finally figured out what had happened. The plane had been essentially commandeered by the President Robert Mugabe of Zimbabwe. He had a meeting in the nation of Malawi, so he had the airline empty enough seats so that he and his entourage could use the plane. He also had them reroute the flight to go to Malawi before going to Kenya and change the departure time so that he would arrive at the proper time for his meeting in Malawi. Well, he, his wife, and a host of officials and newsmen filled the front of the plane. I was in the row just behind his party. They didn't have any special guard keeping people away from the front of the plane, and they didn't even close the curtain between first class and coach. I could have walked up and introduced myself to President Mugabe, but I didn't have a good excuse except, "Gee, I'd like to shake the hand of a president." Only after he deplaned did I think about the ten copies of my book on the will of God that I had in my briefcase. I could have given them to him and told him that I wanted to offer them to him and his advisors because I knew that they have so many important decisions to make. But then it was too late — I had blown my opportunity to have an input into the leaders of an entire nation! When the president deplaned, there was a royal reception at the airport with hundreds of official-looking people including the president of Malawi who greeted him. From the plane window, I essentially had a front row for the full event. But how much more wonderful would it have been if I had been able to have witnessed to them and then been able to see the reception of their souls into the kingdom of heaven! It was a powerful reminder of the significance of the role of witnessing as part of fulfilling the Great Commission.

Speaking of the missed opportunity to witness to a head of state reminds me of a time when we did witness to the Rwandan ambassador to Ethiopia – without even realizing that we were even doing so. Peggy and I were guests in his home because his wife was a member of the church where we were ministering. The ambassador was only a nominal Christian and never attended any of the services; however, we did have times to share a bit with him during mealtimes at the house. On the last night of our visit, the pastor and serval staff members from the church stopped by the house to bid us farewell before our return to the States. During the time of fellowship with the pastor, something totally surprising happened. The ambassador got up from his chair, walked across the room, knelt in front of Peggy, and said, "I want what you have." He had seen enough of Jesus in her life that he realized that he needed to know the Lord in a more intimate way. In essence, she had been an ambassador of Christ (II Corinthinas 5:20) to him.

The second aspect that Jesus enumerated when He defined the Great Commission is evangelism – preaching of the gospel to unbelievers. On all the trips when I take teams with me to the mission field, I always incorporate a significant evangelistic element. For example, when I traveled to Kenya, we were met at the airport by a group of about twenty local Christians – many of whom had taken a week off from their jobs, had traveled from other cities for the outreach and crusade, and had committed to sleep on the floors of the homes of the ones who lived in the area. The plan of each day was early morning prayer, a seminar session, evangelism, and the open-air crusade. There was a local church that was sponsoring the crusade. Each day was focused on a different area around the church. Between the door-to-door visitation and the crusade meetings, there were an estimated one hundred people per day who came to the Lord! In addition, there were a number of healings and deliverances.

There was one funny thing that occurred when we were doing the house-to-house visitation. We started sharing with some people outside their house and, before long, there was a large group of people gathered in the central courtyard of the apartments. Of course, you have to think third-world when I say courtyard and apartments. I'm talking about a dirt and concrete opening between the two-room cement-block caves the people call home. About six or eight of them decided that they would like to accept the Lord. I reached out to pray for the first one in line, and she was slain in the Spirit. The open drain ran through the courtyard, and she was headed right for it. We were all grabbing her trying to save her from falling into the sewer. We did manage to rescue her, but we lost the rest of our little flock. You should have seen them scatter. They all disappeared into their houses as fast as rabbits into their holes!

One of my missions to Belize serves as an excellent example of how we introduce Bible college students to evangelism on the mission field. We began our week by visiting two schools since the school system in Belize is a unique combination of public and Christian education. The government funds the schools which were built by the churches and missionaries, providing an open door for gospel presentations to all the students. We also learned that even the prison system is a novel cooperative between the government and the church in which the inmates are actually given the option of going through a secular twelve-step rehabilitation or a faith-based program. We had the opportunity to minister in two different correctional institutions – a youth hostel where juvenile offenders are held and a regular prison. In both the youth hostel and prison, the inmates were very receptive of the testimonies and ministry of the team.

We spent one morning just walking through the city giving out free sandwiches and ministering to the homeless people in the alleys and the city park. Two particular encounters on that morning stand out. Gilbert was an elderly man who had spent much of his adult life in the United States but had come back to his native Belize in his retirement years and, through a series of events, had wound up alone and lonely. When we met him sitting on a tree stump in the park, we asked how he was doing. His response was, "Well, I'm not doing as well as you are." He then mentioned that he was trying to stop smoking but just couldn't kick the habit. When one of the students asked if he were born again, he responded that he was and told us what church he was part of. Knowing that it was a Bible-believing, evangelical church, we knew that he really understood what we were talking about. When Jeanne asked him if he had been baptized in the Holy Spirit, he responded that he had not. She explained some of the scriptures about the Holy Spirit baptism and then asked him to join her in singing a worship song. As she sang, she soon shifted into worshipping in the spirit in unknown tongues. Immediately, Gilbert was also speaking in a heavenly language! When we walked away to find others in need, we knew that this one man was now free from the power that had held him and now had a new source of victory. The other encounter of the day was with two homeless men who shared not only the same park bench but also the same name. Both of them were named Raymond. In addition, they also shared two other things — they were both alcoholics who wanted to be free from the habit, and they both readily received prayers for salvation and deliverance.

One other outreach in which we had an opportunity to participate was hospital visitation. As we visited the various wards, we had many opportunities to minister to both the patients and their families and friends who were there visiting with them. We not only shared the message of salvation and healing but also the message of deliverance from fear and worry that so often attack those who are suffering and facing surgery and even death. As we prayed, we saw new hope and peace manifest on all their faces. Some of the patients also showed visible signs of the healing touch in their bodies. One gentleman, for example, was unconscious – almost comatose – as we began ministering to him and his family. However, as we moved to the next bed to minister to another patient, we heard some excitement around his bed and looked back to see the patient talking and laughing with his family. One unexpected experience in the hospital was the encounter we had with Veronica, a nurse in one of the wards. As a foreign nurse from Nigeria, she had been praying to be able to get to know some strong believers in her new country. When she saw the Bible college logo on some of the students' T-shirts, she approached them and asked them about the school. They, of course, readily invited her to visit the campus for the special night when I would be teaching. Since she had that particular night off, she accepted the invitation and also brought a friend with her. Both ladies were so excited about what they learned that night that they actually began looking into the possibility of enrolling in the school!

One other outreach was door-to-door visitation in one of the neighborhoods that was particularly under the oppression of gangs and drug lords. As we visited home after home, the one request that was repeated in almost every home was for safety and protection as the people told about how many times their homes had been broken into and how they hear gunfire around them on a regular basis. Everyone was eager to receive prayer, and the young children were especially thrilled to pray to ask

Jesus into their lives. When we asked some of the youngsters if they knew the stories of Adam and Eve, Noah and the ark, or David and Goliath, they all responded that they had never heard these stories. We shared this sad truth with the students at the local Bible school and challenged them to go back into the neighborhood to begin a children's Bible club to recruit these little hearts before the gangs and drug dealers take them.

In Colombia, we were scheduled to minister at a home for children who had been rescued from slave labor on the country's cocaine plantations. Since the building was very crowded, the ministry time was held outside at a park near the facility. This open-air ministry allowed the team to also reach the people of the neighborhood as they passed through the park. The result was that a number of passersby stopped to watch the dramas and listen to the testimonies. One mother and her child accepted the Lord when the invitation was given. In addition, a group of five teenagers on their way home from school stopped to see what was happening. When one team member walked over to them and struck up a conversation, she learned that one of the group was a believer who had been praying for her friends to come to know the Lord. Before the afternoon ended, all four of her friends had received salvation.

The next day, the team planned to go early to the church where they were to minister that evening and spend the afternoon walking through the neighborhood distributing tracts and engaging people in conversation. It was raining when they left the dorms – and as the bus made the hour-plus journey toward the church, the rain turned into a deluge. The streets were transformed into rivers, and the spray from the tires of the buses splashed higher than the tops of the cars beside them in traffic. However, the rains stopped just before the team arrived at the destination, and the skies were perfectly clear the whole time we were canvassing the community. But this wasn't the only time that the Lord stopped the rain during this mission. The rain stopped just in time for the outdoor outreach on one other occasion, and the rains held off until the exact moment the team was concluding another outdoor ministry time. Not only did the Lord close the physical heavens to stop the rain, He opened the spiritual heavens to pour out the anointing as the team ministered on the streets and in the churches. One of the students led four people to the Lord within the first fifteen minutes she was sharing her faith on the street. The special blessing about this experience is that she had never witnessed to anyone or prayed for anyone to receive the Lord before in her life. One student expressed his amazement at how eager the people were to receive the literature that was being distributed, "You would have thought that I was giving out thousand-dollar bills." Others who received invitations to the service as the students visited them in their homes, in the shops, and on the street corners responded by attending the church meeting – and then responded when the call for salvation was given. The street evangelistic outreaches gave us many excellent opportunities to meet people right in the middle of their needs and bring them the hope that is only possible in Christ. As we were sharing with and praying for two ladies on the street in front of a hardware store, the clerk who was running the shop overheard our conversation and came out to the street to ask us to also pray for him. When we invited him to the service at the church that evening, he responded that he had to work but would send his wife to the church to record the message so he could listen to it later. As we were walking through a public park, we noticed a young man and his girlfriend sitting on a bench. Since the girl was wrapping a bandage on her boyfriend's ankle and foot, we approached them and asked how he had injured himself. After he explained that it was a sports injury, we

264

told him that we would like to pray for his foot to be healed. When he granted us permission, we prayed in Jesus' name and saw the pain instantly dissipate. After the miraculous healing, I shared with him that Jesus wanted to heal his heart even more than He wanted to heal his body. Within minutes, both the young man and his girlfriend were praying the sinner's prayer. In the meantime, three young boys had stopped to see what was going on. When we asked them if they would also like to ask Jesus into their hearts, they readily agreed and prayed with us. Just across the park, we met a gentleman who said that he needed prayer for a job because he was out of work due to having an injured hand. After we prayed for his hand, he immediately recognized that something had happened and his fingers were more flexible. Of course, we offered him an opportunity to receive salvation, and he gladly prayed with us.

In Costa Rica, we started our day early by loading the bus by 7:30 AM to head for the Pacific coast. Once we reached the beach, we found a place where we could present our evangelistic dramas and music to the passersby. Even though we weren't able to secure power for amplification, we certainly didn't lack power in our ministry. A few people stopped to watch the dramas, but the action really began once the first person came forward for prayer. As we prayed for him, others started gathering around to see what was happening. They too, began to ask for prayer, and soon every member of the team was actively ministering to someone. Bicyclists stopped to see what was going on, and drivers stopped their cars right in the street, causing a mini traffic jam as they called our team over to pray for them right in their cars. One man who came to the Lord was soon back asking for us to come with him to talk to a gentleman up the street. Excited about his newfound faith, he had already shared with a friend of his who also wanted to know Jesus. Since the man was running a store, he couldn't leave to come to us, so we walked up to his shop and ministered to him. As wave after wave of the ocean rushed to the shoreline on the beach, wave after wave of seekers kept rushing to the students to ask for prayer. In fact, we had a difficult time trying to leave the site to head out for lunch and our trip back to San Jose as more and more people kept coming up for prayer. We saw a number of alcoholics delivered and several instant healings. One man came limping up with a bandage wrapped around his ankle and leg; after prayer he pulled off the bandage and walked away without any faltering in his step.

In Nicaragua, we held open-air crusades in a variety of venues during the village outreaches. One such outreach was held on a little island in the middle of Lake Nicaragua near the ancient capital of Granada. Families rowed in on canoes and rowboats from all the neighboring islands to see the puppet ministry, hear the gospel, and receive the gift packets. The open-air crusade in the outskirts of Granada could probably be termed as a Christian block party as the people filled the entire street, crowding around the team as we ministered. At some locations, we were able to offer free medical clinics to the people from the neighborhood, most of whom suffered from medical problems resulting from their diet, unhealthy living conditions, and impure drinking water. Prior to their interviews with the doctor, all the patients received prayer from the team of students, and many of them reported instantaneous healings prior to their medical examinations. In fact, some of the students testified that they felt that they had crossed a new threshold of faith in their own ministries by being a part of these miraculous healings. The crowds were so large at some of the outreaches that the only possible way we could minister to all the people was to divide our prayer team into two lines facing one another and march the

266

people through the corridor between the prayer team lines. The students only had a second to lay hands on each person and pray a blessing over him; however, we believe that the same anointing that touched people when the Apostle Peter's shadow passed over them also produced some miraculous results in our prayer tunnel. One student reported that he prayed for a cross-eyed baby and watched the baby as its mother carried him through the rest of the line. The baby seemed to be focusing his eyes as if he could see normally after the prayer.

On a home-to-home visitation in the island nation of Trinidad and Tobago, we began by praying for open hearts in each home we were to visit – and God graciously answered our request. The team found the people to be very receptive to the gospel, with individuals – and even whole families – responding to the salvation message in every home. In one encounter, I came upon a group of young men standing with money in their hands, apparently waiting for a drug deal. As I shared the gospel with them, they all responded positively and prayed the sinner's prayer while still holding their drug money. At one home, a young man received the Lord after the presentation of the gospel using a bracelet made of colored beads that illustrate the plan of salvation. As an afterthought as the team was walking away from the young man's home, one of the ladies in the team turned back and asked if he would like to have a couple bracelets to share with his friends. After crossing the street to share with a family there, the team crossed back to visit the gentleman's next-door neighbor. When the man in the house came to the door, he was already wearing one of the beaded bracelets. The new convert had already been to his home and shared the gospel with him!

One of the most amazing stories I can share about our evangelistic ministry occurred during a home-to-home visitation in the Dominican Republic. Since we didn't have interpreters available, we decided to simply take local Christians with us as introducers. When we would visit a home, the introducer would greet the family in Spanish and explain that the international guests were here because they love the Dominican people and wanted to share that love with them even though we were not able to speak their language. The introducer would then ask if anyone in the home needed prayer for a sickness, to get a job, or perhaps a family problem. At that point, we would pray – either in English or in tongues – for those who responded. After the prayer, the introducer would invite the people in the home to come to the church that evening where we would be preaching with a fluent translator. In one home, the mother who had opened the door handed her sick baby to the lady who accompanied me. After the lady prayed for the child in tongues and offered it back to the mother, the mother began to talk non-stop to her. When my friend tried to interrupt with the explanation that she didn't understand Spanish, the mother insisted that she didn't believe her since she had just prayed over the baby in eloquent Spanish!

No matter how insistent I was, my "Please don't do that!" seemed to fall on deaf ears. The next thing I knew the twenty-something-year-old young lady in Scotland was hoisting her father up on her shoulders. I had just prayed for her back to be healed and asked her to do something that she was not able to do before prayer — thinking that she would probably do something simple like bend over to touch her toes. When she explained that she would often pick up her father prior to the spinal compression she had suffered due to a sudden growth spurt in which her spinal column didn't keep pace with the growth of the rest of her body, she insisted that the only way she could verify that she had truly been healed was to pick him up. To the amazement and amusement of the whole congregation, we witnessed the most unusual testimonial imaginable as the young lady's dad took a joy ride around the church on his daughter's shoulders.

When the smile broke across Sharon's face, I knew that our mission in Liberia was a success. The young girl had lived for years under a superstitious bondage that she had to practice certain witchcraft rituals in order to protect herself from a curse that someone had placed on her, dooming her to an untimely death. A string around her waist, a concoction of oil and herbs rubbed on her body, and three magic pellets of mud continually in her possession were her only hope to keep the demonic forces at bay. However, all that changed as soon as we shared with her that, from the moment she had asked Jesus into her heart, there was living inside her a greater one than all the witches in her village, in the whole of Liberia, and even in the entire world. We then led her in a prayer in which she renounced all her dependence on witchcraft and rebuked the devil off of her life and out of her mind. As soon as she said, "Amen," that wonderful smile burst out through the sullenness that had darkened her face up to that point. Sharon then handed us the string, pellets, and bottle of oil as a confession that she was totally free from the captivity in which she had been held for so long. We stepped outside her little house and built a small fire and rejoiced as the emblems of her demonic slavery went up in flames, symbolizing that they had no more power or authority on her.

But this was not the first such incident I had encountered on this mission trip. Just days before we had seen a similar smile of victory erupt on the face of nine-year-old Alethea who had been tormented since she was kindergartener. According to her testimony, she had been secretly inducted into witchcraft without her understanding what was going on. After this initiation, she was instructed to do certain incantations and rituals that resulted in the death of two of her family members. She was totally emotionless as she talked matter-of-factly about her involvement in the occult and the fact that she had essentially murdered her father and sister. We carefully explained to the young girl how she could ask Jesus into her heart and be freed from the guilt and shame of her involvement in these deaths and be delivered from every form of demonic control and influence. She readily repeated the prayer with us, but still seemed almost lifeless with a distant stare and a detached attitude. Then we prayed a deliverance prayer over her and had her join us in verbally rebuking the devil off her life. Next we prayed with her mother and other family members that peace would rest upon their home and that there would be no more fear of demons or witches. But it wasn't until Alethea came back to the church the following morning that we saw it – that bright smile, just like the one on Sharon's face! Alethea was a visible testimony of John 10:10. The devil had tried to kill, steal, and destroy; but she had found life – and not just life, but abundant life!

In Mexico we witnessed a number of miraculous healings, including an elderly lady who had not been able to walk in a year; however, she started walking on her own as the mission team prayed for her. Another testimony is of a boy who had an infection in his ear that affected his eyesight. We prayed for him and the pain in the ear left and his sight improved. Another who had nerve pain from his hip down to the back of his knee was completely healed. Still another miracle took place when a young man sitting out in the crowd was healed of pain and numbness in his foot ever since having been run over by a fire truck. Many of those healed had a look of astonishment on their faces. When the first person testified of her healing to the crowd, people's faith began to increase and then miracles started taking place left and right. A few days after the group left, I met a nurse at the hospital who asked me to pray for a young child in her family who had fractured his skull in a fall. I began to share with her some of the testimonies of healing from the crusade. The nurse said that she had heard about the crusade where all the miracles had taken place from someone who had been healed in one of the services.

In the closing session of a series of meeting in the Philippines, I was asked to give a commission to the delegates. I said that Jesus didn't give a commission to His disciples without demanding that they be baptized in the Holy Spirit. Therefore, I wanted to make sure that the convention delegates were also baptized in the Holy Spirit before He could challenge them to go out to change their world. Suddenly the front of the auditorium was filled with about a hundred of the conference delegates, wanting to be filled with the Spirit – and then Pentecost happened! Scores were slain in the Spirit and all of them received the gift of tongues. After the meeting was finally dismissed, I met a young man in the church lobby (He was not even part of the conference; he was just stopping by the church for another purpose.) But I walked up to him and – without even introducing myself – asked, "Do you speak in tongues?" The startled young man replied, "No." My next question was, "Well, what are you waiting for?" His response was, "The Lord's time." The answer came back, "The Lord's time was AD 33. You are 1984 years late!" At that point, the young man burst into tears and began to fluently flow in a new language. He then confessed that he had received the baptism in the Holy Spirit as a young child at youth camp but something had happened in his life that made him think that he was no longer worthy of this gift from God. This chance encounter had proven to him that that idea was a lie from the enemy.

On that same mission to the Philippines, we met one of the men who had been in the meeting when

Peggy was in the Philippines the previous year. He shared that he had been diagnosed with stage-three cancer but was miraculously healed when Peggy prayed for him. The really exciting part of the story was that he really hadn't been a believer at the time; he had only come to the meeting at the insistence of his daughter and son-in-law. But after the healing, he had truly given himself to the Lord and was now one of the leaders in his church. However, the story doesn't stop there. He was driving a beautiful new car that he had purchased with money that the insurance had given him for the cancer treatment. Even though he had tried to return the money because he didn't need the treatments after he was healed, the insurance company said that the money was his legitimate benefit and that he could keep it and use it as he wished! In addition to purchasing the new car, he also used part of the money to build a small structure on his property that he was using to hold Bible studies and gospel meetings with the vision of birthing a church.

In one particular meeting in Brazil, an overwhelming majority of the congregation stood for prayer – and most of them eagerly came forward to take the microphone and share about their instantaneous results. Pain had left people's bodies from their heads, shoulders, knees, and toes – and every other part of their bodies. As they testified, it reminded me of the little jingle I used to sing as a child in Sunday school, "Head and shoulders, knees, and toes – knees and toes – knees and toes." One woman testified that her joints had been so inflamed that she couldn't bend over to pick up items off the floor and had had to use her feet to move things around her house. After the prayer, she demonstrated to the whole congregation that she could squat and do knee bends. Another woman told us that she had been sleeping on the floor rather than in her bed because of intense back pain. She then added that she had been able to sit through the long service pain-free on the hard, unpadded church pew. One gentleman shared about how he had heard something pop in his back as he was being prayed for. A few days later, we had a chance to visit his home where he showed us a tree that he had cut down and pulled up by the roots as well as two piles of gravel and rocks that he had moved in order to build a driveway. The "punch line" to this story is that he had been unable to do any such physical work for two years because of severe back and shoulder pain! Several other people also shared that they had suffered from pain and/or limited movement due to sports or automobile accidents – many of them, years ago – but that they had been totally restored as they received prayer.

One really amazing story involved three ladies who had attended a service at another church but, as they were walking home, felt impressed to stop by the church where we were having the healing service. The really miraculous thing about this story is that the healing service was a special meeting outside the regular schedule of the church and the ladies were not aware that anything was happening at the church. Each of these three ladies had a serious ailment that had plagued her for years. Miraculously, each woman was totally healed even though they had shown up and asked for prayer just as we were ready to close the service. They had missed the entire message! One unexpected healing came to one of our team members. Gene shared his testimony of having been miraculously healed after an automobile accident over thirty-five years ago. He testified that the doctors had felt that he would never walk again but he was back on his feet within a matter of weeks. During the trip, I noticed that he stumbled a few times and asked him if he was okay. Gene's reply was that he still had a lingering issue with his equilibrium as a result of the accident. After prayer by a couple of the team members, Gene was able to walk a straight line, climb stairs, and maneuver uneven ground without hesitation.

There were many different kinds of healing on that mission trip. As we visited the rehab centers, we saw many lives healed from the brokenness of abandonment, rejection, abuse, and addiction. As we ministered at a marriage seminar, we saw couples and individuals healed emotionally, bringing a renewed hope and courage for their marriages, finances, homes, and families. We saw many lives transformed, both in the churches where we ministered as well as during the women's conference. One couple told me that my message had saved their lives and ministry because they had been so discouraged that they were at the point of giving up. In one church, the sermon in the adult service was on deliverance from demonic activity. During the prayer time at the end of the service, at least eight individuals said that they felt something spiritual lift off them – an amazing result since there were only about twenty-five people in the class. But the story doesn't end there. Without any previous coordination between the team members who were ministering in the adult service, the ones who were working with the children had prepared a lesson based on the story of Legion whom Jesus set free from demonic possession. Additionally, they taught the children a little song to present to their parents after the service, "Shake Off the Devil."

In Colombia, one highlight was the day we spent at a home for girls who were being rehabilitated from drug abuse and prostitution. Most of the sixty young ladies had already received the Lord, but only about a half a dozen of them had been baptized in the Holy Spirit. When we shared with them how to receive this new empowering from God, they all responded immediately. The pastor in charge explained that they had not emphasized the move of the Holy Spirit because the ministry is run by an interdenominational group and that all the churches involved do not recognize the charismatic blessing. He said that we had brought in the missing part. We also had special ministry with several of the young ladies who needed to be delivered from demonic control. We saw dramatic night-to-day changes in their countenances as the demonic control was broken off their lives. After the session, the director of the ministry thanked us for helping him also come to a new level in his understanding of the authority he has as a believer.

Martha was an Ecuadorian orphan girl who had come to live with her half-sister after having lost both her mother and father. Shortly after that loss, her brother also died. In addition to the multiplied grief that she had experienced, there was also anger because she felt that a sister had deliberately not been honest with the brother during the sickness that led to his death. Martha felt that perhaps her sister had wanted the brother to die so she would get more of the inheritance. The combination of all these emotional traumas had devastated Martha and left her easy prey for demonic oppression. When she came forward for prayer, the demon that was tormenting her began to manifest and sent her into a trance-like state. After we took authority over the spirit, Martha regained consciousness and prayed with us to forgive her sister. After prayer for deliverance and emotional healing, a beautiful smile erupted on her face. When we saw Martha in each service after that prayer, she was constantly sporting an ear-to-ear smile.

Tiffany, another young lady in Ecuador, had been subject to epileptic seizures for the full eighteen years of her life and often experienced as many as five episodes per day. When her mother and sister brought her to the meeting, she immediately fell into a seizure. Her mother later explained that being in crowds often triggered these fits; however, this particular episode was exceptionally severe. Although several of the students and some of the local believers spent at least an hour praying for her, ministering to her, and speaking the Word of God over her, Tiffany never regained consciousness. Several team members offered to come to her home the next day to pray for her, hoping that Tiffany would not be so traumatized if she were in a familiar setting away from the crowd. However, it turned out that the local believers actually didn't know how to find her house, so we weren't able to follow through on our offer. When someone was finally able to contact Tiffany's mother, it was too late in the afternoon for us to go the home. Instead, the mother promised to bring her to the service that evening. This was a test of the team's faith since we knew that being in a crowd could easily trigger another epileptic episode. When Tiffany and her family arrived, a small group of the students met with them outside the church. Tiffany's mother reported that she had had only one mild seizure that day — a wonderful improvement! Since Tiffany was alert, the team could easily minister to her and get her responses to all our questions and counsel. When we asked if she was born-again, Tiffany was not able to say that she was certain that she was saved. At that point, we asked the rest of the family if they were certain about their relationships with Jesus. Soon, the whole family prayed, and their bright smiles evidenced that they were now certain about their salvation. After a short time of continued ministry for her healing and deliverance, Tiffany suggested that she wanted to go inside the church for the service — evidence that she had really received her healing because previously going into the crowd would have resulted in a seizure!

Yaniel, a young man in Ecuador, had been totally deaf for all of his fifteen years, yet God had a plan! The service had actually already ended as the congregation there made a special presentation to express their gratitude to the team for coming to minister to them. Yaniel's sister had sung two special songs for the team,

276

church members had presented gifts to the team members, and the congregation was milling about giving farewells to the team. Someone from mission team said that we were willing to have one more time of prayer for those who had any needs. It was at this "last minute" altar call that Yaniel came forward. When the Holy Spirit moved on him, the young man fell to the floor grasping his head as if in excruciating pain. Several team members gathered around him to see what was happening. When he was able to communicate with his mother what had happened, she explained that he was hearing for the first time in his life and that the new sensation was actually causing pain inside his head where there had never been anything but dead silence!

When I prayed with the members of the congregations after the services in Hungary, many reported that pain left their bodies and several said that their hearing began to be restored; however, the most obvious miracle happened in a lady who was bound by depression after the recent loss of her daughter. "Pathetic" is the only word that could describe her when she walked into the service. Carrying a photograph of her daughter, she was "crying on everyone's shoulder" — even strangers whom she had never met before. After prayer, she was smiling, laughing, and rejoicing as she told everyone how God had touched her life! Another young lady who was delivered from a spirit of suicide walked out of the church quoting scripture and exercising her new authority over the devil.

But the story of the daughter of one of the students at the Bible school in India, occupies a special place in my memories. She had been involved in a cultish movement at the university where she was studying. As a result of her association with this group and its teachings, she had fallen into a deep depression. Her father flew her into Chennai for the weekend specifically so I could pray for her. When I prayed for her, she was instantly delivered and left the meeting with a brilliant smile replacing the glum countenance that she had when she arrived. But it wasn't until I had a chance to meet her again several years later that I learned the whole story. Her father had originally booked a train ticket for her, but had a vision as soon as he confirmed the purchase. In the vision, he saw her jump off the train. He immediately canceled the train reservation and purchased an airline ticket. Later on, she told him that she did, indeed, have plans of committing suicide by jumping from a moving train. For a couple years after the prayer, she had been well but later slipped back into her depression. On my return visit, her parents suggested that I come to their home and pray for her. The mother added that the daughter would normally run away when they suggest prayer but that she was happy to hear that I was in town and was willing to come pray for her. She eagerly welcomed me at her home and readily received prayer.

The third element in Jesus' directive to the church is to disciple believers. How? By – as He said in that verse in Matthew that demanded that I have a bigger vision than just Nepal – teaching all nations. Once I realized the impetus of that verse, I soon found myself traveling to country after country to share the good news of the gospel: To teach all nations, in churches, retreats, and conferences. In fact, it was somewhat of a running joke that every time I would get home from a mission and my pastor would ask me how many souls got saved, I'd have to respond, "None." Then I'd have to remind him that I was speaking at a pastors' conference and that all the pastors were already believers.

One thing that I quickly recognized as I traveled through countries in Asia and Africa was that I had to adjust my teaching style in order to communicate fully with my audience. They didn't relate to deep messages about redemption and justification as readily as they did to the simple illustration of how an ugly caterpillar can become a beautiful butterfly. To them the meaning of baptism was not found in Romans chapter six or Colossians chapter two; rather, it was in the simple stories of Jesus and John the Baptist on the shores of the Jordan or Philip and the eunuch at the pool in Gaza. The meaning of communion was not in I Corinthians, but in the Upper Room stories of the gospels. Therefore, I resolved to use lots of illustrations as vehicles to convey my thoughts to the people. For example, I began to illustrate my message on how to receive the gifts of the Holy Spirit by tossing out candy to the audience. Because they had no problem receiving the free candy, it was easy for them to make the transition to understanding that they could also receive God's gifts just as freely. On one occasion, when I returned to the same area where I had used this illustration on my visit several years before, I was greeted as "the candy man" because of the impact of the illustration. Another sermon illustration I used to talk about the importance of what enters into our inner man through our eyes and ears and what comes out of our inner man through our mouths involves my Mister Potato Head toy that I have renamed as "Minister Potato Head." Wherever I use that illustration, I get repeated questions about my friend when I come back to the area — even years later. I discovered that illustrations don't have to be elaborate to be effective. When preaching about spiritual keys, I learned to simply pull my key ring out of my pocket and point to each key as I make the individual points. I learned to stop on the way into the church and pull a couple large leaves off a plant when ministering about Adam and Eve. For a lasting impression on the congregation, I would simply call up a couple from the audience to try to hide modestly behind those leaves. I discovered that messages about the armor of God were infinitely more effective if I brought in some army gear to hold up when I was talking. I did, however, decide that I might have gone a little overboard when I used fireworks to demonstrate a point and accidentally started a fire in the church. Of course, that was always the desire of the old-time Pentecostal preachers – to "set the church on fire"!

On one trip to Colombia, one seemingly insignificant incident started a rather unusual turn of events concerning illustrated sermons. Just before we left the US, a local pharmacy offered M&Ms on a free-after-rebate sale; so, I picked up a bag to give to our host in the county. When I handed him the package, he excitedly exclaimed, "Oh, we've been looking for these!" It turned out that another guest teacher was in town to teach at the local Bible college. He had a lesson scheduled for the following day that was based around an illustration using M&Ms. They had spent hours that very day looking in a number of local markets and stores for the M&Ms, but had not found them any place they had looked. This unusual event demonstrated to us that God was orchestrating our steps – even in what seemed to be very mundane things.

I continually hear pastors say that they wish they could have received this kind of teaching at the beginning of their ministries so that they could have built upon a solid foundation rather than shaky sands. Once a pastor complimented me by saying that my teachings were "simple but not simplistic." One critique that I received from a pastor in Hungary so aptly defined the validity of Mark Twain's observation concerning effective communication, "The difference between the right word and almost the right word is the difference between lightning and a lightning bug." Without knowing anything of Samuel Clemens' quote, the Hungarian pastor commented, "Your messages were like lightning to us."

In Uganda, both Peggy and I ministered on Sunday morning and then at a couples' dinner that evening. We were really impressed by the spiritual hunger demonstrated in the pastors' meetings and the ladies' conferences as the delegates sat for hours drinking in our teachings. Even when we offered them a break, the people insisted that they keep ministering! The theme of the conferences and the topic of most of the ministry was based on my book, *People Who Make A Difference*. Due to the overwhelming response from the local pastors, even though I had brought a large shipment of books – even paying overweight charges to bring them on the plane – the supply was not sufficient to meet the need. Extra copies of the book had to be run off at the last minute at a local print shop, and everyone was thrilled to receive a free copy of the book to go along with the verbal teaching in the class. Both Peggy and I received innumerable comments praising the clarity of the presentation and how the material was so profoundly insightful and relevant. One young man even composed a song based on the focus points in the book. Almost everyone added that the teachings were exactly what they needed to hear at exactly that time!

On one occasion when leading a conference in Hungary, I slipped in a quick example based on the story of the four lepers in II Kings chapter seven even though I was just about out of the time I had been allotted. The next day, a pastor told me that the Lord had spoken to him concerning that story about two weeks prior and he had spent those two weeks wondering what the story was supposed to mean to him. During my short explanation from the story, he got the necessary revelation to apply the message to his own life and ministry. At one church where I spoke on hindrances to answered prayer, I noticed that the people seemed especially intent on the message and that they were all taking lots of notes. When the pastor took the microphone after I had finished speaking, I understood why. He had been teaching a series on prayer and had ministered a message entitled, "We Don't Really Know How to Pray" in the service just two days before. He assured the congregation that he had not talked to me before the service about the current emphasis on prayer in the church.

The pastor at another church specifically asked that I teach on discipleship, so I ministered from one of my recent books and gave him a copy to study. When I saw him the next day, he had already read the full book and had made a decision to implement the program in his church. Another pastor took the book and said that he felt that it was the answer he had been looking for in his ministry among the gypsy groups in Hungary. After one service, a pastor who was visiting from another church called the next day to say that he had spent all morning on the phone calling all his friends to invite them to the next service. In a follow-up meeting with the leadership of one congregation, I was asked why I chose the specific topic I ministered on. The reason they asked such a question was that it specifically addressed the present needs of the church. At another church, the pastor told me that he had been having meetings with his leadership team over the previous few weeks to try to find out why the church had "lost its edge" and that the message I delivered was the exact answer to their question. The founder of a large, well-respected ministry that reaches throughout all of Eastern Europe remarked to the local pastor that he had never heard such preaching before and asked if it would be possible to arrange for me to come into the other countries where his organization operates.

On our closing session together, I had felt directed to minister on the message of "Doors, Windows, and Gates" from my book, Interface. However, I was struggling a bit with that prompting since I had been focusing on the same message in so many recent meetings and didn't want to begin to get into the "one size fits all" rut of thinking that the same message is appropriate for every audience. However, throughout the day, I continued to hear the pastor make references to doors, gates, and gatekeepers. He even made mention of the fact that gates are referred to in Proverbs chapter thirty-one, a passage I had suggested that the single young men read before selecting a wife. Although he had no Idea that I even had a teaching on the biblical significance of gates – much less that I was considering ministering on the topic that evening – he seemed to be peppering his conversation with references to the topic. Just as I was being introduced to minster that evening, Peggy had a prophetic word that again confirmed the message for the night. After the teaching time, Peggy again took the mic and expressed that the Lord was prompting her to ask if anyone needed to be filled with the Holy Spirit. We all were amazed to see the entire group of high school and college age students respond. As they prayed and wept as the Holy Spirit fell upon each of them, the American missionary whispered to me that he had not seen anything like this during his twenty-three years of ministry in the country. After they had all had their own personal encounters with the Holy Spirit, they broke into pairs to pray for one another – a prayer session that lasted until midnight. One other side note to this experience was that we asked the youth to go into a separate room for prayer so that we could continue to minster to the adults. As they were walking into the other area, I felt prompted to ask one particular gentleman to assist in praying for them. He later confided in me that at one time he had been active in ministering to people to receive the baptism in the Holy Spirit and to be healed. Unfortunately, things had happened in his life that had discouraged him and he had stopped that sort of ministry. This opportunity to pray with the students was exactly what he needed to step back into the forefront of leadership within the church – and, with the renewal that is coming in the ministry in Hungary.

Back in Budapest after the camp, we ministered at an all-day conference in one of the local churches. After the meeting had ended, one of the ladies who had not been able to attend the service because she was working in the nursery came to me for prayer. When she mentioned that she occasionally serves as an interpreter for guest speakers, I immediately had a prophetic word for her that she should get ready to see the situation reversed because she would be going to minister in other countries where the people didn't understand either English or Hungarian and she would need people to interpret for her rather than for her to be interpreting for them. When I spoke those words to her, she responded that the exact message had already been spoken over her about two weeks before.

The next day, Pedggy and I ministered at a church where the leadership had read my book on discipleship and made a decision to focus the ministry on discipleship. We ministered to the entire congregation on the importance of discipleship within the Body of Christ and spent the afternoon in personal discussion with the church leadership answering their questions about practical ways to encourage and implement discipleship in the church. When the pastor prayed before I ministered at the service that evening, he petitioned God for open doors – exactly the theme of the message I had on my heart for the congregation. Peggy followed up my teaching with a message on offenses. Most of the congregation responded to the altar call, asking to be healed from wounds they had suffered from offenses. The pastor then confided in us that the sermon was actually a prophetic word for them because the church had just gone through a very painful split two weeks before in which over half the congregation left with two of the associate pastors. Of course, we knew nothing of the troubles within the church before the service, and our visit had been scheduled before the split occurred.

One Sunday morning, I was invited to preach at one of the largest churches in India with an estimated twenty thousand believers in attendance at the service. The Lord had placed a message concerning open doors on my heart for the morning, and the topic was miraculously confirmed as I walked into the building. The first words I heard as I entered the sanctuary were a prayer by one of the staff pastors, "Lord, give us open doors"! After I delivered the sermon, the senior pastor addressed the congregation with a short message in which he quoted the same verse I had preached from and emphasized many of the same points I had brought out, saying, "God has kept an open door before us." In Mumbai, a gentleman testified that he had been asking the Lord to show him if he was on the right path; then, I recounted the story about how Dr. Sumrall had a choice of which route to take on his way to a remote village in Tibet. His guide could take him either around a mountain on the left side or on the right. He felt that the Holy Spirit told him to go around the left side of the mountain, so that's the route he told his guide to take. When they arrived at the village it turned out that bandits, who were hiding on the other side of the mountain, ambushed and killed everyone who came on the right side. As soon as the man heard that story, he knew that the Lord was confirming that he was on the right path. The amazing thing is that I have several stories that I use to illustrate the point about being led by the Spirit, and I generally alternate among stories at that point in the message. However, I just felt impressed to tell that specific story on that particular day.

At a class in the Bible college in India, many of the students came up to express their appreciation for the teaching, saying that they had been grappling with the exact issues discussed in the classes. One young man showed me his notebook where he had written down some of the exact verses that I had discussed in the classes. He then went on to say that he had marked them the previous week and had been meditating on what they could mean in his life. As I taught the lesson, their meaning finally came alive to him. When I taught at one of the extension Indian campuses that had used the videos of my *Finally, My Brethren* class, one student said that all the students were "glued to the screen" during all the teachings. He followed that comment by saying that there is always some turning around and talking during the videos of other teachers.

I had a similar experience in the Turks and Caicos Islands where a pastor showed some videos of Peggy and me teaching on the family. The people in the congregation asked that he try to get us to come to the islands in person for the next year's convention. Of course, we accepted the invitation – who wouldn't be willing to go to a tropical island in the Caribbean to minister! In addition to the believers who joined us each morning at the church and each evening in the sports arena, we welcomed believers from all the islands in the region who joined us by radio for the full eight days of the conference. In fact, when we had some free time to do souvenir shopping, we met several vendors in the market who knew us because they had been listening to the meetings on the radio while they managed their shops that week.

It is always exciting to teach leaders as I am able to share how the scriptural principles of evangelism and disciple making must go hand-in-hand in order to fulfill the Great Commission, and to explain how the church has been robbed of its most powerful tool through the misconception that disciple making requires a special level of qualification and education. I believe that this revelation opens the door to a whole new dimension of effective ministry for these leaders. Many times,

286

delegates approach me after such trainings to express their appreciation for opening their eyes to this biblical principle.

Shortly after we were married, Peggy and I arrived in Sri Lanka to minister in a youth camp that had been arranged for the Christian high school and college students. When our host picked us up at the airport, he announced that we were going to have to cancel the retreat. He then went on to explain that the country was encountering a severe drought and that there was no water in the cisterns at the retreat center. Without water for cooking, cleaning, and washing, it would be impossible to house the group at the camp. I explained that we had spent a lot of money in advance to cover the camp expenses and had flown all the way from America for the event. In my mind, it was impossible to cancel the retreat. There had to be a way to make it work. I asked for just twenty-four hours before he made his final decision. That night we asked the Lord for the windows of heaven to be opened in some miraculous way, and God answered our prayer in an even more dramatic way than I had anticipated! We had the most horrendous rainstorm I have ever experienced. It didn't just "rain cats and dogs"; it was more like lions and wolves. I had never seen anything like it. The rain came down by the bucketsful – no, barrels full. Not only did the cisterns fill to overflowing, the drought that was crippling the nation's agriculture was immediately alleviated. Matthew 5:45 says that God allows it to rain upon the just and the unjust alike. In His goodness, God gave the Hindus and the Buddhists – not just the Christians – the rains that saved that year's crops! It wasn't until I revisited Sri Lanka almost thirty years later and was asked by one of the prominent pastors of the country to preach in his church that I saw proof of the remaining effect of the night that the windows of heaven were opened. That pastor who is now a significant leader in the country was called into the ministry as a high school student in that camp that would have been canceled had God not opened the windows of heaven.

One major aspect of what I try to do on the mission field is to try to make myself unnecessary by awakening the people to the fact that they can learn from the Bible themselves without having to have an outsider come teach them. After training a group in Hungary in the Be Fruitful and Multiply Bible study approach, I prompted them as they did a study on their own in small groups. The passage they were to study was only six verses long, but I seemed to have some difficulty getting the groups to keep progressing through the sequence of questions that are involved in this study method. As I would prod them to move to discussion of the next topic, one gentleman answered me, "The time is too short, because the message is big even when the passage is little." Everyone was thrilled to see how many new insights they received from familiar passages that they thought they already knew very well. In fact, when we had a testimony time later in the camp, I continued to hear references made to the revelations that had been gained during these morning Bible study sessions.

Peggy and I, in addition to our ministry of holding pastors' and leaders' and women's conferences around the world, have also realized that another major aspect of our ministry must be to train others to go into all the world with the gospel. Therefore, we lead several trips each year in which we focus on motivating and equipping others to become missions-minded and missions-hearted.

On one mission to the Dominican Republic, the group of teenagers had to raise over twenty thousand dollars to cover the expenses of the trip, but they were determined to go – no matter what they had to do to make it happen. The kids dedicated their summer to various work projects to earn the money. They had bake sales and garage sales, washed windows, did yard work, painted fences, and even remodeled a kitchen. It was an exceptionally hot summer but the kids didn't let the heat or exhaustion slow them down; they kept working right up to the day that they had to return to school in the fall. By that point, they had over half the cash in hand. Then, they wrote letters to friends and family asking for help. You should have seen the amazement in their eyes each time they received a check toward the trip! By the time winter hit, the money was all in and we began to focus on the trip itself – learning a few key Spanish phrases, preparing dramas to perform in the meetings in the Dominican, practicing singing together, and trying to get over stage fright and shyness by giving testimonies in the youth meetings – but most of all, praying together for the trip. This was not only the first time for most of these students to go outside the country; for most it was also their first time on an airplane. So there were lots of fears to overcome, such as fear of flying and, even more importantly, fear of bugs. These months of preparation had a powerful uniting effect on the youth group. Working together brought them all – guys, gals, black, white, Hispanic – to a place of trusting in and depending upon one another in a way that would never have happened otherwise. More importantly, it was also a time of learning how to trust and depend on God! As for the bugs, rather than running away when we found a tarantula in the dining room, they all ran to see it and even gave it a name!

Finally, Christmas break arrived and we were off on the adventure of a lifetime. Although the trip was short, it was intense and packed with lots of activities. We arrived in Santiago late on Tuesday night and only had time for a midnight snack before settling into our rooms at La Casa Grande. Wednesday was to be a big day in that we were expecting to receive two forty-foot containers of food from Feeding the Nations. Although the containers had arrived two weeks earlier, they had not been cleared because one key agent was on Christmas vacation. Now that he was back, the containers could be released as soon as the extra storage fee was paid. Although the delay was the vacationing official's fault, the missionary was responsible for the late charges. It would take most of the day to get the money transferred, but we didn't worry too much since we didn't need the food until Friday. The teens spent the morning visiting the neighborhood announcing the children's meeting that was scheduled for Friday. This outreach gave them an opportunity to visit in homes and pass out gospel tracts. This was the first time any of our team had ever seen people living in shacks made of scrap wood and sheets of tin with only dirt floors, and it made them thankful for the nice homes they had back in America. Before we completed our sweep through the neighborhood, it started to rain. At lunch we prayed for the rain to stop because the afternoon schedule included an open-air crusade in the city park. The rain stopped just as we got to the park, so we set up the portable sound system and began to sing. As a crowd began to gather, the teens presented a drama entitled "Bondage," which depicts a young lady who wants to come to Jesus but is bound by chains representing lust, greed, and addiction. After the missionary preached, almost a dozen came forward to receive the Lord. The youth team helped pray for the people and went throughout the crowd passing out tracts. After the program, we visited the open-air market and the local shopping area to distribute tracts. That evening we participated in a local church service where the team presented the drama, sang, gave testimonies, and prayed for the individuals who came forward at the altar call.

Thursday we awoke to the news that our containers were still not out of customs. This time there was a problem with one of the documents; the officers had a photocopy of one form but insisted that they have the original. We knew that we had to pray because we could not wait any longer since we had two big food distributions scheduled for the next day. Before the prayer, I shared from Romans 8:26-28 concerning the necessity of having the Holy Spirit's assistance in our prayers. When we don't know how to pray, the Spirit intervenes and prays in perfect alignment with the will of God so that we can know that all things will work out to our best. At that point, several of the students admitted that they had never experienced that kind of Spirit-led prayer but said that they needed it for the present situation and for their lives in general. Our prayer focus shifted from the containers to the team members. As we ministered to each individual, everyone was deeply touched and many began to sob as they experienced deep inner healing. Some testified that the Lord had drawn them into a closer relationship with Himself so that they knew they could now make better decisions and live better lives even around their non-Christian friends and classmates. One girl who was nearing her senior year of high school said that she had no idea what God had planned for her life but that God had used this prayer session as a time to answer many things she had been praying about and showed her what she was going to be doing in her future. After the prayer, we spent time learning some songs in Spanish and went to the supermarket to pass out tracts.

About midafternoon, we received word that the containers were released from customs but that the delivery company wasn't going to bring them that day since it was about a four-hour trip and it was too late in the day to start. Again we prayed, and suddenly we received a phone call stating that the trucks were on the road! We used the rest of the afternoon putting together gift bags for the next day's children's outreach. By divine provision, we had toys with us in our luggage rather than in the containers! When the work was done, the kids had free time for a swim – something they really enjoyed, especially when they remembered that it was freezing back home! When the containers arrived at 7 PM, the drivers told us that it would take until 2 AM to unload them since we were going to do the job by hand. But when the team, along with some local volunteers, jumped into the trucks and started hauling out the boxes, they amazed everybody by finishing the job in one hour and fifteen minutes! Then we turned our energy to getting everything into storage – a job that took the next two and a half hours. The missionary was amazed to hear the kids singing while they worked because he wasn't singing as he labored with the task. He said that the kids' joy was an encouragement to him. Once everything was in storage, we turned our focus to packing the food boxes that were to be distributed at the pastors' conference the following day. It was well past midnight when we folded the last flap on the final box, but the kids were still laughing and singing!

We realized that it was perfect timing that the containers came when they did, not only because they arrived just in time for the two distributions scheduled for the following day, but also because we were able to unload them at night without attracting a lot of attention from neighbors who would have lined up at the gate asking for handouts if the trucks had arrived during the daytime. If the containers had been released when they first arrived, the missionary would have had to unload them without the help of the youth team and the team would not have had the experience of actually moving that much missionary support. In addition, because it was night, the heat was not as intense while we worked.

One thing that we stress when we take out mission teams is the flexibility beatitude, "Blessed is he who is flexible because he will not get bent out of shape."

And we generally have ample opportunity to put that principle into operation — like the time we came to one service prepared to minister to children — with children's messages, skits, and candy — only to discover that it was a teen meeting. Or the time we were to do outdoor ministry in a public park — only to find that the sound system didn't work. After a long time of working with the system, we finally got it working just in time to be caught in a rainstorm as we started presenting the drama. In spite of all the hindrances, we were able to share personally and pray for a number of individuals. One Sunday in Colombia, the team was scheduled to split into three smaller teams and minister at different locations. When the bus arrived at the first church, the pastor there apologized that there was no interpreter because the young woman who was supposed to help had to go out of town at the last minute. However, the few minutes that the team was at the church was just long enough for them to get the report that a man whom they had prayed for the night before was now seeing out the blind eye they had commanded to receive sight. Now, the team had to regroup and reassign the ones who were to minister at that church to the other two teams.

But the lesson in flexibility wasn't over yet. The bus had a flat tire shortly after picking up the students who had ministered at one church, leaving the students at the other church stranded at their church waiting to be picked up. By the time the tire was fixed and the bus arrived at the church, it was too late to stop for lunch before heading to the afternoon service assignment. That was the second lesson in flexibility, but lesson three was still ahead. When the team arrived at the next location, they found that the event was a children's outreach rather than an adult church service as they had been told. They had to totally rearrange the program, substituting children-oriented skits for the adult dramas that had been scheduled, replacing the testimonies and sermon, and frantically blowing up balloons and transforming them into dogs, swords, and flowers before the children arrived. One other miracle of the day was that the leader of the children's ministry had almost stayed back in the dormitory because she had not been feeling well but decided at the last minute to come anyway.

On a different trip to Colombia, we drove two hours from our base in Bogota to minister in a private school in a suburb city on top of the mountain range that surrounds the capital. When we arrived, we received news that the program had been canceled. However, our host stopped by the local parochial school and inquired about the possibility of our presenting a chapel service there. The school administrator gladly accepted our offer and arranged for us to return after a visit that we had scheduled with a nearby orphanage. After presenting skits, playing games, and giving out gifts at the children's home, we arrived punctually at the front door of the school – only to be greeted with news that the school board had overruled the administrator's invitation. However, before we pulled out of the school's parking lot, we received a message that the local public high school had opened their doors for the team to come for the full afternoon of activities with their four-hundred-member student body. We were informed that the director of the school was an atheist; however, she was eager to offer her students an opportunity to interact with native English speakers even though she realized that our intent would be to incorporate the gospel into our time with the students. The team presented a high-energy interactive program including skits dealing with the emotional difficulties that adolescents deal with, a dance routine that the high schoolers could join in with, and testimonies about how Jesus had rescued our team members from issues that these students were also subject to – abuse, peer pressure, drug and alcohol abuse, and promiscuity.

As we concluded the formal presentation, the English teacher – who happened to be a believer – requested that we extend our time to allow the students to practice their language skills by asking questions. Each question proved to be an opportunity for the team members to share more details of their testimonies. When we offered free copies of the gospel of John in Spanish, almost every student eagerly accepted with some asking for extra copies to take home to siblings and parents. At another school, we had several hundred students gather on the soccer field for an afternoon of activities. Just when we got them all on their feet ready for an interactive dance routine, the sound system went out. So, we had to get them all back down on the ground for an alternate part of the program. As soon as they were all seated, the music came on again. So, we asked them to stand up again – just in time for the speaker to go out again. Back down on the ground again, and the sound system decided to cooperate; back up on their feet, and it decided not to cooperate. Believe it or not, this happened five times! But, my team just kept going in spite of the repeated difficulties – doing yo-yo tricks, juggling, and anything else necessary to keep the students' attention as we worked through the problems.

As I've shared about the ministry that Peggy and I have had around the world, I've made a number of references to the books that I taught from and distributed in the many seminars and church services where we have ministered. One major aspect of our ministry has been the writing and distribution of teaching books. I consider that leaving behind tangible written materials for the people's further study is a valuable way of making our impact even more permanent and multipliable. You may remember that my writing career began when I won that national writing contest as a grammar school student, but you may be surprised that I barely passed a creative writing class in college. The ironic thing about the course was that the instructor graded the students on their improvement during the semester. Since I used all the skills that I had learned in the Palmer Writers School when writing my first assignment, there really wasn't much left for the university professor to add during the term. But let me share the most dramatic episode concerning my writing career. On one of our vacations in the Bahamas, we attended a church that we had visited on a previous holiday. This time there was a new associate pastor, whom we had not previously met. After praise and worship, the associate stepped up to the microphone to say, "I know that we will greet all our visitors in a few minutes, but first I have a word from the Lord for this couple," as he pointed to us. Immediately, he began to prophesy to me, saying that I was a writer and that my books would impact nations all around the world. I was "blown away" with the accuracy of the prophetic word and the courage that it must have taken for him to give such a specific word to a total stranger. He then turned to Peggy and prophesied that her ministry of her books would be even more impactful than mine! And, indeed, we have seen her *Women for the Harvest* book translated into far more languages than any of mine and its circulation has outstripped that of any of my individual titles.

I have had the privilege of personally presenting copies of my books to the Vice President of Liberia and the wife of the Vice President of Kenya, and I am happy that many ministers and ministries around the world have seen the value of my writings. For example, in southern India, five thousand copies of the Tamil version of my book on discipleship were printed for distribution among the Christian leaders in the region. When I preached at a large church in the region, the pastor introduced me by quoting from one of my recent books – mentioning the exact point that I had on my heart to minister that evening. He emphasized his point by saying that he was actually busy with something else when he felt led to stop and read a couple chapters from the book. I had not shared with him what I had planned to preach on, and I'm still not sure how he even obtained a copy of the book since it had not yet been made available for distribution. Only a few copies that I had given to close friends were in circulation. A professional counselor who had an office near the church told me that he used the discipleship approach that I outlined in my book to help couples walk through marital problems, families to work out their interpersonal relationships, and individuals to straighten out their personal issues. I was also surprised to discover that a local Christian magazine is using my materials in their bimonthly publication. I was aware that they had published some of my articles previously, but did not realize that they were continuing to translate and use my materials on an ongoing basis. In fact, they had completed a second book which they had published one chapter at a time in their periodical. They also told me that they were planning to combine the chapters and release the two books as entire volumes in the Telugu language and begin to translate a third book in installments for the magazine. At the pastors' conference in Mumbai, one man told me that he had prayed just the night before for a book to help him understand more about the ministry of Paul, then he received the *Maximum Impact* book which is based on Paul's ministry at the meeting the following morning.

When I was in Niger, the top Christian leaders told me that they didn't want me to come back and hold future seminars. You can imagine how that made me feel – until they finished their sentence, "until we can find a way to get your materials into print for our pastors." Of course, it also works the other way around – sometimes the books open the door for ministry rather than serving as a follow-up. For example, when I walked into the office of a church where I was to preach in Kenya, the pastor showed me a copy of my *Finally, My Brethren* book and said that he had gotten hold of it a couple years before. He then said that ever since he had read the book he wanted me to come to Kenya and preach in his church. In the Philippines, one lady was so moved by the message in Peggy's book that she bought four hundred copies of it to distribute to her friends and business associates.

One surprise advantage of the focus on literature came when we decided to extend our ministry behind the Quran Curtain. The internet posting shouted, "The US government ordered the evacuation of non-essential staff from its consulate in ___ on Friday due to the threat of attack, with the State Department also warning US citizens not to travel to ____." Thus, just days before Peggy's scheduled departure to that country, we had to re-evaluate the decision for Peggy to travel into this region without any male traveling companions. As we watched the situation closely, hoping to see an improvement, we actually witnessed it deteriorate with even more violent terrorist activities.

Eventually we were forced to make the decision to cancel the trip. However, the decision came only after Peggy's book, *Women for the Harvest* was already translated into the national language and three thousand copies had been printed in the country. Even though we were disappointed that we lost the price of the tickets and the opportunity to enter the country, we were thankful for the timing of the travel advisory. Had it come any earlier, we would not have invested in the publication of the materials that impacted the country since Peggy would not have been there to teach it. The translator wrote that he found the book to be a very practical guide, based on all that Peggy had learned from her ministry in many countries around the world. He and his ministry team saw the distribution of the book to be a launching pad for new women's ministries in unreached villages and a

298

corrective to the attitude of most of the senior pastors in the country's church, who have taught women to remain silent. He reported that he had received many very positive comments from those who had a chance to read the book. One call came from a lady of high position in one of the leading Muslim hospitals in the country. She testified that even though she is the daughter of a prominent pastor and the wife of another leading pastor, she had never heard any teaching like what she found in the book. She then added that she could see that everything in the book was correct according to the Bible and that she is now a big "fan" of Peggy Shirley! In Peggy's absence, the translator's wife boldly preached and shared from the book in women's meetings around the country. At the first seminar, all the ladies present were very touched by the words and decided to continue with weekly meetings for prayer and Bible study. They wrote, "We are very much thankful, Miss Peggy Shirley, for publishing this book in our country to awake the women here who are working under pressure and doing hard labor all their lives."

A couple years later, I was first contacted by another Christian leader in this same Islamic-dominated country with the request that my book *People Who Make A Difference* be translated and published in his nation. At first, I questioned if it were even feasible or prudent to do so. After several communications with the gentleman, I discovered that he had a large underground network of pastors and Christian workers who were eager for more training and that he felt that the teachings in the book were exactly what they needed at this time. Just a few weeks before the book was released, several gospel workers were arrested in the very city where the initial distribution of the book was scheduled. There was a lot of chaos among the Christian community over these arrests, but the situation soon settled down and the gentleman who was leading the project was able to return to the city to finalize all the details for the release of the book – an event that drew five hundred participants from sixty different congregations from three different Muslim ethnic groups.

But this rally was just the beginning; our contact continued to distribute the book to pastors in other parts of the country. He wrote concerning the impact that he was seeing from the release of the book, "We believe that God will work out the leadership training of these gospel leaders through this book, and they will become the ones to bring change in this nation." Even though I did not get the opportunity to personally visit this Muslim country, I know that the Lord has given me the privilege of having an impact there through the distribution of the book. The gentleman who did the translation work requested copies of more of my books and wrote, "Personally, I have received blessings and guidance from reading this book and many new things have dawned to me and many questions have been answered. It is my prayer that the good Lord will help you to visit this nation and we want to see a wave of spiritual awakening in this nation. We want to see the church leaders mobilized and understand the great commission in its real essence and be part of spreading the hope of salvation and there should be a change in the community because of their efforts." Peggy and I are actually discipling an entire nation even though we have never set foot on its soil!

I can't close this section without sharing at least one story about the hard work and dedication behind getting the books in the various languages of the world. One of my students at the Bible college was so impacted by the *Finally, My Brethren* class that he translated the book into his native Portuguese for his own personal benefit. When he received the call to move back to Brazil, he determined to get the book published and distributed in the country. Unfortunately, the disk with the translation was damaged in the move. Undaunted, he demonstrated unwavering commitment and started from "scratch" to re-translate the book after arriving in Brazil. This time, he encountered some unexpected difficulties that had not presented themselves when he was in the US. First of all, he discovered that the spoken Portuguese had gone through some transformation during the fifteen years he had been away, meaning that he had to relearn some of the basic grammar rules before he could do the work. Secondly, he discovered that the Portuguese Bible did not read the same as the English Bible he had been using for all those years. Since the book is titled after the English translation of Ephesians 6:10, he turned to his Portuguese Bible for the wording of the title. He was surprised to find that the most common translation in use in Brazil read only, "my brethren," and the second most common translation said, "finally." He was left with a dilemma of how to translate even the front cover – much less, the rest of the book. Furthermore, all the Portuguese versions substitute the word "fight" for "wrestle" and add a second reference to fighting in verse twelve where both the English and Greek leave out the verb. Moreover, the whole concept of wrestling is unfamiliar in Brazil since they don't practice that sport in the country. Unstopped by all the challenges, he continued with the project until he was able to present the finished project at a special celebration during my visit.

Even though humanitarian work is not the focus of our ministry, Peggy and I know that it is the second part of the Great Commandment – to love our neighbors as much as we love ourselves – and that love is the very nature of God. Therefore, we have always been sensitive to respond to the physical needs of those to and with whom we minister. I've already shared a few stories of how we built a house and office for the director in Nepal, but I didn't share that we also bought him a car. I've also told the stories of how we responded to the tsunami in South Asia and about our biggest challenge of all – the earthquake in Nepal. But our humanitarian efforts started on a much smaller scale with simply buying musical instruments for a needy church in Kenya. Unfortunately, when we arrived in the Nairobi airport, the duty officer wanted to charge us a very steep customs fee. Just when we thought that there was no resort other than to pay, the duty officer's superior stepped out of his office on the way to the restroom and noticed that there was a bit of a confrontation at the customs desk. He walked up and told the agent to let us go though with no fee! In Zambia, Peggy and I felt directed to refurnish the office of the pastor we were working with since everything he had in his office was worn out and broken down. When we went to the office supply store, we found that the prices were far higher than what we had expected. Since everything had to be imported and since there was only one store in the city that carried office furniture, the dealer felt justified in inflating the prices. The sales clerk and I began a bit of bargaining over the price as I told her that I was a missionary and asked for a charitable discount. Eventually, she offered me a fifteen percent discount. Still, I continued to press for more by telling her that she was dealing with an individual who had learned to bargain in India and was accustom to negotiating deep discounts. At that, she responded that she had offered me the maximum discount that she was permitted to give and that I'd have to talk to her manager if I wanted anything more. I then asked to see the manager and jokingly suggested that she tell him that he was about to enter into some Indian negotiations. The clerk disappeared to the back offices and returned a few minutes later with her manager who – to my surprise – was an Indian! Well, I was still able to negotiate an extra five percent discount!

Let me just mention some of the other opportunities we have had to demonstrate the Lord's compassion around the world, such as a camera for Uganda, a printer-copier-fax machine combination for the Congo, a motorcycle for Sri Lanka, helping to rebuild the home of missionary friends in Belize after they took a direct hit from a hurricane, and putting a roof on a school in Zimbabwe. Just about one year after a team from Teach All Nations had the privilege of traveling to the Turks and Caicos Islands to hold a week-long conference in the island paradise, Hurricane Irma ravaged that island to the point that it could more easily be mistaken for purgatory rather than paradise. It looked like a war zone. About eighty percent of the city where we had ministered was destroyed but some of the surrounding areas suffered one hundred percent destruction. Fortunately, the family of the pastor who had hosted our team survived the storm, but the same cannot be said about their physical property. Half of the church building was destroyed, and the roof was ripped off of the other half. The pastor's wife had invested all of her life savings into building a kitchen in the church to feed the people, and all of her years of efforts were destroyed in minutes – even before she was able to celebrate the grand opening! But things got even worse when a second hurricane – Maria – swept through within a month, destroying everything that Hurricane Irma had left standing. As soon as we received the news about the catastrophe, Teach All Nations responded with an offering to help them begin to rebuild. The first project in the recovery effort was to rebuild the feeding center. An organization donated a generator so that – even while the city was still without electricity – they could prepare and provide meals for the community. The pastor summed up the situation with, "God has turned the destruction into an opportunity!"

In our travels around the world, working with men and women of God on every continent, we observe first-hand the dedication of the missionaries and national pastors who serve in the nations we have visited. Along with this, we also note the sacrifices that their families have had to make because of the demands of the ministry. Therefore, we decided to dedicate a portion of all our organization's income to assist these families with the expenses of sending their children to college. We have been blessed with the privilege of sending students from Nepal, the Philippines, the Dominican Republic, and the Turks and Caicos Islands to college to prepare for a brighter future.

Saturday Mornings in the Workshop

Dr. Sumrall used to tell the story of a woman who asked him to ordain her so she could do missionary work in India. Knowing that her husband and none of her half a dozen or so children were believers, he used a play on words to respond to her, "First, you go home and get your own tribe of Indians saved – starting with that big chief!" Although this answer was a little gruff – typical of Dr. Sumrall – it was actually good biblical advice. Abraham – the first man in history to be given a global mission when God told him that every family in the whole world would be blessed through him (Genesis 12:3) – was chosen because God knew that he would first instruct his own family (Genesis 18:19). Peggy and I, also, have always realized that our first priority and responsibility had to be to the family that the Lord entrusted to us; so, we decided to raise our boys "by the book"!

You may remember that we had to move up our wedding from after my seminary graduation in June to my spring break in March because of my mother-in-law's trip to China. However, the honeymoon was already scheduled for June and we couldn't move it earlier to coincide with the new wedding date. The result was that we were actually surprised during our honeymoon with the possibility that Peggy was already pregnant with our first son Jonathan, who had been conceived just six weeks into our marriage. Our second son was "supposed" to be a girl. Well, at least that is what the ultrasound showed. Of course, those were the very early days of ultrasound technology and the systems were not very sophisticated. In fact, they were so inaccurate that the expectant parents were not allowed to see the images and only doctors were permitted to interpret the pictures. We actually had "It's a girl" birth announcements and a "Mommy's little girl" dress to bring "her" home from the hospital that I had to go exchange once Christopher was born. Our third son almost didn't come because I was certain that our quiver was full with just two boys. (Psalm 127:5) However, Peggy was insistent that our quiver would not be complete without that little girl that she had been "cheated out of" with Christopher. She kept hinting – well, much more than just hinting – and I kept resisting – well, maybe I was a little more stubborn than simply resistant. (At any rate, finding baby dolls tucked into my bed each night didn't convince me.) However, during one of my trips to Israel, I was asking the Lord to clarify some decisions that I needed to make concerning my future when He answered that one more child was part of His plan. So, needless to say, Peggy was happy that she was right – or at least partially. When we went in for the ultrasound exam, the nurse told us to go ahead and start shopping for Barbie dolls, but Peggy asked her to please make certain since she didn't want a repeat of the scenario with Christopher. After a second look, the nurse responded, "No, on second thought, maybe you should get some GI Joes" because our third son Jeremy was on the way.

When we were young parents, the most popular parenting book on the market happened to be *The Strong-Willed Child* by Focus on the Family's James Dobson. Since Jonathan had always resisted going to bed at night and would climb out of his crib and stand at his bedroom door pleading for us to come let him out until he would fall asleep at the door, we assumed that he was the perfect candidate for all of Dr. Dobson's strategies. It turned out that Jonathan is actually the most easy-going and compliant of all our boys – perhaps a testimony to the success of Dr. Dobson's training, but more likely because it is his inborn nature that we simply misdiagnosed. At any rate, he was raised under very strict conditions – in fact, such stringent restrictions that when he became an adult we felt that we should apologize to him. We realized that in raising him "by the book," we had not necessarily raised him by the Book. Therefore, we refocused our parenting style, making the main focus just being there as part of their lives. Peggy made a practice of having a "mother-son date" with one of the boys each week – a time to go out for an ice cream, visit the toy store, or just find some other way to let him know that he was special to her. By the time Jeremy came along, we had abandoned the strong-willed child model so completely that Jonathan and Christopher noticed how much we had changed our technique and actually accused us of letting their little brother "get away with murder."

My job at the Bible college was very demanding. I was at the school all day every day and usually there for night school at least one or two nights each week. The church ministry required me to be in all the services: Sunday morning, Sunday evening, and Thursday evening, all the elder board meetings, and all the special events – which we had a lot of! Essentially, I had only one day each week to spend with the boys – Saturday, which also happened to be my fix and repair day. Therefore, one thing that I programed into every week so that I could spend some father-sons time with the boys was Saturday morning in the workshop. I've often said that I never aspired to be a bicycle or small appliance repairman, but I became a master in both fields simply because my aim in life was to be a good husband and father. It has never ceased to amaze me how many broken things accumulated on my workbench by Friday night each week or how there was always some new project that Peggy had placed on the "to-do list." So, Saturday was the official fix-it day – and a great opportunity to bond with my boys. I took them into the workshop every Saturday and taught them a few handyman skills – how to use all the tools, how to figure out what was broken and strategize how to repair it – and all the simple rules that make things work right: "Measure twice and cut once," "If it's worth doing, it's worth doing right," "Always measure each individual cut, and never use one thing that you've cut as the pattern for another cut"… Of course, I could have repaired all the broken stuff a lot quicker had I been alone at my workbench, but that wasn't the point. My objective wasn't to make bicycles and small appliances work again; it was to pass on my life to the three boys that God had entrusted to me. As the title of a book by S. Truett Cathy – founder of Chick-fil-A – says, "It's Better to Build Boys than Mend Men." By working side-by-side with me, they not only learned how to use tools, they also learned all-important life qualities such as competence and confidence – quality traits that showed up in more places than in a workshop.

As soon as our chores were finished, we were four kids ready to play – a bike ride to the nearby ice cream parlor, heading to Grandma's lake house in the summer, or snow sledding down Erskine Hill in the winter. Oh, and did we ever have fun with all these adventures – like the time when Jonathan and I didn't even realize that we were out in twenty-degrees-below-zero weather until we came back home or the time that Jeremy cut right in front of a speed boat on his Uncle Bill's wave runner, putting his life and mine within inches – or maybe even millimeters – of ending! One of our favorite adventures was building a treehouse in the woods behind our house. It was a spacious project that could accommodate all the kids in the neighborhood, and it was accompanied with a very high rope swing that made even adults a bit queasy since it swung so far out. Of course, the boys' go cart and all the trails that we carved through the woods also helped make the Shirley home the most popular house on the block.

Because we lived only a couple hours' drive from Chicago, we could make one-day trips into the city for museums, the aquarium, and the zoos. One thing that we especially enjoyed was the official inauguration of the Christmas season with the parade and the lighting of the Miracle Mile. It was a spectacular event as the decorations on each block would illuminate as a special motorcade of celebrities would pass down Lakeshore Drive. One year we arrived just as the lighting was to begin. Of course, it was next to impossible to find a parking place in Chicago at any time – much less during such a special event, and especially at the last minute. However, we simply followed the policemen as they directed the city traffic in preparation for the parade. In some freak turn of events that I have yet to figure out, a patrolman waved us onto Lakeshore Drive just as the motorcade began its process. He had essentially placed us as the lead car in the parade! When we finally realized exactly what had happened, we decided to just play along and slowly cruised the street, waving at all the people who had lined the streets to watch the parade and celebrating the illumination of the Second City's Christmas lights as we approached each block.

In all our fun and games, there was always time for learning – like lessons on centrifugal versus centripetal force while standing in line waiting our turn to ride the up-side-down roller coaster at Six Flags, stops to examine cocoons and talk about the metamorphosis of the life cycles of moths and butterflies, late-night trips to Indiana Dunes to lie on the beach and watch shooting stars during the summer meteor showers, trips to Uncle John's farm to learn about the differences between the bulls and the cows...The list could go on and on, but I can't stop without mentioning the time that I "pulled rank" as a member of the school board to get my boys out of school during the solar eclipse. While all the other children were locked inside because of the principal's fear that they might look at the sun and damage their eyes, my boys were the only ones who got to go outside and look through the protective glass of my friend's welding mask to watch the astronomical phenomenon of the moon "gobbling up" the sun.

I also enjoyed reading to the boys every night before putting them to bed – a time for them to learn a wealth of facts and develop a real curiosity about the world around them. This expansion of their interests has served them well in life, making them conversant in almost every field of interest. But the benefits of this book-reading practice didn't just help the boys. It also provided me with one unexpected little bonus. It began with our first family cruise experience, which occurred not long after seeing the movie *Titanic*. We all recalled the dramatic scenes from the movie as we took part in the initial activity on board the ship – an emergency evacuation drill, complete with life vests and orderly assembly at our assigned muster stations, which Jeremy called the "mustard station." After that cruise experience, he wanted me to read to him about famous shipwrecks – pirate ships in the Caribbean, gold-laden Spanish galleons in the South Atlantic, the Titanic in the North Atlantic, and ghost ships in the Great Lakes. Soon after having finished one particular book, Peggy and I traveled on a mission trip. As we were returning home, the final leg of our trip was the flight from Chicago to South Bend. The stewardess on the flight announced that they were going to have a contest sponsored by one of the passengers on the plane – the owner of one of the most exclusive restaurants in Chicago. He had offered to give dinner for two to the passenger who could guess the depth of Lake Michigan that we were flying over. Well, since one of the stories in Jeremy's book was about a ship that rested in the depths of that same lake and since the book had specifically mentioned exactly how far the divers had to explore beneath the surface of the lake to find the sunken ship, I knew the precise answer to the question – earning Peggy and me a wonderful night on the town in Chicago!

Another important key to nurturing my boys was to take them to church and all the children's ministry events such as Vacation Bible School and summer camp. Some of our fondest memories were forged at the father-son camps where we learned all sorts of outdoor skills from archery to sailing – including how to capsize a sailboat. But that was just the crust of their spiritual education; the meat was our nightly Bible reading and prayer time where they learned that they could relate to and trust their Heavenly Father the same way they could relate to and trust their earthly father. And then there was one bold prayer that I prayed over my boys – a prayer that I've never heard of anyone else praying: "Never get away with anything!" I'm not sure what inspired me to pray such a radical prayer other than the fact that I didn't want them to ever develop the attitude that they wouldn't have to face the consequences of their actions. I don't know for sure that my prayer worked with every bit of mischief that they got into, but it was effective enough that they all learned how to take responsibility for all their deeds. Needless to say, I had to accompany them to the principal's office on more occasions that I care to remember, and even before the judge's bench. But that's a story all its own, and I expect that the boy involved will have to share it on his own. However, the thing that always impressed me when we were faced with such situations was that my sons were always able to handle themselves with a maturity far beyond what would be expected of boys their age. I've always considered their ability to calmly and confidently stand before intimidating authority figures to be a result of the skills and principles they picked up in those Saturday morning sessions in the workshop. Today, all my sons are mature young men, and there is something significant in their lives that was placed there during those Saturday mornings in the workshop. Yes, they all have certain handyman skills and problem-solving abilities that they gleaned from our little projects together – but more importantly they have some of my personality and character that rubbed off during our time together.

As a mentor to my boys, I understood that my job was to help them think properly so that they could act, live, and mature properly. Proverbs 23:7 proclaims, "For as he thinketh in his heart, so is he." Notice that Solomon used the word "as," indicating that it is <u>how</u> we think – not <u>what</u> we think. That determines who we will be. If <u>what</u> we think about was the determining factor, all American boys would become convertible sports cars by the time they were sixteen; by the time they reached twenty-one, they would all have turned into girls; and they would all be a million dollars by age thirty. In raising my sons, I was constantly aware as they were going through these stages of concentration on cars, girls, and money but I knew that no matter how much they meditated on these things, they would never become them. On the other hand, I was keenly aware that the <u>way</u> they were thinking about those topics would determine who they were to become. Therefore, I saw that my role as their father was to guide them in <u>how</u> to think about cars, girls, and money. Thinking <u>about</u> cars would never make them actually become automobiles, but the <u>way</u> they thought about cars would determine the kind of drivers they would become. I knew that I needed to focus on helping them think of cars as something other than toys, status symbols, and weapons. Otherwise, it would be dangerous to be on the road at the same time with them – and I would never be able to afford the insurance premiums! Thinking <u>about</u> girls would never make them actually become women, but the <u>way</u> they thought about girls would determine the kind of husbands they would become. Consequently, I knew that I needed to focus on helping them think of girls as something other than sex objects or ego enhancers – otherwise, they would become abusive husbands with no hope of happy, stable marriages. Thinking <u>about</u> money would never make them actually become dollar bills, but the <u>way</u> they thought about money would determine the kind of spenders and investors they would become. Therefore, I knew that I needed to focus on helping them think of money as a tool to accomplish their goals and as seed for sowing into the future – otherwise, they would be facing a future characterized by unhealthy greed and debilitating debt.

I was especially pleased with the amount of maturity that one particular son developed concerning material possessions. When some boys from a nearby neighborhood began to befriend the boys on our block, we thought that it was good that our kids were expanding their circle of friends. However, it didn't take us long to notice that these new boys seemed to be a bit "street smart." And before long, bicycles – including our son's – came up missing. When we began to investigate, a policeman friend of mine told me that the boys worked for a man in their neighborhood who had them steal bikes so he could strip them down and sell the parts. Unfortunately, even though the police knew what was happening, they weren't able to get the hard evidence needed to arrest him. Even though my young son was heartbroken over the loss, he faced the loss with his chin up. Later, as a teenager, he took a serious fall while mountain biking and had to leave his bike hidden behind some bushes while a passerby picked him up and brought him home to get bandaged up. When we went back to pick up the bike, we spotted a car driving off with the bike sticking out of the trunk. Unfortunately, we couldn't get to the scene fast enough to catch the thieves. Again, he was devastated at the loss of an expensive bike, but he also took this loss in stride. And then there was the time that he sold a laptop on eBay to a customer who was actually running a scam by paying with a hacked PayPal account. By the time that PayPal reversed the funds, the computer was already shipped off with no way of retrieving it. Again, there was a momentary anger and frustration, but it was soon replaced with the awareness that it was only a material object that he could eventually replace. His biggest loss was when someone stole his four-wheeler out of the driveway and escaped down a dirt road near our house. Because he used this backroad, the police were not able to locate the culprit. Unfortunately, we discovered after the fact that the vehicle was not covered by our homeowner's insurance. Again, he took his loss with a positive attitude that far exceeded what would have been expected from a young man of his age.

I'd like to compare these experiences with an incident that happened to one of our other sons. When our boys were in kindergarten and grade school, Peggy and I were actively ministering in Nepal by taking annual trips. Since colleges usually end their school years earlier than other schools, we always found it convenient to travel as soon as the school term for the Bible college ended. That way, the boys would be in school part of the day and the sitter only had to take care of them for the other part of the day. The one thing that we overlooked (We actually weren't even aware of it.) was that there would be a graduation ceremony for the kindergarten class while we were gone. Of course, the sitter took care of all the details and took photographs of the event for us to see as soon as we got home. We, of course, "made a big fuss" about our son's accomplishment, but somehow missed the fact that our absence from this event had actually made a huge emotional scar upon his little heart. It wasn't until he was an adult that he opened up and shared with us about how much he was hurt by our absence and how it had affected him during his developmental years. Of course, there are many differences that have to be taken into consideration. The kindergarten incident happened to him at a much younger age than the age at which my other son was when he experienced all the thefts and the different temperaments of the two boys. However, I believe that the real difference was the fact that one boy lost things: bikes, a computer, and an ATV while the other's loss was the presence of his mom and dad – the one thing that he had learned, through those Saturday mornings together in the workshop, to be the most significant element in life.

All my boys are heroes in their own rights. One Sunday evening, Christopher reached under the church pew and picked up a loose gemstone he saw on the carpet. He whispered to his mother, "I'm a rich man! I have a diamond!" She, of course, thought that it was just a rhinestone that had fallen out of someone's costume jewelry and tossed it into her coin purse. The next day at work, I looked up from my desk to notice a lady from the congregation walking around the church with a flashlight. I jokingly told her that when Jesus said we should be the light of the world He didn't mean for us to walk around carrying flashlights. When she explained that she was looking for the diamond that had fallen out of her wedding ring, I told her that my son had found it and invited her to stop by the house after school so he could return it to her. I wanted Christopher to be there to hand her the diamond and know that he had done something that really made a difference in someone else's life. Interestingly enough, this same son also found a wedding ring for a honeymooning couple who were swimming off a pier in Tahiti. When the bride came out of the water in a panic, Christopher dove down to the sandy bottom and came back up holding the lost wedding band. On another occasion, Christopher actually saved my life by pulling me ashore when I ran out of energy while swimming in the Bahamas. And Jonathan saved his uncle's life by pulling him to safety after the uncle suffered a heart attack while riding a wave runner in the middle of the lake. Again, I always credit the lessons in the workshop on those Saturday mornings toward making them the heroes they became.

It is often said that the family that prays together stays together. This is certainly true, but there is an even more powerful spiritual dimension which the Lord has made available to help protect and strengthen our families. In my own personal life, I have discovered that God has given me a really wonderful Helper to enable me to fulfill my responsibilities and accomplish my expectations as a husband and father. He is the Holy Spirit. When Jonathan was in that transition stage in life and beginning to take on adult responsibilities, we had to leave him behind as we left for our family vacation because he couldn't get time off from his job. Even though he was missing the "trip of a lifetime" in Tahiti, he relished the idea of being his own man since this would be his first time in the house with no parents or sitter. It was probably more difficult for us than for him for exactly the same reason – this was his first time in the house with no parents or sitter. We, of course, missed him but had a great time anyway. One day while snorkeling through the emerald green waters of this tropical paradise, I had a sudden awareness that my son was in danger and needed my intercession. While still surrounded by an array of gorgeously colored tropical fish and beautifully tinted coral reefs, I whispered a prayer for him. When we were able to call home, I received the news that an elderly gentleman, blinded by the late afternoon sun, had failed to stop at a red light and plowed into my son's car as Jonathan passed through the intersection with a green light. We later calculated that, due to the time zone differences, his green light and my prayer in the green waters were at exactly the same minute! It was a very serious accident

316

which totaled Jonathan's car but left him essentially unscathed. When we viewed what was left of the car upon returning from our trip, we were all amazed that he had not been killed or at least seriously injured. He had been protected by the prayers from thousands of miles away, prompted by the Holy Spirit.

We serve a wonderful God who wants to bless us with the desires of our hearts, and He has the most unusual ways of doing so! A number of years ago, I had a desire to take my family on a vacation to Europe, but such a trip was nothing more than a "pipe dream" on our budget. However, we could afford a trip to Florida because my mother-in-law had a home there. All we had to pay for was the airline ticket, which I was able to get at an almost unbelievable discount. We made it as far as Atlanta, but were told that the flight from there was overbooked by five seats – just the number in our party. When I offered up our seats in exchange for a later flight and compensation toward future travel, the airline agent went to work to rebook us. After a good while at her computer, she looked up and explained that the other flights she wanted to get us on were also overbooked. My response was, "Well, just bump us off of those flights too." Before we left her desk, we had free dinner vouchers, a hotel room in Atlanta for the night, free breakfast vouchers, and three thousand dollars' worth of free airline travel! When we added in the mileage points we had earned for the trip and the points we earned from buying the tickets on our credit card, we were able to fly to Europe for free! Now, to put this miracle in perspective, the airline statistics for that particular year showed that only one out of every five thousand travelers was bumped off a flight. Of course we have to remember that there were five of us bumped off of two consecutive flights, making the probability more like one in fifty thousand! Imagine that! Our God certainly knows how to work the odds in favor of His kids! When we started working on our plans for the dream vacation to Europe, we decided to travel through Switzerland, Italy, and Greece on the Eurorail because they offer a pass that allows the passenger to go anywhere the trains travel, boarding and disembarking as often as he wishes. As you might expect, the train system was offering a special for the exact dates that we were to be traveling. We wound up traveling for sixteen days for less than the normal ten-day fare! So, we made our plans and booked all the tickets.

But that's when we got a major "monkey wrench in the gears." Just a couple weeks before the trip, as my boys and I were enjoying our Saturday afternoon adventures together, we were building ramps for doing acrobatics with our bikes. The boys were all enjoying "getting some serious air" when I decided to show off my skills as well. The next thing I knew is that I was on the ground in excruciating pain. When I realized that I was unable to move my right arm, Peggy decided that it was time for a visit to the emergency room – where I was diagnosed with a broken shoulder blade. Since all the muscles that control the arm are anchored to the shoulder blade, the injury left me without the ability to move my arm more than a couple inches. This was especially bad news since we had planned to carry only backpacks on our Europe trip to make it easy to jump on and off the train at all the various stops that we planned to make and to get around as we toured all the cities that were we hoped to visit. With a broken shoulder blade, I would not be able to wear a backpack. With an incapacitated arm, I would not be able to carry anything or even hold the handrail to get on and off the train. With the excruciating pain that shot through my body every time I moved my arm, there was no possible way I could have endured – much less enjoyed – the trip. It looked as if our dream vacation was about to go "down the tubes" – except for the fact that we serve a miracle-working God.   Shortly after the accident, I had an occasion to be with R. W. Schambach, an evangelist who had an amazing healing ministry.   Knowing that Bro. Schambach could be really rough with the people he prayed for, I was really reluctant to ask him for prayer, but I really believed that God had allowed me to be with him at this specific time because of my very serious need. I began by telling him about the accident and was careful to make sure that he understood that I could only move my arm about four inches without excruciating pain. At that point, he took my hand and carefully moved my arm, asking me if this was as far as I could move it. When I affirmed that that was the limit, Bro. Schambach did exactly what I was afraid that he would do – he jerked my arm all the way above my head. And, I was instantly healed! In a bold act of faith that would have killed me had I not been instantly healed, the use of my arm was immediately restored and I was able to do everything that I could ever do with that arm – including carry a backpack all over Europe!

That day, I was able to show my boys not only how we could fix bikes and kitchen appliances in our workshop on Saturday mornings but how we can take the broken things in our lives into God's workshop and let Him fix them for us – the most important lesson I could ever hope to teach my sons!

Epilogue
In the Fullness of Time

As you have read through the story of my life, I hope that you have seen the one theme that has been woven through all the experiences I have recounted – God had a plan. He prepared and equipped me for it, and then He worked in my life to make His plan a reality. Allow me to conclude with a bit of theological background to confirm that this is His intent for all of us. My hope is that it will encourage you to allow Him to do His mighty exploits in, for, and through you as well!

When John the Beloved recorded the Great Commission, he remembered the words of Jesus stating that He was sending the church into the world in the same way that the Father had sent Him.

> Then the same day at evening, being the first day of the week, when the doors were shut where the disciples were assembled for fear of the Jews, came Jesus and stood in the midst, and saith unto them, Peace be unto you. And when he had so said, he shewed unto them his hands and his side. Then were the disciples glad, when they saw the Lord. Then said Jesus to them again, Peace be unto you: as my Father hath sent me, even so send I you. And when he had said this, he breathed on them, and saith unto them, Receive ye the Holy Ghost: Whose soever sins ye remit, they are remitted unto them; and whose soever sins ye retain, they are retained. (John 20:19-23)

There may be many ways to interpret exactly what He meant by this statement, but I would like to suggest that we can find some powerful meaning for the wording by looking at Paul's writings in Galatians 4:4-5.

320

> But when the fulness of the time was come, God sent forth his Son, made of a woman, made under the law, To redeem them that were under the law, that we might receive the adoption of sons.

Although these verses are packed with great theological truths, let's limit our discussion to the one phrase, "in the fullness of time" because this phrase actually speaks of the way in which the Father sent His Son. Before we actually turn to the study of the concept of the fullness of time, I'd like to lay just a bit of groundwork. Why did God wait so long to provide a way of salvation for all mankind if He had a plan all along? While I can't say that I have a real answer to that question, this verse helps us to understand that there was a specific season that the Father had in mind for His intervention in the human saga — a point in history when the times came to their fullness. Scriptures also indicate that He had this whole agenda orchestrated even before He created the earth. (Matthew 13:35, 25:34; John 17:24; Ephesians 1:4; Hebrews 4:3; I Peter 1:20; Revelation 13:8, 17:8)

When we look at the world condition at the time of Jesus, we see that so many factors came into perfect convergence at that one pinpoint in history. The Roman Empire, which ruled the world at that time, had imposed one political system throughout the civilized world — Pax Romana. This system allowed the countries under Rome's control to exercise a certain amount of autonomy as long as they did not violate the general authority of the empire. One of the provisions of Pax Romana was free passage between the individual cities, states, and regions under Roman rule. There were no visas or passports required as travelers made their way through the empire. In addition, the Romans built the most elaborate road system known up until that time. This extensive roadway system connected even the most remote parts of Africa, Asia, and Europe in a network so expansive that the proverb, "All roads lead to Rome," has endured to modern times. The superior quality of the construction technique of the Romans is evident today in roads and bridges that are still usable some twenty centuries later.   I have personally ridden on two-thousand-year-old roads that are still in service in Israel and crossed a two-millennia-old bridge in Rome that today carries modern vehicular traffic safely from central Rome into the Vatican. God was waiting for the Caesars to unify the nations and connect them with an outstanding transportation network, providing safe and dependable passage to the very ends of the world. Had He sent His Son before the rise of the Roman Empire, the possibility of the spread of the gospel to the far reaches of the globe would be hampered by lack of transportation and innumerable border restrictions. As it was, the gospel was able to spread rapidly because the Roman Empire had eliminated almost all such hindrances.

When Alexander the Great died in a drunken stupor in 323 BC, he was lamenting that at the age of thirty-three there were no more worlds for him to conquer. No other military or political leader in all of human history has ever made such a claim or left such a legacy of bringing the total civilized world under the control of one individual in a single lifetime. As his armies swept their way around the Mediterranean and into regions of India and Africa, one deposit they left behind was the Greek language. Every territory that came under their power was required to adopt Alexander's tongue and become part of the unified language system he imposed. The genius of this language is that it is the most precise tongue ever spoken on the planet. With the intricate conjugation structure of the verbs and the elaborate declination system for the nouns, there is no question as to what a sentence is intended to say; the precise meaning of each statement is contained not only in the definitions of the specific words used but also in the forms in which those words are used. The Father used this uniquely fitted language to be the universal medium through which the message of His Son would be communicated. Even though Jesus did not personally speak the Greek language, those who recorded His sayings and documented His life took what they knew and communicated it with accuracy in Greek and then went forth to proclaim it in the one universally accepted tongue understood in all regions of the earth.

At the same time that Jesus was living on the planet, the entire world of religion was going through a state of flux. Even though Hinduism predates Christianity by almost a thousand years, it was in the same time frame that the Christian faith was spreading around the world that the Hindu religion was defining itself and codifying its teachings. Even though Siddhartha Gautama, the Buddha, lived some five hundred years before Jesus, it was only at the time of Christ that his teachings were being collected and organized. The religions of the Greeks and Romans were in the process of shifting from direct deity worship to a more philosophical interpretation as myth and legend rather than absolute factual interpretations. The Jewish faith as it had existed for centuries was also going through a major change as the teachings and traditions of the rabbis, rather than the Old Testament scriptures, were becoming the measure of the faith. What the rabbis said about the scriptures became more authoritative than the scriptures themselves. It was at this exact period of history that such rabbinical teachings were being recorded and preserved in the Talmud, Mishnah, and Midrash. God specifically timed the coming of His Son to be at a time when men all around the world and from every form of religion were reevaluating what they really believed. Their hearts were ready and their souls were ripe for a new word from God — the Living Word. Both Jews and pagans were questioning what they had traditionally believed, and they were ready to respond quickly to the gospel. (Acts 6:7, 14:1, 19:27)

One other factor that figured into the rapid spread of the gospel is that God sent His Son just at the time of the great dispersion of the Jewish race from Israel. The Jews had already been scattered among all the nations of the earth to the point that the first century BC geographer Stabo said that there was no single place that had not received Jews. This spread of the Jews escalated with the Roman Empire's conquest of Palestine and the destruction of the city of Jerusalem in AD 70. At that time, the Jews were forcibly evicted in what has become known as the diaspora or the dispersing of the race throughout the world. Because the Jewish faith and practice were essentially omnipresent, there was a ready platform upon which the Christian message could be presented around the world. Notice how the book of Acts repeatedly attests that the gospel was first introduced in the synagogues as it spread from city to city. (Acts 13:14, 14:1, 16:13, 17:1, 17:10, 17:17, 18:4, 18:19, 18:26, 19:8, 22:19, 26:11) Paul clearly states that it was his deliberate plan of operation to go first to the Jewish community before moving to the gentiles. (Romans 1:16)

On another level – and likely the most important level – the Father was waiting to send His Son at the precise moment in which the message would be recorded with the unique quality that makes the New Testament truly the Word of God. Because of the unique timing of the coming of Jesus, it was years after His life, death, and resurrection that the gospels were written down. There were several reasons why people, particularly the Jews, did not write their life stories during the period of the early church. First of all, not much of anything was written down at that time. Most of the people were illiterate; therefore, most of the learning in this period was oral. First Corinthians 1:26-27 confirms that not many of the early Christian believers were educated. In fact, it is only in recent history that education has become widely accessible, a reality that Daniel spoke of as a sign of the last days. (Daniel 12:4) Secondly, Jewish scholars were cautious about writing down their teachings for fear that they would be considered to be attempting to equate themselves with the prophets and their work, which was written in the Bible. The Jews said, "The last prophet was Malachi, and there are not any prophets in the world today." In addition, oral teaching was considered nobler than teaching which was communicated second-hand in a written format. Scholars of the time said that the living voice was much richer. Memorizing and reciting the works of the ancients and the teachings of the contemporaries was considered an honorable activity. One of the contemporaries of Jesus boasted to have learned forty-eight books of Homer by memory. When a rabbi would give a teaching, the students would memorize it verbatim. They memorized everything he was saying as he said it. After the class, two students would get together and quote the lessons back and forth to each other. If one of the students said one word different from the way the other one remembered it, they would stop and discuss the point until they both came into agreement of exactly what that rabbi said word-for-word. A third reason that the gospels were not immediately written down was because printing was very expensive. Until the invention of the printing press some fourteen hundred years later, books had to be handwritten one at a time. At the time of Jesus, it cost twenty to twenty-five denarii to transcribe about sixteen syllables. To get a perspective on what that meant, we can turn to the story that Jesus told in Matthew chapter twenty where vineyard workers earned a denarius for a day's wage. In other words, hiring a scribe was like hiring a highly skilled professional who got many times more than an average working man's daily wage. A fourth factor that kept the early Christians from recording the gospel stories immediately was their belief that Jesus was coming back in the Second Coming almost immediately. They took certain statements of Jesus such as Matthew 16:28 and Matthew 10:23 to mean that He would return so soon that there was not any reason to make copies of his story when they could just repeat the message by word of mouth. They felt that it was a better use of their time to go out and proclaim the message rather than to take the time to sit down and write.

However, within a few years, things began to change. The church realized that they needed reading material for their church services. The first century church took its form of worship directly from the Jewish synagogue because most of the first-century Christians came from Jewish backgrounds. In the synagogue worship, one of the most important parts was the reading of the Torah, the Old Testament Law. Since the church followed the pattern of the Jewish ceremony, they needed a written part of the scriptures to read. They would read the Old Testament, but they also wanted the teachings of the apostles and of Jesus Himself. As early as 67 AD, Justin Martyr referred to reading the letters of the apostles for such church functions.

There was also a missionary intent behind the writing down of the gospels. Try to read the gospels through as though you had never heard the story before. Just sit down and read them like they are a new novel you just picked up at the bookstore. Do not think about all the sermons that you have heard about Jesus. As you read, you will become enthralled with the life of the man. You will want to know more and more about Him. You will find that He always demands you to make a decision. You will either say, "This guy is a lunatic. He's absolutely

326

crazy. He's berserk!" or you will decide, "These people are liars to make up such erroneous lies about such a man!" or you will say, "He has to be Lord." Out of the American Revolution grew the expression, "The pen is mightier than the sword." It was this same reality that drove the early believers to take the time to record this sharper-than-a-two-edged-sword message. Additionally, the church needed a source for catechetical teachings. The Old Testament leaders set up landmarks so children could ask questions and receive instruction. (Joshua 4:6) In the Jewish Seder service each Passover, the Jewish children always ask questions of the elders for the purpose of instruction, "Why is this night different from all other nights?" Christians realized that they needed a similar codified way of prompting children to learn about the faith of their fathers. The gospels were to be for answering the questions raised about Jesus. Heresy among adults was just as important a factor as was inquisitiveness among children. The gospels were to guard against heresy that was developing in relationship to the life story of Jesus. The pseudepigrapha, or imitation gospels that began to be circulated at this period, were full of examples of fantasy stories that soon began to be circulated as if they were the true gospel stories. One other motivating factor was the need to establish a direct link to the men who personally knew Jesus. (I John 1:1) The church needed to establish a direct chain with as few links as possible between Jesus and the existing church; therefore, the gospels were recorded by apostles who directly knew Jesus or disciples of these apostles.

The result of this lag in the production of the written gospels was that when the written product did appear, it was reflective history inspired by the Holy Spirit rather than historical documentation of news events. Some people conceive the inspiration of the Holy Spirit working in the gospel writers as though the authors were in a trance. Some view it like an instrument — as a man blowing a trumpet. These people believe that the gospel writers were like the trumpets and that they had nothing to do with what came out of them as the breath of God flowed through them. However, the inspiration was not of this nature as can be seen when we read through the different gospels. You'll see that there are different points and different influences in each book. This is because of the human nature of the person who was writing. The same Word of God was given by each writer, yet we can tell characteristics of different personalities as they bring forth the message. The writers were writing about a historical event. They were the eyewitnesses who had seen it and experienced it, yet the Holy Spirit helped bring to their remembrance what went into the gospel at this point. (John 14:26) The Holy Spirit chose what was significant and gave the interpretation for it. To emphasize that one writer's personality shows up here or there does not in any way detract from the fact that the Holy Spirit inspired it. The Holy Spirit did inspire it. There are no errors in the gospels because everything was Holy Spirit inspired. But because the gospels were not written the day after the events occurred, the accounts are not history in the sense of a newspaper report of an event. It is not like a television news reporter's "on the spot" news. It is a spiritual understanding of the event, written years later by men who had time to reflect and years for the Holy Spirit to quicken them to really know what that event was all about. If you think about something that happened to you years ago, you will only remember what that event was all about but not the minute details. God knew the exact moment in history to send His Son so that His story would be more than history; it would be the Word of God. The contemporary philosophy of oral as opposed to written teaching guaranteed that the gospel would not become a textbook history lesson, but a message of

God's mercy reported after years of reflection in the writers' lives.

God sent His Son in the fullness of time when all aspects of politics, engineering, religion, and philosophy were totally lined up so that the message of the gospel would have the maximum impact in the shortest amount of time. Just as history was in the crosshairs when God sent His Son, Jesus sent His disciples out when all the conditions were exactly right for their success as well.

Two intriguing verses in the story of Jesus seem to focus on the concept that He entered human history at a very specific moment in time. In Luke 1:36 we read Gabriel's message to Mary concerning the conception of John the Baptist. He mentions Mary's cousin Elizabeth and says that she was called barren. Notice that he does not say that she was barren, only that people considered her so. The message behind the angel's wording is that there was a specific time at which John the Baptist was to be born. Since he was to be the forerunner of Jesus, he could not be born until it was almost time for Jesus to come on the scene. Therefore, Elizabeth had to wait until an advanced age to give birth to him. In other words, even though she was not barren, she could not give birth until the fullness of time. The other intriguing verse is John 4:4 where it is recorded that Jesus "must needs pass through Samaria" on His way from Judaea to the Galilee. The truth is that He actually didn't have to pass through Samaria at all. In fact, most Jews at this time in history had such animosity against the Samaritans that they avoided traveling through Samaria even though it was the most direct route between Judaea and Galilee. They regularly traveled through the Jordan River Valley in order to bypass Samaria. Jesus could have easily followed this well-established route; however, there was something else at play in His decision that day. It was the fullness of time. There was a Samaritan woman who would be at the well at the exact time Jesus' journey would bring Him to that exact spot. The Father knew that she would be there and that she would be ready to hear what Jesus would have to say to her. He also knew that she would become a catalyst to bring revival to the whole city. Because of that, the Father compelled the Son to take that specific route at that specific time. Convergence was destined because it was the fullness of time for the woman at the well and for the city of Samaria.

When we are sent out to take part in the Great Commission, we can be assured that He is orchestrating everything in His precise timing; there is nothing that will happen by accident or random luck. When the football team is in the huddle, the quarterback may tell one of the runners to go down the sideline and turn around when he reaches the twenty-yard line. That's because he knows exactly what's in his mind for the next play. If the other player will only follow the quarterback's instructions, he will discover that just as he turns around at the twenty-yard line, the ball will be ready to fall into his arms. When it comes to the Great Commission, God has each play planned out in even more detail than the world's best quarterback. When He says that He's sending us, He has a doable plan in mind.

www.ingramcontent.com/pod-product-compliance
Lightning Source LLC
LaVergne TN
LVHW051038080426
835508LV00019B/1577